29323

NEW DIRECTIONS
IN
NEW TESTAMENT STUDY

DATE DUE

NEW DIRECTIONS
IN
NEW TESTAMENT STUDY

PATRICK HENRY

SCM PRESS LTD

Grateful acknowledgment is made to the following for the use of copyrighted material:

Harcourt Brace Jovanovich, Inc., and Faber & Faber, Ltd., for quotations from T. S. Eliot, "East Coker", in *Four Quartets*. Used by permission of the publishers.

The New Yorker Magazine, Inc., for quotations from "The Great Span", in The Talk of the Town. © 1975.

Scripture quotations from the Revised Standard Version of the Bible are copyrighted 1946, 1952, © 1971, 1973 by the Division of Christian Education of the National Council of the Churches of Christ in the U.S.A., and are used by permission.

334 01114 0

First published 1979 by The Westminster Press, Philadelphia
First British edition published 1980 by
SCM Press Ltd
58 Bloomsbury Street London WC1

Typeset in the United States of America
and printed in Great Britain by
Richard Clay Ltd, Bungay, Suffolk

In 1521 the Elector Frederick of Saxony "wished to be enlightened as to the meaning of Scripture, and appointed a committee. But the committee could not agree."

Roland H. Bainton, *Here I Stand: A Life of Martin Luther* (Abingdon-Cokesbury Press, 1950), p. 203

CONTENTS

PREFACE

What is going on in New Testament study? Is the field headed in new directions? These are questions that may be asked by biblical scholars themselves, by students beginning the study of the New Testament, by ministers and priests who find little time for scholarly reading in the daily round of congregational and parish life, by laypersons sharing in the recent revival of interest in serious biblical study in the churches, or by persons who simply want to know what is happening in one of the oldest of all scholarly disciplines.

Whatever may be the significance of current New Testament study, there is a great deal of it going on. There are at least 450 books a year in the field, and articles appear at the rate of a thousand or more a year in about 400 journals. In the face of this flood of writings, the effort to "keep up" may appear futile, and the temptation to read the Bible only in terms of "what it says to me" can become overwhelming. In a sense, of course, "what it says to me" is all the Bible, or any book, can mean. NEW DIRECTIONS IN NEW TESTAMENT STUDY is written in the conviction that the New Testament can say much more *to us* if we understand the insights being made available today by New Testament scholars.

For much of this century New Testament study has been carried on in effective isolation from the liveliest developments in the humanities and the social sciences. While psychology, anthropology, and literary criticism have been increasingly sensitive to myth as a positive and irreplaceable way of fashioning and interpreting experience, New Testament scholarship has been preoccupied with the effort of demythologizing. Leading New Testament scholars have adopted a particular philosophical judgment about the human

13

situation—that of the existentialists—and have probed the New Testament from that perspective. What they have found is an intensely individualistic gospel, for which the prior community of Israel and the subsequent community of the church are both largely irrelevant. In the meantime, sociology as a way of approach to human experience has been affecting nearly all disciplines, and the existentialists' "myth" of individualism appears to be in at least as much need of "demythologizing" as the "three-storied universe" of the New Testament.

The new directions of New Testament study are being determined, in large part, by New Testament scholars' moving beyond the obsessively theological preoccupations of recent decades. It may come as a surprise that the lowering of theological intensity actually enhances the direct significance of New Testament study for the life of the church. This book will argue not only that New Testament study is becoming more conversant with the liberal arts generally but also that New Testament study as it is now being done offers new possibilities for Christians who, out of obedience to God, are committed both to the church and to rigorous thinking.

In writing this book I have become vividly conscious of the range of my intellectual debts, going back at least to undergraduate days. My teachers, especially George Buttrick at Harvard, Henry Chadwick at Oxford, and Jaroslav Pelikan at Yale, will detect unacknowledged echoes of their lectures and conversation. Books read long ago, as well as ones read more recently, have become part of my intellectual capital, and while I have indicated sources of my ideas whenever I am aware of them, I am sure that much of what I have found in my mind is drawn on accounts whose names and numbers I have forgotten.

The genesis of this book was a series of lectures I delivered at Pendle Hill, a Quaker Study Center in Wallingford, Pennsylvania, during the spring of 1975. I am grateful to the staff at Pendle Hill for the impetus to start getting my thoughts in order, and to the audience, who challenged me with their questions and encouraged me to prepare the lectures for publication. The response of the Pendle Hill audience, together with my experiences over several years leading adult groups in the (Episcopal) Church of the Redeemer in Bryn Mawr, Pennsylvania, and in the church of which

I am an elder, the Swarthmore Presbyterian, has persuaded me that there are many persons outside the academy, as well as within it, who are eager to know what is going on in studies and libraries.

The lectures have been thoroughly revised and considerably expanded. Most of the additional work was done on a leave of absence from Swarthmore College, during which time I was a Fellow of the Institute for Ecumenical and Cultural Research, affiliated with St. John's Abbey and University, in Collegeville, Minnesota. I am grateful to Swarthmore for the time off (as well as to my students at Swarthmore, whose inquisitiveness and intellectual commitment are a constant stimulus to their teachers), and to the Institute for its ideal working conditions, its dialogues and criticisms, and its determination to bridge the gap between academic research and the life of the church. I owe special thanks to the Institute's executive director, Robert S. Bilheimer, whose acute questions were matched by his encouraging words. Bob Bilheimer comes at questions such as the ones this book is about with a mind fully capable of grasping the academic abstractions—and a holy impatience with letting the matter rest there.

Friends and colleagues, some specialists, some nonspecialists, have read all or part of the manuscript, and I appreciate their suggestions: Fred Carney, Pat Collins, Melvin Endy, Jerry Frost, Leo Garrett, Drusilla Gillespie, Gay Grissom, Grant Grissom, Marion Hatchett, Thomas Hoyt, James Johnson, Howard Kee, Katherine Meyer, Sally Mowris, David Page, Valerie Prescott, Donald Swearer, Linwood Urban. I wish I had the nerve of my friend John Meagher, who ends the preface to one of his books by listing his readers and then saying: "If you are not totally satisfied with this book, don't blame me. I did what I could. Blame them."[1] I am unable to upset the conventions of preface-writing in that way, but perhaps I can innovate by thanking lifeguards and fieldhouse custodians, who make pools and tracks available. Were it not for regular swimming and running, the writer of a book might eventually get stuck in the chair, and hence be unable even to carry the manuscript out of the study.

My wife, Patricia, has read with the careful eye of a trained scientist, and has shown an uncanny knack for knowing when to console with "You'll get it done" and when to cajole with "You'll *never* finish it!"

The book is dedicated to my parents on their retirement from forty years of ministry to the Northway Christian Church of Dallas, Texas.

P.H.

Swarthmore College
  Swarthmore, Pennsylvania

Institute for Ecumenical and Cultural Research
  Collegeville, Minnesota

CHAPTER
ONE

THE NEW CONTEXT
OF NEW TESTAMENT STUDY

A second-century writer summarized the questions he thought a religion should be able to answer: "Who we were, and what we have become, where we were, where we were placed, whither we hasten."[1] Such questions arise also in the realm of scholarship itself, and since the beginning of the twentieth century the development of New Testament studies has been punctuated by books and articles that take a look at the state of the field and attempt to answer the questions "Where are we? How did we get here? Where are we going?"

For an academic field to "study itself" may sound like little more than professors wandering through a hall of mirrors in an ivory tower, but self-awareness is no less healthy for a profession than for an individual, and furthermore, the Christian community has—or ought to have—an interest in knowing what New Testament scholars think they are up to. Matters of academic interest are never all that the church is concerned about, but they are not beside the point. "The church is always more than a school; . . . but the church cannot be less than a school."[2]

I. THE NEW ACADEMIC CONTEXT

There is one particularly striking difference between the effect of New Testament study on those who practice it today and the effect it had a hundred years ago. In the nineteenth century, numerous scholars moved through their New Testament researches, and took many readers with them, into various degrees of dissociation from the church, some with relief, more with regret and even anguish. Such occurrences are of course not unknown today, but there is scant literary record of scholars in the last generation or two who have found their New Testament research as such creating insuperable problems for their faith.

The main reason that scholars are not finding New Testament study a huge stumbling block to faith is that critical method itself has reached a stage of maturity where it is becoming self-critical. "Maturity" is not a term that appears in every account of New Testament scholarship these days. Recent analysts have used such terms as "dead end" or "crisis of confidence" to answer the question "Where are we?" and have suggested that the historical approach to the New Testament is the answer to "How did we get here?" The diagnosis is "exhaustion," and the remedy must be either complete rest or some new miracle drug. That New Testament study is in a period of significant transition is undeniable, even by those, such as myself, who suspect that every period can be described as one of "transition." I see the transition being generated, not by some miracle, but by scholars' reflecting more carefully on their own methods.

Is it not presumptuous to make a judgment that any field of scholarship, and particularly one so vast as New Testament study, has reached "maturity"? I want to guard against misinterpretation of my use of the term. Our time is mesmerized by anything that is thought to be unprecedented, and I believe theology has been skewed by declarations that the world has "come of age" and that "modern persons" are some radically distinct form of creature from those who have gone before. Our own increasing awareness of the deep continuities between the period of Renaissance and Reformation on the one hand and the period that they contemptuously called "the Middle Ages" on the other hand should make us hesitant to indulge in a similar cultural high-handedness and shortsightedness, or what C. S. Lewis called "chronological snobbery."[3] So, when I say that New Testament scholarship is showing signs of maturity, I am saying only that the element of reflective self-criticism is becoming more prominent.

It is increasingly clear that the way we have become accustomed to seeing New Testament study done is itself a novelty; what has seemed to be an irresistible tendency in New Testament scholarship, toward more and more radical conclusions and an ever-widening gulf between academic understanding of the New Testament on the one side and the life of the Christian community on the other side, is something of a historical curiosity. The current state of New Testament study gives promise of new relationships between academic analysis and the life of the church—or rather, of renewed relationships, since during most of Christianity's history the serious study of the New Testament has been the business of the church and for the church.

Two cautionary notes must be sounded at the outset. First, I am not talking about warfare between the church and the academy, with the prize of battle being occupation of the New Testament territory. To some observers it may seem that nothing short of the imagery of combat can describe the relationship between true believers and professors; there are enough sorry instances of ecclesiastical censure of biblical scholars to make such a portrayal partially credible. It is to the church's disadvantage, however, to frame the issue in these terms, because when ecclesiastical authority, "protecting" the purported interests of the church, has denounced the results of scholarly inquiry, the church has nearly always made a fool of itself. The church is not in our time "recapturing" the New Testament from the academy. The academy is gradually realizing that an adequate *scholarly* understanding of the New Testament requires appreciation of the *community* which produced the books of the New Testament, and for which they were produced. To neglect that community, both in its original forms and in its current manifestations, is to rip the New Testament out of its context.

But even if the scholars are now seeing that the New Testament belongs in and to the church, the church has no cause for complacent satisfaction, for just as professors too easily make their own abstractions into absolute criteria, the church too easily assumes that its life today is the criterion for proper understanding of the New Testament. In return for the church's reminder to the scholars that the New Testament is a book by and for a community of faith, the scholars remind the church that its reading of the New Testament may be seriously distorted by conformity to this or that cultural or sectarian pattern. The proper relationship of church and academy is one in which each reminds the other of what it tends, by virtue of its primary commitments, to forget.

The second cautionary note: While to say that things are changing does not generate any discussion, to say they are changing in the direction suggested by this book is to make a judgment with which not all practitioners of New Testament study would agree. The migration of biblical study from theological seminaries to departments of religious studies during the past two decades has been rapid and extensive, but there has not been much formal analysis of its implications. Most of the persons who have reflected on the shift have suspected that it means a further deterioration in what was left of the family relationship between theological scholarship and the church.[4] With the ending of the institutional connection it has been feared (or hoped, depending on the ax being ground by the analyst) that the scholar's tenuous sense of obligation to speak in a way intelligible to the faithful and useful for the church would wither away completely.

I am arguing that these projections are, in the main, wrong. I see evidence that the treatment of the New Testament in the new academic context is not driving the wedge between the church and the scholars deeper. I am arguing that even some scholars who have cut all personal ties with the institutional church are reaching conclusions, on the basis of their critical approaches, that are of positive value for the very institution they have themselves rejected.

The picture is not uniform, of course. Some conclusions, either overtly or subtly, would challenge fundamental aspects of the church's self-understanding. But in general I see a tendency toward a cautious affirmation of the New Testament as a book which, in the words of Augustine (Bishop of Hippo Regius in North Africa, A.D. 396–430), "offers itself to all in the plainest words and simplest expressions, yet demands the closest attention of the most serious minds," or, to use the more picturesque language of Gregory the Great (Bishop of Rome, A.D. 590–604), "is a kind of river, in whose shallows a lamb may wade, and in whose depths an elephant may swim about."[5]

II. The New Ecumenical Context

Coinciding with the shift of biblical studies into a new academic environment, there has been another shift taking place—one with potentially even deeper significance for the understanding of the New Testament. Yet it is a shift almost unnoticed by most North American and European Christians. Very rapidly, the numerical weight of Christianity is moving to the southern hemisphere. The authority of "North Atlantic" theology is no longer uncritically accepted by church members in Latin America, Africa, and Asia, and there are already strong voices in those areas insisting that the way the New Testament has been interpreted by European and North American scholars is more thoroughly culture-bound than the scholars, with their ideal of "objectivity," have on the whole been willing to admit.

There is not yet a tradition of New Testament scholarship in the southern hemisphere, but as those areas of the Christian world become increasingly—and very rapidly—self-conscious and self-reliant in theology generally, they are bound to make contributions to New Testament study of a sort we in the West cannot predict, precisely because our predictions presuppose our own situation and experience. Even though prediction would be foolhardy, mention of a few features of the new ecumenical reality of the church might help give a sense of the potential for impact.

There is of course no more justification for lumping "southern hemisphere" churches together than there is for speaking grandly of "Western" churches, but some parts of the developing world provide for the church very different contexts from those familiar to us. How will the New Testament be interpreted for persons who are as yet only minimally affected by industrialization and other social dislocations of the "modern world"? What will be found in the New Testament by scholars who represent churches that face governmental and religious hostility? What emphases will emerge in New Testament study done in cultures that are not steeped in the tradition of the Bible and Christian theology?—even the most "secularized" Westerners are familiar with the basic themes and concepts. It will be interesting to see how the New Testament is studied in areas where the Bible is something of a cultural intruder (as it was in the Roman Empire), where the non-Christian audience are not "post-Christian" Westerners but devout Buddhists, Hindus, Muslims. Africans criticize Western Christian theology for offering little that touches the depths of the African soul; can we in the West have our own souls deepened through African interpretations of the New Testament?[6]

The questions multiply, and they are genuine questions—it is too early to say what the answers will be. But the questions should make clear how potentially volatile an age lies immediately ahead for New Testament study. It is highly unlikely that a survey of the state of New Testament study in the middle of the twenty-first century will be able to devote itself, as previous surveys have done and as this one will, almost exclusively to activities of Europeans and North Americans.

In one respect, the impact of the new ecumenical reality on biblical study can already be felt. Southern hemisphere Christians have different priorities from those of us in the northern, and the development of "liberation theology" is, among other things, a challenge to read the Bible in a new (or long-neglected) light. Black Americans, too, find the Bible's central message in the theme of liberation, and together with the oppressed in other parts of the world they have insisted that while the New Testament may fulfill the Old Testament, the Old Testament, with its governing image of liberation from bondage and with its concern for "the people" more than for "the individual," is the best interpreter of the New Testament. As we shall see, a new appreciation of the Jewishness of the New Testament and a new awareness of the social dimensions of early Christianity have emerged within New Testament study apart from the impetus provided by liberation theology, but it is likely that the new ecumenical situation will encourage these new scholarly developments, and will help prevent their being simply a passing fashion in the ever-changing academic world.[7]

There are three other dimensions to the new ecumenical context of New Testament study, a form of intellectual activity which has been carried on largely by liberal Protestants. The recent flowering of Roman Catholic biblical scholarship is a subject of such importance and interest that an entire chapter of this book is devoted to it.

A second new dimension is provided by Eastern Orthodoxy. Critical study of the Bible has not been characteristic of Orthodoxy, and the contribution to date of Greeks, Russians, and others to New Testament scholarship has been minimal. However, there is a deep stirring of intellectual life within Orthodoxy today, brought about in part by contacts through the World Council of Churches and by the challenge posed to many Orthodox churches by governments and societies that are expressly antireligious. Orthodoxy has much to offer New Testament study, and can make at least one crucial contribution: the recognition of the ecclesiastical *community* as the focus of and arena for reflection. Indeed, Orthodoxy may be able to provide a storehouse of tradition to support the new liberation theologies, at least in their insistence on taking the reality of "peoplehood" seriously.[8]

The rise of evangelical Christianity to cultural prominence in recent years provides the third new ecumenical dimension to New Testament study. Evangelical scholars are gaining an academic hearing not only because the churches they represent are growing and powerful but also because much of their own scholarship is no longer defensive and reactionary. Those conservative evangelicals who insist on the inerrancy of the biblical text cannot, of course, make any compromise with the tradition of critical scholarship, but they are by no means unchallenged from within their own churches, and some of the challengers are showing how the analytical techniques which have led to radical conclusions can lead in a more conservative direction. Or, to put it more accurately: they are finding evangelical implications in radical conclusions. For instance, the young British New Testament scholar James D. G. Dunn, whose sympathies are clearly evangelical and even Pentecostal, demonstrates as unflinchingly as any liberal scholar the extraordinary diversity of the New Testament, and he finds within that diversity solid grounding for the continued relevance of the apocalyptic and pentecostal perspectives within the Christian community. Indeed, Dunn sees the church in the New Testament period as more ecumenically diverse than it has ever been since.[9]

The prediction of a convergence of South American Catholics and black American Baptists and Greek Orthodox and British Pentecostalists in their impact on New Testament study may strike the reader as fanciful, but the new ecumenical situation is real, and for most of us it is very strange. We will have to get used to "the fanciful" becoming "the order of the day."

III. THE PLAN OF THE BOOK

At the conclusion of "The New Testament in Current Study" in 1960, Reginald Fuller ventured to make some predictions about impending developments, but prefaced them by noting that no one could have foreseen the new directions determined by Karl Barth's commentary on Romans in 1919, or by Rudolf Bultmann's essay on "Jesus Christ and Mythology" in 1941, or by Ernst Käsemann's call for a reopening of "The Question of the Historical Jesus" in 1953.[10] It has been characteristic of our time, and of our time's understanding of itself, to see both faith and scholarship as matters primarily, or even exclusively, of individual concern: the person alone before God, the scholar alone with the sources. There will likely be major individual voices in years to come; someone will, like Barth, be groping in the dark, grab a rope, and discover that it is tied to a bell in the tower that will rouse the entire town.[11] But prediction today of where New Testament study will be tomorrow is difficult, not so much because we cannot know in advance who will break through to a new insight, but because the entire context in which New Testament study takes place is new and thus far largely untried.

New Testament scholars now inhabit offices on corridors with classicists, anthropologists, linguists, psychologists, philosophers, historians of art, literary critics. And just as the church can no longer be thought of as the ecclesiastical aspect of North Atlantic culture, with colonial extensions around the world, so can serious New Testament scholarship not any longer be considered the special preserve of liberal Protestants. With New Testament scholars out in the academic open, and with the church's moving into a new age of ecumenical maturity, something is bound to be happening. This book is an attempt to describe what is going on, and to assess what it means.

Chapter 2 will set forth the book's basic point of view—that thinking historically has positive implications for spiritual life, and that historical thinking, with a proper degree of self-criticism, is the most appropriate way to get at the New Testament. Chapter 3 suggests that several of the main questions confronting New Testament interpreters today were already apparent in the early centuries of the church's life, and while ancient answers may not suit us, we at least have to admit that our situation is not unprecedented. The two following chapters (Chapters 4 and 5) discuss developments in the study of major religious, cultural, and intellectual factors in the shaping of early Christianity—Judaism and Gnosticism—both of which now appear much more complex than they used to. Then come chapters (Chapters 6 and 7) on two leading figures of the New Testament—Jesus and Paul—each of whom has undergone extensive and unexpected reappraisal in recent years. The chapters on Jesus and Paul are followed by evaluations of sociology (Chapter 8) and comparative religion and psychology (Chapter 9) as ways of approach to the New Testament, and by an account of the truly astonishing development of Roman Catholic biblical scholarship in the past thirty years (Chapter 10). The book concludes (Chapter 11) with a consideration of what all this means for an understanding of the New Testament as the Christian era draws near the beginning of its third millennium.

CHAPTER TWO

THINKING HISTORICALLY

I. HENRY FORD AND KARL BARTH

What do we care what they did 500 or 1,000 years ago? . . . It means
nothing to me. History is more or less bunk. It's tradition. We don't
want tradition. We want to live in the present and the only history
that is worth a tinker's dam is the history we make today. That's the
trouble with the world. We're living in books and history and tradition. We want to get away from that and take care of today. We've
done too much looking back. What we want to do, and do it quick,
is to make just history right now.[1]

Henry Ford's remarks were made in an interview with a *Chicago
Tribune* reporter in 1916, and the interview was brought up in the
course of Ford's libel suit against that newspaper in 1919. In an
editorial the *Tribune* had called Ford an "anarchist" and "ignorant
idealist," and despite the fact that Ford was plaintiff in the case, the
judicial process came to a climax in a merciless eight-day interroga-
tion of Ford himself. At one point the *Tribune*'s attorney asked:
"Do you recall that you were announcing to the world that you did
not believe in history, that it was only tradition, and you didn't care
anything about it? That is true, isn't it?" Ford's reply was less
grandiose than his claim three years earlier that books, history, and
tradition were "the trouble with the world." He said simply,
"Never served me very much purpose."[2]

In the very same year as *Henry Ford* v. *Chicago Tribune Co.* there
appeared a much longer but no less stunning verdict on history. It
was Karl Barth's *Epistle to the Romans,* which, as we noted in Chapter
1, signaled a revolution in theology. For the young Swiss preacher
and many others in his generation, the First World War, which had

fueled the fires of controversy between Ford and the *Tribune,* had shattered the foundations on which their earlier view of history was based. History could no longer be seen as the record of the steady growth of the kingdom of God, conceived as social and political and material betterment. History now had the aspect of judgment; indeed, of the wrath of God. In its own way, Barth's opinion of history is as harsh and uncompromising as Ford's. Barth draws a sharp line between the Word of God and the world; or more precisely, he fixes a great gulf between them. Barth is of course much more subtle than Ford, and his historical learning is convincingly displayed in the footnotes to his *Church Dogmatics.* Still, in his theological onslaught against any compromising of the absolute freedom of the Word of God, Barth is not far from saying that history as such is more or less bunk.

It may well be that Henry Ford and Karl Barth have never before appeared together on the same page, and they do make a curious pair. But they illustrate two important influences in the shaping of American religious attitudes during this century, influences that have strongly affected biblical interpretation.

It is often argued that historical thinking, which developed explosively in the nineteenth century, is what makes belief difficult and faith uncertain for people in the twentieth century, just as natural science created particularly acute problems for those in the seventeenth and eighteenth centuries. The nineteenth century is littered with discarded creeds, and in many cases the creed was abandoned in the face of the historical criticism of the Bible. Matthew Arnold heard the "melancholy, long withdrawing roar" of the ebbing tide of the sea of faith, and in his opinion it was to be "the Bible as Literature," immune to erosion by historical and scientific criticism, that would be left upon the shore.[3]

The problem of "the historian and the believer," and especially of "the believer as historian," is a real one, and raises acute questions of what Van Harvey has called "the morality of knowledge."[4] What does it mean to make *honest* claims on the basis of historical conclusions? Do Christians have the necessary warrants to support their claim to *know* what they say they know about the past? Harvey's questions state clearly an issue that has, in one form or another, preoccupied Christian intellectuals for decades.

Henry Ford's evaluation of history as "more or less bunk" serves to remind us that we would rather not be bothered by history. When we want the reassurance of answers, the past bombards us with questions. Indeed, one reason people shy away from history is that the past when understood is more complicated and ambiguous than we usually perceive the present to be. It is commonly thought that people flee from a chaotic present to a simpler, neater past, and there is undoubtedly a great deal of nostalgic romance in America currently. There is much going on from which people might well want to escape: familiar patterns of society and thought are disintegrating, virtually all authority is distrusted, "new theologies" come and go almost as fast as the latest clothing fashions. But genuine historical thinking is no easy way out of the current situation; on the contrary, by attending to the complexity of the past, the historian raises the suspicion that the present too is not properly grasped by the clear-cut categories that most of us use when interpreting our experience.

Much Christian theology and New Testament study in the twentieth century has been shaped in response to "the problem of history." The ambiguity of the past has seemed to many thoughtful persons so out of phase with the need for confidence in God that they have followed Karl Barth in the uncompromising distinction between the Word of God and the world. Barth has many spiritual children, and their sibling rivalries can be fierce, but whether they are theologically conservative or theologically radical or something in between, they share the conviction that what matters religiously is God's encounter with human beings here and now: in Henry Ford's terms, "We want to live in the present." A conservative church in Texas collapses nineteen centuries of ecclesiastical history by declaring on its cornerstone: "Church of Christ / Established in Jerusalem / A.D. 33 / This Building Erected / A.D. 1951"; and Rudolf Bultmann, the most influential New Testament scholar of this century, and himself a contemporary of Barth's, said he could calmly let the critical fire burn because all it was consuming was "the fanciful portraits of Life of Jesus theology." For Bultmann, even if some historical point could be established beyond dispute, it would be improper to rest faith on that point, since faith would then be a "work" designed to establish our own righteousness, and thus no longer faith. It would be faith in "Christ after the flesh," and, according to Paul, we no longer know Christ in that way.

Bultmann declares bluntly: "The 'Christ after the flesh' is no concern of ours." Both the Texas cornerstone and Bultmann are making much the same point as Henry Ford.[5]

When major theologians are saying that history is too uncertain a basis for faith, and that *even if* it were certain, it would distort faith; when these same theologians say that God's word to me comes in the decisions I must make every day, and that every decision is an either/or proposition—I choose either authentic existence or inauthentic existence—then I will hardly think it worth my time and energy to puzzle over the past, and I am apt to be dissatisfied with the historical form of theological study and reflection, for it multiplies options.

The person thinking historically knows that Luther's "Here I stand. I can do no other. God help me" is exceptional, and that the puzzlement of Tevye in the musical play *Fiddler on the Roof* is common: "On the other hand . . . . On the other hand . . . . On the other hand . . . ."[6] The person thinking historically may well suspect that Tevye's faith, which even in severe crisis does not deny options, is at least as appropriate a clue to the understanding of the New Testament as is Luther's forthright declaration.

Thinking historically is not an exclusively intellectual activity. To put it more exactly: historical thinking is an intellectual activity that shapes attitudes and feelings, and they in turn shape the intellectual activity itself; the process of interaction continues, so the personal life of the historian as it develops plays an important role in determining what is seen in the evidence from the past. Historians, reflecting on their own lives extended through time, increasingly understand that faith has to do with persistence, with loyalty through ambiguity and doubt, with spiritual nurture and discipline, and not simply with isolated, staccato crises of decision, and this understanding is affecting the way the past is treated. The judgments on history pronounced by Henry Ford and Karl Barth are no longer the starting point of New Testament study.

II. THEORY AND METHOD

Apart from what is said in this chapter, there will be little sustained discussion of issues in the philosophy of history. However, this book itself is an expression of a kind of "working theory" of history. The way the book is constructed, the way arguments are presented and interrelated, the angle from which critiques are made—all reflect the current state of a particular individual's historical thinking. And "thinking historically" is going on in this book at several levels simultaneously: thought is directed toward the New Testament, toward the tradition of its interpretation, and toward one's own life as a historian in history. My argument that "thinking historically" has positive implications for spiritual life is not an abstract one, but concrete: my argument is this book itself.

The author, no less than the reader, is eager to get on with the main business; and yet, while a full-scale discussion of philosophy of history is not necessary, there are still features of historical thinking that need to be mentioned. In popular opinion, the historian is a curious (and rather inconsistent) blend of scientist and magician: historians are believed either to gain sure knowledge of the past or to construct a past out of their own overeducated and overheated imaginations, so that the best that could be said on their behalf is a wry comment of Samuel Butler's: "It has been said that though God cannot alter the past, historians can; it is perhaps because they can be useful to Him in this regard that He tolerates their existence."[7] What are historians looking for? What do they know? Why does history have to keep getting rewritten?

In 1960, the year Reginald Fuller delivered in San Francisco the lectures on "The New Testament in Current Study" referred to in Chapter 1, a series of lectures was delivered in London by several scholars to celebrate the inauguration of a new theology professorship at the University of London, and was published subsequently under the title *The Church's Use of the Bible: Past and Present.* The British series takes a characteristically long view, but does not dwell on the past for its own sake; the lecturers knew that there is no simple means of making the past speak to us, that making the past relevant to the present is a challenge as well as a temptation. In his survey of the treatment of the Bible by the Greek fathers of the church, Henry Chadwick faces squarely the temptation of relevance. He mentions some of the ways in which the fathers

illuminate our debates, but we must beware of assuming identity of standpoint. . . . We must not let our hearts run away with our heads.

When the apparent similarity is at its greatest, we need to be most cautious lest, in our effort to make these dry bones live, we clothe the dead with too much of our own flesh and blood. In short, it may be true (I think it is) that the Fathers being dead yet speak. It is equally true that though they speak they are also dead.[8]

I agree with Chadwick that "no simple transference is possible," but there are certain questions and problems posed by the New Testament that are integral to it and its role in the Christian community, questions that are never definitively answered because they are not the sort of question designed to have "an answer." History is always being rewritten not simply because our experience changes and permits us to see new things in old evidence but also because the past itself is not a "brute fact" to be dissected and analyzed. The past, through its voices—written, drawn, painted, carved, constructed, discarded—is constantly confronting us with options and possibilities that had not occurred to us. Our journeys into the past are voyages of discovery, and we limit the potential value of the voyage if we restrict in advance the range of things we are willing to notice.

A. From Ranke to Sandmel

Samuel Sandmel, a rabbi and professor of New Testament at Hebrew Union College in Cincinnati, has demonstrated time and again the capacity of Jewish scholarship to illuminate the New Testament. His general editorship of the Oxford Study Edition of the New English Bible is testimony to the high regard in which he is held by biblical experts. Sandmel's good sense and sound judgment will attract our notice at a number of points in this book; for now, what he has to tell us is the story of his own development as a historian.

Sandmel began his scholarly career with "the thought of some day trying to write a definitive study of the first Christian Century in Judaism and Christianity." He assembled materials for three decades. "The box is now well filled, and my impulse toward creating a synthesis is still present, but I no longer feel an urge to write something 'definitive.' " Sandmel suggests several reasons for this change in his intention, and his book *The First Christian Century in Judaism and Christianity: Certainties and Uncertainties* is an examination of the most basic reason for the change:

> As I observed view clashing with view [among the scholars], I came to suspect that some, or much, of the difference and divergency in the illuminating scholarship was possibly due to the wish of the scholars to know more than could be known. This reactive feeling led me to try to clarify for myself, beyond what the scholarship asserts, what it is that scholarship does not know, or does not know for certain.[9]

Sandmel is saying, in effect, that students of New Testament are still haunted by a ghost they would all claim to have laid to rest—the ghost of Leopold von Ranke (1795–1886), the "father" of modern historical study. Ranke was dissatisfied with the use traditionally made of the past as a storehouse of evidence and examples with which opponents in argument would beat one another over the head. Ranke set out systematically to put history on a sound scientific footing. He developed techniques by which one can make judgments about documents; there is nothing closer to the heart of the historian's job than those judgments, and to that extent we are all children of Ranke.

However, Ranke went further, and declared the historian's task to be that of presenting the past "as it actually happened."[10] As a corrective to earlier polemical history, Ranke's ideal can be embraced. But Ranke has planted in the entire historical enterprise an ideal that can tempt the practitioner to forget the severe limits on what we know for sure. It would be hard to find any historian today who would admit to holding Ranke's ideal as a practical goal; few would even admit it as a theoretical possibility. But Sandmel has suggested that whatever disclaimers are made, New Testament scholars have not really exorcised Ranke.

> The more I work in that [first] century, the more persuaded I become that scholars have in significant part deceived themselves about the possibilities of exact and responsible conclusions. The bent among scholars seems to me that of knowing more than can be known; they seem to be certain—where I find myself tantalized by uncertainties. Scholars very often seem to consider themselves able to solve problems which, perversely, remain continuing enigmas to me.[11]

Sandmel points to many areas in New Testament scholarship where the possibility-probability spectrum has been shifted so that

it lines up probability-certainty, and as we consider the current state
of New Testament study, we shall see Sandmel's critique, either
directly or indirectly, helping to nudge the spectrum back to where
it belongs. It is important to realize that Sandmel is not declaring
history to be totally arbitrary; we have knowledge of the past, but
we have to be clear what kind of knowledge it is. "What I have
stressed is the limitation on our knowledge, or rather, the limitation
on our *precise* knowledge."[12] There may be various reasons we
would like our knowledge to be more precise; it is salutary to notice
that Sandmel, who has no Christian ax to grind, has found his
practical experience as a historian steadily diminishing the realm of
"precise knowledge."

B. Jesus Under the Microscope

It is not far wrong to say that the phrase "historical criticism of
the New Testament" suggests to most people the investigation of
the Gospels and the assessment of the evidence for the life and
teaching of Jesus. The attention given to Jesus in the nineteenth
century is astonishing: Albert Schweitzer had more than 250 books
piled around his desk as he wrote *The Quest of the Historical Jesus* and
those books were of course drawing on others. In our own century
the development of new techniques of investigation, most notably
form criticism (to be discussed in some detail in Chapter 6), has
further intensified the historical analysis of the Gospels. Doctoral
dissertations devoted to single paragraphs, or single sentences, or
even isolated words, have proliferated.

The focusing of so much attention on Jesus and the Gospels
has, to be sure, resulted in fresh and penetrating insights, but
another result has not been so fortunate. The capacity of historical investigation to give us a comprehensive (but not precise)
knowledge has been diminished. There is a widespread opinion
that "historical" means "destructive" or "reductionist." And the
effect is not simply on popular attitudes. New Testament scholars themselves have practiced the high-powered focusing of
their historical microscope for such a long time that they can
slip right past the point at which something might be seen in
perspective. For example, at a recent symposium on the relationships among the Gospels, a classical historian remarked that he
had studied carefully the second-century evidence for the tradi-

tion that Mark's Gospel reflects directly the reminiscences of Peter, and had concluded that he would be thoroughly delighted to find such solid evidence for some other ancient historical tradition; hence he was puzzled that nearly all New Testament scholars treat that tradition about Mark's Gospel with severe skepticism.[13]

There are many signs that the historical investigation of the New Testament is operating increasingly with a wide-angle lens. As will become clear in Chapter 6, this has the unexpected result of helping to get Jesus himself in clearer focus. It has other unexpected results, too: the relationship between Jesus and Paul becomes more complex (and closer), through a new understanding of the nature of the very earliest Christian community; old distinctions within Jewish and Hellenistic society that could be utilized by earlier scholarship as though they were established facts are blurring almost beyond recognition; insistence that Christianity is a religion, against certain recent theologically motivated efforts to put it in some other category, has opened the way to a new appreciation of the rich meaning of the sacramental life portrayed in the New Testament. These and other developments will be the substance of succeeding chapters; they all reflect, and to some extent depend on, a reduction in the intensity of attention paid to the figure of Jesus, an intensity that actually distorted the historical enterprise as applied to the New Testament.

C. "So Much the Worse for the Facts"

The philosopher G. W. F. Hegel, whose thought dominated German intellectual life for much of the nineteenth century, is reported to have said, when asked what he did when he found historical facts not squaring with his theory of history, "So much the worse for the facts."[14] In the light of such philosophical imperialism, it is easy to see the merit of Ranke's protest, but the relationship of "the facts" to historical theory is highly intricate. However, it is important to say, or perhaps even to reiterate, that one must not opt for a particular theory of history before patiently sorting through the evidence.

It is not widely understood that historians are severely limited, in the story they can legitimately tell, by the chances of the preser-

vation of documents. Anyone whose acquaintance with history con-
sists mainly of high school or college "introductory textbooks" may
have little idea of the kind of work that underlies what is said in such
survey accounts. The "flesh and blood" with which the "dry bones"
of the past are clothed in history books is not just any flesh and
blood, but the bones with which the historian works—chronicles,
letters, diaries, official papers, literary writings, paintings, statistics
(when they are available), tombstones, buildings, and dozens of
other bits and pieces littering the shore of the past—are initially
"very dry," and are very, very far from providing a complete
skeleton of any period. As Sandmel insists, it is incumbent upon the
careful historian to admit how sketchy our knowledge is.

One whose days are spent sorting through the materials of the
past and trying to make sense of them is likely to be suspicious of
any theory that claims to account for everything. One may be
tempted on occasion to agree with the book of Ecclesiastes and say
that there is nothing new under the sun, that everything happens
over and over again in a wearying and never-ending cycle, but
further work with the documents will usually make it clear that
one's agreement with Ecclesiastes was more a product of a particularly low mood than of an insight into history. The magnificent
architecture of Hegel's scheme, in which Absolute Spirit comes to
full self-consciousness in the ever-upward movement of history, is
inspiring, but despite Hegel's dismissing the facts, the failure of the
evidence to confirm the theory hardly encourages confidence in the
theory's explanatory power. Marx's analysis of history, which is
Hegel's analysis turned around (or, as Marx himself said, Hegel's
analysis set on its feet), is subject to so many qualifications, even
among committed Marxists, that the historian is wary of adopting
a Marxist stance.

The opposite extreme is not attractive either. We might be
tempted to characterize history as "just one damn thing after another." There are historical sources known as chronicles, which set
out to do little more than record "one damn thing after another."
We can usually detect some sort of principle of selecting and ordering at work in ancient chronicles, but the writing of history involves
something more self-conscious and artistic than that. The historian
attempts to tell a story, one that is faithful to the evidence and one

that may make one or more points about the nature of human experience.

Any points of that sort will of course reflect something of the historian's assumptions, but those assumptions need not be embedded in a full-blown theory of history. A midway position, between vast schemes on the one hand and chronicle on the other hand, is suggested by a book known more for its humor than for its scholarship: *1066 and All That,* a hilarious spoof of English historians and their writings. What is history? the book asks, and answers: "It is what you can remember."[15] The authors mean to refer mainly to the situation of an examination, in which for the student the only practical meaning of history is what can be remembered in the next hour or two. But the definition suggests a profound insight: that the work of the historian is an extension of the human faculty of *remembering.*

We all know that our memory has in it more than we are conscious of at any one time (and often less than we would wish at a particular time), that our memories play tricks on us, that memory is a dynamic combination of treasure house and carnival fun house, with spooks and distorting mirrors. Because memory is not easily subject to classification into neat categories, because memory is, in the imagery of Augustine, a great deep,[16] the historian who sees the truth in "history is what you can remember" will shy away from using ready-made charts of the great deep.

D. Working Assumptions

In the course of reflecting on this process of remembering, I have developed several working assumptions, which do not constitute a "philosophy of history" but which help to shape the conclusions to which I come. Some of these assumptions are at odds with views widely held among New Testament scholars.

1. The differences between the past and the present should not be exaggerated. Of course we do not live in the first century A.D., and there is some warrant for speaking of that period as "another world." But there is an untested assumption in the following statement by Paul J. Achtemeier, a statement that sums up what has become a starting point for much twentieth-century study of the New Testament. Achtemeier is characterizing the different kinds of

contact between an interpreter and a text; some sort of contact is
essential if any transference of meaning from the text to the interpreter is to take place.

> The contact may be as tenuous as simply a knowledge of the language
> in which a text is written, or it may be so total as to include the
> interpreter's whole being. This latter is the case, for example, when
> we read a local newspaper. We do not raise the question of how
> understanding is possible in that situation. We simply understand it,
> because we share the same world with it. Our contact is total. When
> such total immersion in the same linguistic and cultural world is
> lacking, however, the problem arises whether or not the text is under-
> stood. Then the question must be raised about the kind of contact
> between us and this ancient text, as in the case of the Bible, which
> makes understanding possible.[17]

No one could doubt there are problems in transferring meaning
over a space of twenty centuries. What one can doubt is that "our
contact is total" when we read the local paper. Every day the paper
tells about situations at home and abroad that I can scarcely claim
to "understand." Only by the greatest stretch of my imagination
can I even faintly grasp the meaning of a suicide in a prison or a
riot in a ghetto or a corporate decision to take over another company. Women in our society are telling us men that we have been
deluded by our assumption that we understand their world when
we treat it as part of our world. And anyone who takes the trouble
to read more than one local paper is quickly brought face up against
the difficulty of interpreting contemporary texts.

There is no particular comfort for the interpreter of ancient texts
in recognizing that the present may be comparably difficult to understand, but the student of the New Testament should not be
overwhelmed by confident declarations that bridging the gap between that ancient text and "modern persons" is a task different in
kind from the general human endeavor of making sense. It is at
least theoretically possible that we could come to "know" and
"understand" the first-century world of the New Testament better
than we "know" and "understand" our own neighbors.

2. Historical thinking is not so foreign to most people as they
believe it is. It follows from the definition of historical thinking as
a special, and expanded, form of remembering that anyone who has
reported to husband or wife on the day's activities, or who has

"read between the lines" of a letter, or who has made a judgment about the bias in an editorial, has engaged in the activity of the historian, if only in a rudimentary way. The distinction between "yesterday" and "antiquity" is great, but it is not absolute; the story the historian tells of the first century and the story you tell of what happened last week have more in common as human activities than most of us suspect.

Recognition of this similarity can influence one's reading of the past. For instance, I do not find in persons I know (including myself) the kind of thoroughgoing consistency that some interpreters of the past demand of people long since dead. If letters attributed to Paul say contradictory things, my tendency is to see this not as a direct confrontation requiring a solution in the form, "Which letter is Paul's and which is not?" but rather to wonder, "What else would one expect?" Of course one must not hope to mix, bake, ice, have, and eat one's cake all at the same time, and there are often choices that must be made; but attention to the similarities between regular human thinking and historical thinking makes me skeptical when it is announced that "these evidences cannot be reconciled."

3. Increasing acquaintance usually leads to awareness of complexity. This is simply a generalized formulation of the experience reported by Samuel Sandmel, but it has a corollary in much everyday human interaction. Colleagues, students, friends, relatives, children—all can throw us off guard, for just when we think we have them figured out, they will often reveal some hitherto hidden complexity in themselves, and a whole new scheme of thought is necessary to account for what we now know.

The careful interpreter of an ancient text is always discovering new significances, nuances previously undetected, unrecognized connections. And when new evidence is suddenly made available, as we shall see in the case of two major manuscript discoveries of this century (the Dead Sea Scrolls, in Chapter 4, and the Gnostic library at Nag Hammadi in Egypt, in Chapter 5), it usually leaves in its wake more new questions and uncertainties than solved problems.

Reflecting on the intricate interlacing of many elements in my own life and in that of persons I know, I am predisposed in favor of those scholars who detect complexity in the New Testament. For instance, recent studies that set out a variety of *kērygmata* (*kērygma,* plural *kērygmata,* is the technical Greek term for preaching or proclamation), as against the presumption that there was only one original *kērygma,* seem to me plausible. We shall deal, especially in Chapter 6, with this changing direction in the understanding of early Christian preaching; a new awareness of the variety in what early Christians believed about Jesus opens the way to theological reflections that had been ruled out by the predominant view of the past thirty or forty years, a view that judged all other New Testament evidence in terms of what was singled out as the authentic kerygma. In the light of that one, everything else was seen as more or less a distortion.

4. As many things happen by accident as by design, and designs themselves often get fouled up. This may seem so obvious as not to need saying, but just as historians often portray the dead as more consistent than the living, so do they often attribute to the dead a deliberateness and degree of control over events that no one we know could hope to have.

Recognition of the power of accident and the weakness of design is especially important when one begins to think about the apostle Paul. We know him extremely well; there is hardly anyone in antiquity who reveals as much of a personal sort. And yet that very openness of Paul tempts us to forget how fierce a partisan he was and how many opponents he had, who themselves had their own arguments which are lost to us. Everybody "knows" that Paul's letters were "occasional pieces," but it is very easy to slip into assuming a kind of deliberateness in their composition entirely out of character with their "occasional" nature.

5. We are limited in the story we can tell not only by the somewhat haphazard collection of materials at our disposal but also by the fact that certain viewpoints are not represented at all. There is an extraordinary interest currently in the question of the New Testament's attitude toward women. But no matter what new insights are gained by studying Paul's language and Jesus' actions, it remains a fact that the sources are all (as far as we know) written by men.

It is clear that women played a significant, maybe even dominant, role in the early Christian community, but it remains true that we have no account *from them* of the meaning of their Christian experience. The historian can say that first-century Roman society did not encourage literary production by women, certainly not by the class of women who were active in the Christian movement. But the historian should also recognize the limit to the reconstructed story, and not forget that what we call "the early Christian attitude toward women" is in fact derived from the writings of men. We do not know the attitude of early Christian women toward Christianity, or toward early Christian men, or toward themselves as Christians. And men today, who are learning (or should be learning) that women are challenging fundamentally our portrayal of their attitudes, thoughts, desires, ambitions, ought to be wary of assuming that what the Gospel of Luke, for instance, tells us about early Christian women can be taken at anywhere near face value.

In summary: historical thinking is both more familiar and more strange than we suppose it is. It is part of the common human activity of remembering, and partakes of the elusive "now you see it, now you don't" quality of our memory. As soon as we think the past is dead and gone, a new interpretation comes along to bring it back to life. The historical approach to any subject, including the New Testament, is bound to frustrate those who want precise knowledge and absolute answers. Thinking historically about the New Testament will not do for anyone who wants an immediate, direct answer to the question, "How can I apply this or that New Testament passage to my life today?" The chief effect of current New Testament study is the creation of an exploratory, tentative, questing frame of mind, prepared for surprises and capable of a kind of growth that is stifled when answers are too swift and neat.

CHAPTER THREE

QUESTIONS
ANCIENT AND MODERN

There are three general questions that anyone who would try to understand the New Testament must deal with one way or another. These were burning issues in the first centuries of the church's history, and they are at the center of scholarly concern today:

1. The relationship of Christianity to Judaism, or "The Question of Continuity and Discontinuity"

2. The character of the apostolic age, or "The Question of Diversity and Unity"

3. The nature of biblical language, or "The Question of Text and Meaning"

Each of these questions is a name for a set of many questions, and clearly the sets themselves have areas of intersection. The purpose of this chapter is to have us begin to think historically about these questions which were alive in the formative Christian centuries, and which not only have not died but have not even faded away. These three questions will weave in and out of our analysis in subsequent chapters, and will provide the main linkages between the various subjects discussed.

I. The Question of Continuity and Discontinuity

Those who wrote the books of the New Testament had no New Testament. It might be thought quite unnecessary to remind anyone of so obvious a fact, but even New Testament scholars can forget that the first two or three generations of Christians had little by way of their own literature, or can at least forget how much difference having such a literature at a later stage meant. It is quite impossible for one to grasp what is going on in the New Testament

unless one has taken with full seriousness the early Christian identification of the Hebrew Scriptures, what we know as the Old
Testament, as the word of God. There can be no sharper break with
early Christian belief and practice than the neglect into which the
Old Testament has fallen in many churches today. But, as we shall
now see, such neglect has a long heritage.

A. The Answer of Discontinuity

We tend to think of the apostle Paul as a single-minded man. He
is almost a Hamlet of indecision, however, compared to a second-
century follower of his, Marcion, who claimed that Paul alone, with
his distinction between gospel and law, recognized the radical new-
ness of the message Jesus came to bring. If there were passages in
Paul's letters that said complimentary things about Israel, that was
no problem; after all, Paul himself had complained of "Judaizing"
opponents, and surely they could have tampered with the manu-
scripts of his letters, inserting their own views and thus making the
apostle speak their words. The Gospels, according to Marcion,
were likewise faulty guides to the truth, for they reflected the
opinions of inept followers of Jesus who thought he was the fulfillment of Jewish hopes for a Messiah. Luke's Gospel, supposedly
written by a companion of Paul, had some claim on Marcion's
attention; its author had at least been in touch with one who had
seen the light.

Using a critical method governed by a ruthless logic, Marcion
purged Paul's letters and Luke's Gospel of all "taint" of Judaism,
and established these "purified" texts as the authoritative norm for
the large number of communities around the Roman world that
acknowledged him as their leader. Marcion's movement was no
marginal, splinter group; it may well be that in the middle of the
second century half the people in the Empire who would have
identified themselves as Christians were adherents of Marcion.[1]

Marcion claimed that Jesus was an emissary from a hitherto totally unknown God. The Jewish Scriptures told about the creator
god, whose character was presented in those books as at best "judicial" or "judgmental," and at worst as genuinely vindictive: "the
author of evils, a lover of war, inconstant in judgment, and contrary
to himself."[2] Jesus appears suddenly, unannounced and unanticipated, to reveal the true God, the God of love. Those who

understood the truth would engage in unremitting warfare against the lord of creation and all his servants, including those who would try to trap Jesus in the net of covenant and law.

Marcion's jettisoning of the Old Testament and of any Christian documents that tied Christianity to the traditions of Israel had an almost irresistible appeal to people who liked neat solutions to knotty problems. For Marcion, the demonstrable historical continuity between Israel and the church was the result of a terrible mistake, a failure on the part of most of Jesus' followers to understand what he was doing. Just as Jesus had come to rescue the children of the true God from the clutches of the creator, so Marcion had the task of rescuing the church from the clutches of that creator's servants. The intricate spiritual, intellectual, and social problem of figuring out what it meant to be a member of a "new" people while living in continuity with the people "chosen" two millennia before, the problem that Paul in Romans (11:16–24) had sought to solve with the imagery of horticultural grafting, was one from which Marcion sprung you free: there was simply no connection whatever between the old and the new.

The appeal of Marcion is not a relic of the past. Traces of his attitude can be found even at the scholarly level today, when it is suggested that the only statements of Jesus that can be treated as surely authentic are those which cannot be paralleled in some rabbinic or other Jewish writing. In defense of this suggestion it could of course be said that it is only a device for determining what is *surely* authentic, without prejudicing the case that other statements *may* be authentic. In practice, however, such distinctions subtly, and almost inevitably, lead to a portrayal of Jesus as more sharply at odds with his own Jewishness than is historically plausible.[3]

At the popular level there are evidences of lingering Marcionism even more damaging to the Christian community than are the traces to be found in scholarship. When a sharp line is drawn, as it so often is in sermons and discussions, between the "God of wrath" of the Old Testament and the "God of love" of the New Testament, the spirit of Marcion is close at hand. There are many reasons for the continuing appeal of "the answer of discontinuity," some of them calling for analysis of the social and psychological sources of anti-Semitism. For purposes of our study, there are two main explanations.

First, people simply do not pay very close attention to the texts. It is hard to imagine a more profound commentary on the definition of God as love than the prophecy of Hosea, and many a student is perplexed on first encountering the reason Jesus gives for speaking in parables (Mark 4:11–12; Matt. 13:13; Luke 8:10): it is so that people will not understand, because if they did, they might turn and be forgiven. The portrayal of God in *both* the Old Testament *and* the New Testament is highly complex.

Second, the "God of love" extracted and abstracted from the New Testament is particularly congenial to persons at the upper end of the social and economic scale. No note sounds louder and clearer through the movement of liberation theology than the insistence that the "God of wrath," the "just God" of the Old Testament be restored to Christian thought. The theme of judgment is certainly present in the New Testament too, but today the oppressed are interpreting judgment there in the light of the presentation of judgment in the Old Testament, and in so doing they are reminding us that when Jesus referred to his Father, he was referring to the God of the Old Testament. Marcion's theory of discontinuity is especially appealing to the comfortable, and it is perhaps not beside the point to note that Marcion was extraordinarily wealthy.[4]

B. The Answer of Continuity

There was one major barrier to complete confidence in the claim of continuity between Judaism and Christianity: the vast majority of Jews rejected the claim. That was for Paul a source of intense anguish—"I could wish that I myself were accursed and cut off from Christ for the sake of my brethren, my kindred by race" (Rom. 9:3). For subsequent generations it was a problem with increasingly formal and decreasingly personal dimensions, but the debate over rights to the Hebrew Scriptures could not be evaded.

The history of Christianity in the first and second centuries is in large measure the story of attempts to establish and explain the continuity between Israel and the church, and here we can only sketch the main outlines of the development. Basically there were three answers: that of Jewish-Christianity; that of messianic interpretation; and that of allegory.

1. Jewish-Christianity

In one of history's more striking ironies, the form of Christian belief and practice with the most plausible claim to be in the tradition of the first followers of Jesus was, by the end of the second century, being declared heretical by persons speaking on behalf of the largest and most powerful churches. The Jewish-Christians, themselves a diverse lot, had not been conscious of a decisive rupture with the Jewish past, or even with the Jewish present. There was not for them, as there was in the Gentile mission, need for a cultural translation of the gospel; the story of Jesus was the story of things that had happened in places and contexts with which they were familiar. They literally walked every day where Jesus had walked and talked in days of not so very long ago.[5]

If the Romans had not decisively put down successive Jewish revolts between A.D. 66 and 135, disrupting all social and religious patterns in Palestine, the Jewish-Christian community might have remained strong enough to survive as viable testimony to the possibility of a practical blending of Judaism and Christianity. In the middle of the second century Justin Martyr, a Christian teacher in Rome, was willing to consider that those who "hope on this Christ of ours" while continuing to follow the regulations of the Jewish law must be treated as "of one family and as brothers," as long as they did not try to force other Christians to follow the same rules. But Justin admits that not all Christians agree with him, and it was not to be long before his tolerant attitude would be forgotten.[6]

2. Messianic Interpretation

Early Christians found predictions of the Messiah all over the Old Testament, and if Jews did not see the texts in that way, the Christians had a ready answer: the Jews were simply obstinate and hardhearted, as ancient prophets said they were and predicted that they would continue to be. Even the generous-spirited Justin was not above accusing the Jews of having tampered with the Hebrew text of the Old Testament so they could counter the claims that Christians were making on the basis of the Greek translation.

Down even to minute details the Scriptures were made to yield up direct testimony to Jesus. For instance, the belligerently antiJewish Letter of Barnabas, dating from the early second century, insists that Abraham's 318 warriors in Genesis 14 are a prophecy of the Christian gospel, since the figures for 318 *in Greek* are the letters *IHT*, the *IH* being the first two letters of the name "Jesus" and the *T* being a clear reference to the shape of the cross.[7]

Some Christians were content to say that the Jews had been basically faithful to God's call until they turned against Jesus, and it was only in recent times that the hearts of the people had been hardened so that they could not understand their holy book. Others declared that the Israelites were inveterate apostates, that it was only by some miracle that any truth had been preserved among them at all, and the church, the New Israel, was attached to a very thin line of tradition that stretched back through a few lonely and persecuted prophets to Abraham. If the messianic expectation is virtually severed from the full historical reality of ancient Israel, then there is little besides habit or inertia to keep one from falling into Marcion's camp, since, according to this view of messianism, what the Jews expected and what actually came were different to a degree that amounts to a difference in kind. The marginal theological benefit gained by holding on to the Old Testament is outweighed by the psychological and social liberation to be gained by divorce between the Testaments. The messianic interpretation as a method of explaining and maintaining continuity is, in short, unstable.

Despite the inherent instability of messianic interpretation, it still has a good deal of practical effect among Christians who tend to single out for special Christian attention those passages of the Old Testament which, with more or less plausibility, are thought to be predictions of the Messiah. There is a major force working against this tendency in many churches today. The movement of liturgical renewal gives prominent place to cycles of Scripture readings in worship, and in the course of several years faithful attenders of services will hear virtually the entire Bible read publicly. As a result, Christians who go to church regularly may find themselves less and less content with a superficially "Christian" reading of the Old Testament.

3. Allegory

With the historical demolition of Jewish-Christianity and the inherent instability of the messianic interpretation, it remained for the principles and practices of allegorical interpretation to keep the church's grasp fixed on the Old Testament—a document which, despite ambivalence and difficulties, the church seemed determined to retain as a Christian book.

Paul himself, by using allegory in his treatment of the Old Testament, had sanctioned the method. When he wrote to the Galatians (4:24) that Hagar the slave and Sarah the wife, by each of whom Abraham had sons, were "an allegory: these women are two covenants," he opened the way to discoveries of hidden messages everywhere in Scripture. The interpreter was free to assume that whenever the Bible talks about something, it is really talking about something else.

The lifework of Origen (A.D. 185–254), a Christian teacher of Alexandria, was the attempt to find meanings in, around, and above the text of Scripture. It was Origen who first undertook systematically to comment upon all the books of the Bible, both Old and New Testament, and to do justice to the Old Testament he went to the rabbis and learned Hebrew. The continuity between the Old Israel and the New Israel was for Origen a given fact: it had been decided by the church in the struggle against Marcion, and Origen endeavored above all to be faithful to the church, though he had the misfortune to be declared a heretic (at least in part for things he never said) three centuries after his death. The whole effort of perhaps the most productive scholarly life a Christian has ever lived was devoted to working out the implications of the continuity between the Testaments and between the communities that produced them.[8]

Origen's energetic, speculative mind was not content with the mechanical application of any one method to the interpretation of texts. He was concerned to think through critical theory as well as to practice criticism, and he refined into a useful tool the principle that every text of Scripture has a hidden meaning, while some, indeed most, have a literal meaning as well. And there was flexibility in allegorical theory. Augustine, who looms as large in the Latin Christian tradition as Origen does in the Greek, held a view strikingly different from Origen's. "I do not censure those who have succeeded in carving out a spiritual meaning from each and every event in the narrative, always provided that they have maintained its original basis of historical truth."[9]

As a device for maintaining continuity between the Old Israel and the New Israel the allegorical method was of course ideal, and served, in its various forms, to keep Christians aware of the connections, or at least of the need for connections. If you read in Joshua (15:63) that "the Jebusites dwell with the children of Judah in Jerusalem unto this day," you need not engage in the hopeless task of deriving spiritual instruction from the literal sense; rather, "as in the Gospel the tares are suffered to grow together with the wheat, in like fashion also here in Jerusalem, *that is,* in the church, there are some Jebusites, persons who live a debased and unsatisfactory life, who in faith, in deeds, in all their conversation, have gone astray."[10] But if the method solved the problem of connections between the Testaments, it threatened to sever another connection: too liberal a use of "that is" to designate the *true* meaning of a passage would cut the Bible loose from history altogether.

Origen recognized the peril, and late in his life he found it necessary to insist that he believed that the Evangelists—Matthew, Mark, Luke, John—had used straightforward narrative prose in recounting the story of Jesus. They were telling about things that had happened.[11] The trouble with allegory is that allegorists want to pick and choose the applications of their method, and this arbitrariness makes allegorical interpretation, like the messianic interpretation, fundamentally unstable.

It is highly unlikely that there is anyone today practicing allegorical interpretation in quite the way Origen did it, although as we shall see in Chapters 9 and 11 there are several current ways of treating the Bible as a code book of secret meanings. More widespread is a form of interpretation that has certain affinities with allegory, although at first glance it appears quite different.

When the first question we put to a text is, "What does this say to me here and now?" we are in effect making the text an allegory of our own experience. We read into (or out of) the text meanings that are already part of us; the text may appear to be about people who lived in Galilee nearly two thousand years ago, but what it is *really* about is *my* experience. What the text might have meant to different people in different times, and how that meaning might open up possibilities of growth for us, is of secondary interest or no interest at all. We are not so far removed from the tradition of allegorical interpretation as we might have thought we were.

C. The Current Search for Connections

Reginald Fuller's account of "The New Testament in Current Study," of the year 1960, was dominated by the figure of Rudolf Bultmann. At that time Bultmann's students had already developed several lines of criticism of their teacher, but it was still true that New Testament study could be mapped most economically by indicating where scholars stood in relation to the tradition centered in Bultmann. In the nearly two decades since Fuller's lectures a great deal has happened. Divergencies among Bultmann's students have become increasingly pronounced. Bultmann himself has recently died, having lived into his nineties. Most significant in altering the scene from 1960, however, is the reemergence of questions about New Testament interpretation that were shunted aside by the Bultmann program. One of these is the question of the continuity between Judaism and Christianity.

Bultmann's theology, which concentrates on what it means to be a historical being but neglects our experience of living in a historical tradition, diverted attention from Christianity's openness to the past, and directed attention to the individual Christian's openness to the future. A Christian need not define herself or himself in relation to Judaism, or even to traditional Christianity; the only question that matters is how one responds to God's radical call to obedience in each concrete moment.

In addition to this theoretical breakaway from concern for the connections, there was also Bultmann's own reconstruction of *Primitive Christianity in Its Contemporary Setting,* in which he argued that a redeemer myth was the central motif in earliest Christianity. This myth, according to Bultmann, had various Oriental, mostly Iranian, roots, but had little or nothing to do with traditional Jewish attitudes and beliefs.[12] Very few New Testament scholars have been willing to go all the way with Bultmann in his reconstructed pre-Christian "heavenly redeemer myth," but he did establish an expectation that the decisive formative influences on Christianity would be found outside the Jewish context.

There are many reasons for the new interest in the connections between Judaism and Christianity. The discovery of the Dead Sea Scrolls has certainly played a part, by throwing open the whole question of the varieties of Judaism at the time of the emergence of Christianity. Some connections (though faint) are once again being detected in that character who for so long was thought to have been safely laid to rest, the historical Jesus. The rapid development of Jewish self-consciousness following the Nazi holocaust, the establishment of the State of Israel, and the Six Day War of 1967, have helped to create a whole new context in which Christians cannot easily get away with disregard of the continuity/discontinuity question.

The effect of the new context is apparent both in the popular realm, where dialogue between Jewish and Christian groups is becoming more frequent, and in the academic realm, where more and more New Testament scholars are finding themselves working closely with Jewish scholars of Judaism, and not simply with Christian scholars of the Old Testament. Finally, and most generally, the recovery of interest in the ancient question of continuity and discontinuity reflects a better application of historical thinking to their subject by New Testament scholars. The almost total abstraction of the formative Christian events and message from their Jewish context, an abstraction that has characterized much New Testament study in recent decades, is simply unlike what most historians do when they tell the story of the past.

The fact that New Testament scholarship is turning its attention to Judaism can be of major importance for an understanding of the New Testament itself, and beyond that, for Christian theology. New Testament scholars may come to believe that the Old Testament demands far more attention than they have given it, and we may move away from a time dominated by outlines of "the Scriptural basis for Christian theology" that make not a single reference to the Old Testament.[13]

As we shall see in the next chapter, the Judaism to which New Testament scholars are turning their attention is now perceived as much more complicated than earlier opinion held it to be. Distinctions that used to make classification easy are blurring almost beyond recognition. A simple dichotomy of "Jewish or Greek" will hardly do for anything anymore, and the more finely honed "Palestinian-Jewish" and "Hellenistic-Jewish" and "Gnostic" and "Greek-philosophical" and "Oriental mystery" are themselves becoming increasingly chipped and dulled as they are used to carve up the evidence. An appreciation of the early Christian use of the Hebrew Scriptures is only part of the result of this new direction of New Testament study, for while Judaism was already, in practical terms at least, a "religion of a Book," the Book, as Sandmel has forcefully insisted, was already subject to a bewildering variety of interpretations.[14]

II. THE QUESTION OF DIVERSITY AND UNITY

Even a quick reading of Paul's letters makes it clear that not all Christians in the apostolic age agreed on all major points of belief and practice. The arguments were fierce, and the amount of apostolic authority persons possessed usually amounted to the sum of apostolic authority that others were willing to grant to them. The book of Acts is a portrayal of the first Christian generation from a later vantage point, and in Acts we can see already the picture of a harmonious "golden age" of the earliest church well on the way to formation. But the New Testament itself shows us Christians who were at sharp odds over the very fundamentals of the faith.

During most of the second century the question of a specifically Christian Scripture was very much an open one. Writings, many of them under the names of apostles, and presenting virtually every conceivable viewpoint, were circulating, and an appeal to "Christian texts" to settle a dispute would have resulted in hopeless confusion. It may be that Marcion forced the issue by publishing his edition of Luke's Gospel and Paul's letters; it is often said, in any case, that Marcion produced the first "canon" (that is, a restricted body of writings as the authoritative documents of the faith—the word "canon" is the Greek term for "rule" or "measure" or "standard"), though few subjects are more obscure in their details than the process by which what we know as the New Testament canon of twenty-seven books developed. But we can say that before the New Testament was assembled and generally accepted toward the end of the second century, the problem of the diversity of the apostolic age was a live and ever-present issue. The question of diversity and unity in the New Testament, a question that poses itself squarely to New Testament interpreters today, is as old as the church itself.[15]

A. Paul and the Jerusalem Church

One important influence in the shaping of early Christian theology is something that did not happen. The New Testament strongly suggests that most Christians in the first generation believed Christ would return in their lifetime, and that his return would constitute the establishment of the kingdom of God. The texts, particularly Paul's letters and the Gospel of John, contain evidence of the effort to think through the implications of the delay of the Return.

To the historian of early Christianity there is another nonhappening that is in historical terms as puzzling as is the nonreturn of Christ in theological terms: the striking neglect of Paul's writings by most second-century Christians. The New Testament book known as 2 Peter, which probably dates from the middle of the second century, says that "there are some things" in Paul's letters "hard to understand, which the ignorant and unstable twist to their own destruction, as they do the other scriptures" (3:16). Perhaps the specific issues Paul dealt with were different enough from those of the second century to make his letters appear irrelevant to people a hundred years later, people who were trying to carve out a place for the church in a world that stubbornly continued to exist despite earlier Christian predictions of its imminent end.

Marcion's drastic use of Paul made the apostle suspect, and the appeal made by many Gnostics (persons who, in ways more or less like Marcion, distinguished the God of redemption from the god of creation) to Paul's distinction between spiritual milk for babes in the faith and spiritual solid food for those (like themselves) who were mature (1 Cor. 3:2) did not help his reputation either.[16] In any case, whatever the reasons for the neglect or avoidance of Paul, if the New Testament had been lost and we could reconstruct it only from references to it in second-century writings, Paul would not have anything like the prominence he has in the New Testament as we know it.

It is hard for us to imagine what it would be like to treat Paul as peripheral to the main Christian message. The apostle has triggered many of the decisive revolutions in Christian theological history: Augustine, Luther, Kierkegaard, Barth—all heard God speaking to them directly through the words of Paul. Each insisted that it was Paul who really taught him to know Christ, but we can wonder whether Paul taught them to know Christ the way Peter and James and John knew Christ. That question loomed large in the nineteenth and early twentieth centuries. One writer presented Jesus as an Essene monk who becomes temporarily a wandering preacher, and survives the crucifixion. He returns to the monastery and is discovered some twenty years later by Paul, who has in the meantime constructed a religion of resurrection and redemption on the basis of stories about Jesus. Paul, sensing the threat posed by Jesus to Christianity, kills him.[17]

In the past decade the understanding of Paul has taken a dramatic turn. Scholars have begun to look very carefully at what Paul says about his opponents, and there is a growing consensus that the "Judaizers" who dogged his heels, trying to undo his missionary work, were not emissaries from the Jerusalem church, but rather were local Christian troublemakers, very likely not even converts from Judaism. The implications of this for the understanding of diversity and unity in the apostolic age are far-reaching. Paul's claim that what he preaches is essentially congruent with the gospel of the Jerusalem church appears more plausible and less a case of special pleading. The portrayal of basically amicable relations between Paul and the Jerusalem "pillars" in Acts becomes less of a historical romance. In short, it begins to appear that modern critical scholarship is moving toward what might be called a more conservative view of unity in the apostolic church than was possible even in the second century, when the identity of Paul's opponents had already faded from the church's consciousness.

B. Discrepancies Among the Gospels

At the end of the second century Bishop Irenaeus of Lyons (in what is today southeastern France), who has clearly been challenged to justify the church's use of four Gospels—no more and no less—answers the challenge in the following way:

> The Gospels could not possibly be either more or less in number than they are. Since there are four zones of the world in which we live, and four principal winds, while the church is spread over all the earth, and the pillar and foundation of the church is the gospel, and the

Spirit of life, it fittingly has four pillars, everywhere breathing out incorruption and revivifying persons. From this it is clear that the Word, the artificer of all things, he who sits upon the cherubim and sustains all things, being manifested to human beings, gave us the gospel, fourfold in form but held together by one Spirit.[18]

The argument is, from our point of view, rather strained, to say the least, but it tells us something important about our subject: that Christians were aware, already in the second century, of the differences in the Gospels—indeed, they recognized the sharpness of the differences to such an extent that they believed a special activity of the Holy Spirit was required to hold the four Gospels together.

Irenaeus clearly believes that Jesus planned that there would be four Gospels. Each Evangelist emphasizes a particular aspect of Jesus and his significance, although none of the Gospels, if properly understood, gives a warrant for the partial views of Jesus put forward by one or other of the Gnostic sects.[19] Irenaeus believed that each Evangelist was working out a plan determined by Jesus, but he believed further that Jesus' plan included the peculiar role of each Evangelist as a theologian. And indeed, Irenaeus' view is a striking anticipation of a "discovery" that has shaped all study of the Gospels in the last hundred years: the recognition that the Evangelists are *primarily* theologians, not concerned to present biographies of Jesus, but to drive home theological claims about him.

Attention to the discrepancies among the Gospels was quite common among early Christian writers. Both pagan critics and puzzled church members were disturbed by the inconsistencies, and a pastoral theologian of the stature of Augustine devoted much effort to demonstrating that the Evangelists were really telling the same story.[20] While it is likely that many Christians avoided the problem by choosing whichever Gospel they found most congenial and disregarding the rest, most Christians in antiquity and even today have probably functioned with a kind of rule-of-thumb "harmony of the Gospels," in which, for example, both the shepherds (from Luke) and the wise men (from Matthew) come to the stable, the difference between Matthew's "Blessed are the poor in spirit" and Luke's "Blessed are you poor" is overlooked, and the question of whether it was the Last Supper (Matthew, Mark, Luke) or the crucifixion (John) that took place on the Passover never arises. A full-scale "harmony" was constructed at the end of the second century by Tatian, a Syrian Christian, and his work had wide-ranging influence for centuries through its translation into numerous languages. But one need not have heard of Tatian to recognize the appeal of his way of dealing with the Gospel discrepancies.

The differences among the Gospels, which Irenaeus saw as an asset in the fight against heretics in second-century Gaul, were, and have remained, a stumbling block to lay piety, and most people, almost inadvertently, have solved the problem by failing to notice it is there. Every year teachers of New Testament, particularly of undergraduates, see compelling evidence that scholarly interest in the interrelationships of the Gospels has remained isolated not only from the wider culture but also from the church. Each year we receive shock waves from our students, many of whom have been brought up in the church, as they work their way through Gospel Parallels. For some, there is the discovery that the Gospels are far more interesting documents than they had ever realized. For others, there is the disturbing suspicion that the church has not been honest with them, that it has hidden from them problems with which it cannot adequately deal.

Perhaps the church should take a cue from Irenaeus and be more open about the "fourness" of the Gospels through which the one Spirit works, instead of encouraging the view that the one Spirit is like an editor at *Time* or *Newsweek*, who takes the various reports of the staff in the field and works them up into the final, homogenized story. And anyone who has seen the movie *Z* will find the Gospel discrepancies not primarily a problem to be overcome, but rather an indirect testimony to the basic soundness of the Gospel tradition. In that movie, the prosecuting attorney knows his case is clinched when the suspects all tell *exactly* the same story—clearly they have got together and made it up.

C. Scripture and Tradition

Irenaeus' insistence on four Gospels was a declaration that unity must be sought on the far side of diversity, but it was also a sharp line drawn against further diversity. There were many other gospels, some claiming apostolic authorship, clamoring for the attention of the Christian world, and Irenaeus is saying that the four are sufficient as well as necessary. To sort out competing claims to the authentic tradition going back to Jesus and his first followers was a matter of extraordinary intellectual and political complexity. Indeed, the interplay of Scripture and tradition as the process by which unity was derived from, or imposed upon, the diversity of the apostolic age is probably the most intricate subject in the history of Christianity. Disputes about the nature of the process remain the deepest sources of division among the churches.[21]

The question of diversity and unity was for Christians of the second century *the* question about their own situation, and they answered it in several different ways. Some attributed the diversity to the work of Satan (and/or the machinations of proud and ambitious persons), while others said it was part of God's providential plan. But that there was diversity—extensive and pervasive diversity—no one could doubt.

And the question of diversity and unity is at the center of New Testament study today, with surprises for everyone. Paul and the Jerusalem church are now in league against the "Judaizers"; Luke, who among the Evangelists used to be considered a theologian of only moderate talents, is now being hailed as a major creative thinker, while the Gospel of John has been snatched from the Hellenistic orbit into the Palestinian one (but a Palestinian one itself far more deeply Hellenized than was previously thought); and on a critical issue which has divided them bitterly for four and a half centuries—the issue of Scripture and tradition—Catholic and Protestant scholars are sounding more and more the same.

III. The Question of Text and Meaning

We come now to the most fundamental of the three "Questions Ancient and Modern," and we come to it last in the series for a reason: New Testament scholars in recent decades have been preoccupied with this question in isolation to such an extent that they have failed to take continuity with Judaism and diversity in the apostolic age seriously enough in their interpretation of the New Testament. They have posed so starkly the "predicament" of "the modern person" to whom the meaning of the New Testament must be conveyed, they have drawn such a sharp contrast between the condition of persons today and their condition at any other time, that they have been compelled to concentrate almost all their efforts on the attempt to pry loose from the New Testament some word that is not tied to the particularity of Judaism or confused by partisan battles among the apostles.

It is the contention of this book that the new direction of New Testament study amounts to a more adequate and better balanced understanding of the three "Questions Ancient and Modern"— more precisely, the new direction amounts to the recognition that this third question of text and meaning cannot be properly dealt with until the first two have been worked through. The process cannot, of course, be neatly compartmentalized ("This week we do history, next week we figure out the meaning"), but for a long time the doing of history among New Testament scholars has been governed too exclusively by particular answers to the question of meaning, answers that have themselves been based on a rather restricted notion of who "the modern person" is.

A. The Problem in Antiquity

We have already seen instances of the ancient recognition of interpretation problems: 2 Peter says Paul is hard to understand; the tradition of allegorical reading of texts was an attempt to "make sense" of material that did not appear to "mean anything" if taken literally. Several recent studies have shown that the frontline combat between the Gnostics and their opponents was over the interpretation of texts; the first known commentary on a New Testament book is the Commentary on John by Heracleon, a Gnostic, and another Gnostic, Ptolemy, wrote a letter in which he provided a set of principles for interpreting the Old Testament, taking into account different kinds of literature within it. Indeed, the "heretics" were so good at biblical interpretation that Tertullian, a churchman of Carthage in North Africa late in the second century, warned his "orthodox" friends against trying to establish points of doctrine in argument by appealing to the interpretation of particular passages. In his experience, apparently, he had found such contests always ending in a draw.[22]

We have made reference already to Origen as a practitioner of allegorical interpretation. Origen believed that the biblical text itself compelled one to look for hidden meanings; he even went so far as to say that in order to convey some truths the Scripture wove into the story something which did not happen, occasionally something which could not happen, and occasionally something which might have happened but in fact did not. [And this applies not only to the Old Testament], but because he is the same Spirit and proceeds from the one God he has dealt in like manner with the Gospels and the writings of the apostles. For the history even of these is not everywhere pure, events being woven together in the bodily sense without having actually happened. . . . And the careful reader will detect thousands of . . . passages like this in the Gospels, which will convince him that events which did not take place at all are woven into the records of what literally did happen.

For Origen, some elements of Scripture were impossible "scientifically"—for example, Satan's literally showing Jesus all the kingdoms of the earth in a single view from the top of a mountain in the story of the temptation in the wilderness; while some were impossible "morally"—for example, some of the descriptions of divine wrath and apparent arbitrariness in the Old Testament. These difficulties were not for him hindrances to finding "meaning," but incentives to look for it.[23]

Augustine wrote an entire treatise on the interpretation of the Bible, and, significantly, he called the book *On Christian Teaching;* the title can even be translated *Christian Education.*[24] Interpreting texts is what educated people did in the ancient world, and Augustine is declaring that Christians can hold their own in educated discourse, both because they have a text full of meaning and because they can employ sophisticated techniques to get at and convey that meaning.

Biblical interpreters in the ancient and medieval church were of course influenced by philosophical assumptions, especially those of the Platonic tradition, that are hardly in vogue today. But even if we cannot read the texts the way they were read fifteen hundred or a thousand or even five hundred years ago, we can learn two important lessons from interpreters long since dead. First, they were aware of the "hermeneutical problem," that is, of the difficulties of determining the meaning of ancient texts (after all, the New Testament was already an "ancient text" to persons in the fourth and fifth centuries; and was Augustine's "world" much less different from the world of the apostles than is ours?), and while their solutions of the problem cannot be our own, their formulations of

the problem can be instructive. Second, most of the biblical interpreters of the ancient and medieval church were bishops and
monks, not professors. Bishops then were much more pastoral and
much less administrative than they are now, and monks have nearly
always had extensive contact with the society around them. The
acquaintance of bishops and monks with the "modern persons" of
their own time was intimate, and the relationship of the Bible to the
religious community was for them an assumption, not a proposition
requiring to be substantiated. It might turn out that the "strangeness" of the interpretations of many centuries ago is a result not
only of their different philosophical assumptions but also of their
being directed to a community of all sorts and conditions of persons, and not simply to students and professors.

B. "The New Hermeneutic"

A scheme of interpretation that has been influential in Germany
in the past couple of decades, and that is becoming increasingly
known in America, challenges the usefulness not only of interpretations from the Christian past but also of many parts of the New
Testament itself. "The new hermeneutic" insists that the New Testament is, in large part, a record of misunderstandings of the Christian faith.

This result follows from a starting point that has similarities both
to Bultmann's existentialist understanding of the human condition
and to a good deal of currently popular "human potential" psychology.[25] There are many steps in the analysis, and a brief summary
cannot indicate all the nuances in the approach, but the heart of the
matter is this: self-realization is the process by which we become
truly human; we realize our self authentically as we make decisions
about the future, which comes to us as open (though limited)
possibility; we are restricted in the range of our self-understanding
by the horizons of our language; the only use a past event can
possibly have for us depends on its being graspable within the horizons of our language experience, and on its providing clues to the
way we today can make decisions that will enhance, and not dimin-
ish, our realization of true selfhood. What this boils down to is the
following pointed question: Did Jesus demonstrate, under the conditions of historical existence, the possibility of true self-under-

standing? And that forces the even more pointed question: What was Jesus' self-understanding?

As we shall see in Chapter 6, the effort to get at "Jesus' self-understanding" is a feat that surpasses the abilities of the historian. And the proponents of "the new hermeneutic" are entirely forthright in admitting that for them, New Testament ways of speaking about Jesus and his significance that do not mesh with their understanding of the character of human existence are the result of failure on the part of many (even most) of Jesus' followers to comprehend his radical insight into the human situation.

As Paul J. Achtemeier, in *An Introduction to the New Hermeneutic,* has pointed out, these scholars have far more in mind than making sense of the New Testament. Hermeneutics is for them not a matter of making sense of texts; it is "the interpretation of human existence," and the method ranges into all areas of theology. One might say, then, that "the new hermeneutic" is not centrally a business of New Testament study; but there is no doubt that it has direct impact on an understanding of the New Testament when it claims sure knowledge of the "true" meaning of Jesus, and proceeds to dismiss everything else as distortion.[26]

The practitioners of "the new hermeneutic," with a thoroughness surpassing that of the church fathers of the fourth century, have determined, on the basis of their theory of human nature, what a redeemer *must have done,* and have then declared that that—and only that—is exactly what Jesus did. And as Achtemeier notes, there is an unresolved question at the heart of the new hermeneutic's appeal to Jesus' self-understanding, for basic to the theory's description of human existence is the irreducibly *bounded* nature of every human existence. There ought in theory to be no way Jesus could be of any use to us, for even if he showed the possibility of authentic self-understanding under the conditions of historical existence, those were the historical conditions of his time and place, not ours.[27]

C. Structuralism

Structuralism shares with the new hermeneutic the conviction that language is what distinguishes human beings from other creatures, and that a critical analysis of language is necessary for insight into the meaning of our experience. But there is a major difference between what the new hermeneutic says about language and what structuralism says about it. The former talks of language as our "fate," as that which limits our experience: the hope for authentic existence lies in the possibility of breaking through the limits of language—which of course leads to the creation of new language, which will become part of the "fate" of the next generation. For the new hermeneutic, language and existence are always in tension. To the structuralist, however, language is itself "fated" or bound by the fundamental structure of the human mind, and the hope of the structuralist is not to break through language, but to uncode it, to discover what it reveals about the way we are put together. If the new hermeneutic insists that we are bound by the language available to us, structuralism insists that the available language is bound by the structure of our thinking.[28]

Structuralism has become in recent decades a highly refined system of analysis, with enormous influence in the field of anthropology. Its practitioners have made a strong case for cross-cultural similarities at a deep level, beneath the surface of texts and traditions that at first glance appear literally worlds apart. A fully worked out structuralist analysis of a text sometimes looks like nothing so much as a model of a molecule in organic chemistry, and the very elaborateness of some of the "structures" prompts suspicion that the line between insight and cleverness has been crossed. Another source of suspicion is the imperialist claim implicit in the structuralist program: in theory, at least, every text should be reducible to one or more of a limited number of basic patterns characteristic of all human thought, and until one has detected those patterns, one has not got at the meaning of the text.

The patterns found by structuralists have to do mostly with polar opposites that human beings have to come to terms with in one way or another: life/death, male/female, one/many, self/other, and so on. This brief catalog suggests immediately that the New Testament provides rich territory for the structuralist, for a good deal of its language is almost transparently of this polar sort. But structuralism goes far beyond noticing that the New Testament speaks in these terms. The structuralist sees the polar opposites not as the true subjects of discourse themselves, but as clues to the structures of the minds that produced the texts. When life is said to overcome death, what that *means* is not that the dead shall be raised to new life, but that a resolution has been found to the tension created in human thinking by the recognition of the facts that there is life and there is death. If a text tells us that "something happened," what *really* happened (and what the text is *really* telling us) is that somebody found a scheme for resolving a tension fundamental to human thought.

It should be apparent that structuralism, like the new hermeneutic, is much more than a method for interpreting texts. It is the working out of a theory of the nature of human existence, although structuralism can buttress its theory with an extensive array of anthropological field data, while the new hermeneutic is necessarily restricted to the intrinsic force of its own description of the human situation. The sweeping claims of structuralism are not unchallenged, however, despite the impressive evidence. Within the field of psychology, and particularly in that part of the field which overlaps linguistics, there is sharp debate over the question whether there is a "structure" of the mind that precedes and underlies language. And one can ask whether, even if the structuralist patterns are at the base of what we say, we are unjustified in claiming to have grasped the meaning of a text before we get to the structural level.

D. The Significance of Paul Ricoeur

The current diversity of approaches in New Testament study makes it unlikely that in the near future we will see the clear dominance of one line of interpretation, but there are signs of the increasing influence of one particular theoretician of interpretation, Paul Ricoeur, of the University of Paris and the University of Chicago. Ricoeur himself would insist that he is only part of a larger pattern of influences: he has appropriated into his own philosophical development the findings of existentialist and phenomenological philosophy, Freudian psychology, structural linguistics, and sociology. His publications are characterized by development and self-criticism, so that to be a follower of Ricoeur is not to have a fixed base from which to operate, but to be aboard a moving vehicle. He contends that the enterprise of interpretation is by its very nature incomplete, and the tentativeness of his conclusions

stands in marked contrast to the certainty with which recent interpreters have announced their discovery of *"the* Christian understanding of human existence."[29]

Ricoeur provides a philosophical analysis of the activity of interpretation ("hermeneutics"), and what he proposes has significant
implications for the understanding of the Bible—what sort of thing
the Bible is, how it speaks, how we should listen to it. Ricoeur has
the potential for becoming a major force in New Testament study
for at least two reasons. First, he is himself directly interested in
matters of scriptural interpretation. He is a professed Christian, so
the relationship of his general philosophical and scholarly position
to theology, and more particularly to the Bible, is a matter of
personal as well as professional concern. Second, the wide sweep
of his intellectual curiosity, and his extensive learning in several
fields, has led him to attempt a philosophical critique and synthesis
of many of the disciplines that are having specific impact on New
Testament studies. This is not to say that everything fits neatly
(Ricoeur would himself be immediately suspicious if that were to
happen), but it is to say that in Ricoeur's scheme of interpretation
there is the possibility that practitioners of New Testament study
can see themselves, and be seen by others, as engaged in a common
enterprise.

Ricoeur is concerned above all with the interpretation of *texts.*
He has given a careful account of what happens when speech is put
into writing: the entire context of the language changes, for the text
becomes an object in its own right, which can create audiences the
writer never imagined, and the discourse in the text can no longer
be governed by the situation of a speaker and a listener, in which
meaning is controlled by countless refinements of gesture, intona-
tion, and by the fact that speaker and hearer share the world immediately surrounding them.

To recognize what happens when *speech* becomes *text* is to lay the
groundwork for interpretation, and the scheme of interpretation
which Ricoeur advances allows for genuine *historical* understanding, an intermediate position between antiquarian history ("What
did the text mean to those who first read it and wrote it?") and
contemporary relevance ("What does this text say to me here and
now?"). Ricoeur recognizes that both of these questions are important, but that they are incomplete in isolation from each other

(something most serious interpreters have known for a long time), and that they are incomplete even when taken together (something very few interpreters have understood).

The fault in antiquarian history is that a fundamental, irreducible uncertainty lurks at the end of every attempt to reconstruct "What the text originally meant," since the very production of the text itself cuts the discourse loose from its original situation. To be sure, we are not completely in the dark. In broad strokes we can describe the "thought world" of a given era in the past, we can discern horizons within which thinking, and perhaps even feeling, were confined. But the effort finally to penetrate "behind the text" to what the author "really meant" is misdirected; by committing what they have to *say* to *writing,* authors themselves set up a barrier to our knowledge of what they meant in the original act of discourse.

The fault in the rush to contemporary relevance is the confinement of the horizon of the text within our own horizon. If we come to the text only with our questions, we lose the chance for growth and for fresh insight, which the text offers us, and which it offers precisely because it comes out of a strange, foreign, perhaps even forbidding world. To impose our own limits on the text is to assume a specious "contemporaneity or congeniality" between us and the text; it is to overlook the fact that true understanding is "understanding at a distance." The *appropriation* of the meaning of the text —that is, "the movement from the alien to the proper"—can be accomplished only through the recognition of the distance separating reader and text.[30]

Is the interpreter, then, in an impossible situation—unable to know the intention of the author, and forbidden to subject the text to modern questions? This is precisely the kind of quandary Ricoeur likes to find himself in, for he believes that the human situation is best characterized by paradox, by the incentive to growth that comes from the need to find ways out of apparently locked boxes. And Ricoeur has found, in the concept of "the world of the text," a key that opens the interpreter's box.

If authors, in the very act of expressing themselves *in writing,* close off certain avenues to a knowledge of their original meaning, they at the same time genuinely *create.* The text presents, or proposes, a "world" of its own, with a particular structure, with its own symbolic coherence, and with the capacity to generate its own audiences. Anonymous works (which most of the biblical books are) can interest us precisely because our attention is arrested by "the world of the text." The "intention of the author" remains forever a theoretical construct, since we know nothing of the author apart from the text. And even when we know a good deal about an author, we can never have enough information to get "behind" the text. Ricoeur directs our attention to the "world" that is "before," or "in front of," the text, and suggests that it is this world which is the intermediate link between the past and the present.

"The world of the text" is not itself a "brute fact," capable of being once and for all mapped and categorized. It occupies the space between author and reader, and the relationship between those two human beings (or more, when we are dealing with communities, as we usually are in matters of religious texts) is one of lively possibilities, not dead certainties. But the world of the text does occupy that space; it is not simply a copy of the author's intention or the projection of the reader's concerns. The world of the text has been created by the author, and in the act of creation set free; and the reader sees that world in a particular way, but is not free to make it over from scratch. Ricoeur has said (or rather, written) that "the hermeneutics of the text tries to grasp [the text] in [the] moment of grace" between its being understood in its original context and its being made of use for our current context.[31] There is, then, a fundamentally *elusive* quality to meaning.

I see three implications of Ricoeur's work for the study of the New Testament:

First, Ricoeur has given a plausible account of what historians actually *do*. He springs us free from the trap of "objectivity" vs. "subjectivity," and describes that curious, dynamic process of conversation with the texts which we are actually engaged in, whatever theoretical knots we may tie ourselves into. And what follows from Ricoeur's analysis is a principle of self-criticism, what Ricoeur calls a "hermeneutics of suspicion." We know, he says, as historians that we are part of a tradition, but since the Enlightenment of the eighteenth century we have tried to act on the pretense that we are free of prejudices in the attempt to know the historical past. In Ricoeur's terms, incompleteness and the need always to revise opinions are not simply the unfortunate results of our limited sources and finite intelligences, but are built into the very nature of the activity of understanding itself. Our inability to give a final and complete interpretation is not a liability that we would ideally be able to overcome; it is, on the contrary, a necessary condition for any activity of interpretation at all. The minute we knew *exactly* what a text meant, the text's meaning would vanish.[32]

Second, Ricoeur insists that the Bible be taken as a whole. For Christians, the early church's refusal to give up the Old Testament, and its canonization of a highly varied collection of books as the New Testament, sets a barrier against the attempt to find the meaning of the Christian faith in the New Testament alone, and especially in one or another part of the New Testament. The Bible is proposed to us as a whole by the church, and what we are called upon to interpret is the world that the Bible presents—in all its paradoxes and contradictions, with all its loose ends and jagged edges.

Ricoeur has himself spoken to the problem of the discrepancies among the Gospels, in different language from that used by Irenaeus, but in a way that the second-century bishop of Lyons would have appreciated. "In the case of the New Testament, I am grateful that the primitive church did not choose, but took the stand of a kind of hermeneutical freedom, saying we have several traditions, and all four gospels contain the tradition, complete with its inconsistencies."[33] For Ricoeur, it makes no sense to single out this or that piece of early Christian tradition and say the meaning resides there, whether it be the kerygma extracted by Bultmann, or the ethics of the Sermon on the Mount, or Paul's justification by faith. That is to pretend that we can get "behind" the text to what is "really going on." What we have is the text, and the whole text. To explicate the "world" of that text is the job of interpretation: nothing less than demonstrating how that world in its totality and its complexity suggests possibilities for our own life. "When people say, 'But these things are dead,' I have no answer, except that it is not true. It may be that our work is to demonstrate this."[34]

Ricoeur's argument goes even deeper. Not only must we take the whole Bible seriously, we must also recognize that the way the Bible speaks is itself inseparably part of the message. The Bible does not put forth as an abstract proposition a definition of God as the shaper of history. It proposes a world, *through its account of history,* in which God is an active force. Philosophical criticism of course has to be brought to bear on questions raised by the Bible, but it is important to notice the nature of biblical language, and to take seriously its use of narrative forms. Ricoeur is proposing an extension of a principle espoused, and often followed, by interpreters of the Bible in the era of the church fathers and in the Middle Ages: they said that Scripture was its own best interpreter, and you should always try to explicate a passage by reference to other passages. Ricoeur says that understanding requires attention to the whole shape of Scripture; indeed, he would say that the world of the text is the necessary framework for the proper interpretation of the text's constituent parts.

Third, once Ricoeur is through the door of a discipline, that door cannot be easily closed against the host of friends he brings with him. The friends can be identified in the footnotes to his works: there are anthropologists, linguists, sociologists, students of comparative religion, advocates of phenomenology in philosophy. Ricoeur is critical of some of his friends, particularly the structural linguists, who have wrested the text too completely from the author, and have obliterated the essential distance between author and reader. Analysis of the *structure* of a text is an important step in interpretation, according to Ricoeur, but it does not get to the level of the discourse that is going on in a text. Ricoeur warns biblical interpreters, however, that they "must first catch up with Structuralist method in order to defeat its ideological claim"—the claim, that is, that structure and meaning are identical.[35]

If Ricoeur and his friends continue to work their way into the texture of the footnotes in articles and books by New Testament scholars, and even more, if their way of approaching texts becomes familiar in the teaching of biblical subjects to laypersons and to future scholars and clergy, the results could be momentous. The isolation of New Testament study from other disciplines (even from study of the Old Testament, which has had remarkably little impact on recent New Testament interpretation) will be over, and the full range of life expressed in the world of the biblical text will begin to become accessible. New keys to the meaning of the New Testament will turn up, but anyone claiming to have found *the* key will immediately fall under suspicion.

All will not be easy or comfortable for the churches in these new developments. Many of the disciplines that Ricoeur calls into play

in biblical interpretation have a strong sense of their own auton-
omy, and sometimes what is put forth as an explanation will have
all the appearances of "explaining away." But Ricoeur is right to
suggest that most scholarly disciplines are moving in the direction
of a chastened tentativeness about the adequacy of their accounts.
Interestingly enough, it is the natural sciences, and especially physics, that have led the way in this movement toward intellectual
humility; it is time New Testament study joined the trend. If we
abandon the search for certainty and turn our efforts instead to an
exploration of the world of the biblical text, we may find we have
gained more both intellectually and spiritually than we have given
up.

E. New Ventures

The shaping of New Testament study by the impetus of Ricoeur
and others who come at the material from fresh angles will not
happen overnight. The way universities and scholarly associations
are set up does not encourage the kind of "breaking free from the
way one was taught" that is required for shifting the direction of
a field as venerable and as widely practiced as that of New Testament study. But there are new ventures. A Center for Hermeneutical Studies in Hellenistic and Modern Culture was established in
1969 by the Graduate Theological Union and the University of
California, "in the belief that (1) team effort is essential for real
growth in these fields [Hellenistic studies, post-biblical Judaica, and
early Christianity], and that (2) methodological breakthroughs will
likely occur where scholars of a variety of fields encounter each
other seriously in pursuit of common interests." In addition to
practitioners of the traditional disciplines in the three named fields,
the Center "brings together faculty members of the departments of
Classics, Comparative Literature, English, Folklore, History, Law,
Near Eastern Studies, and Rhetoric."[36] A group for the study of
Christian origins in the light of modern social scientific methods has
been organized within the American Academy of Religion. And a
new journal, called *Semeia: An Experimental Journal for Biblical Criticism,* is providing a platform for new kinds of investigations. It is,
of course, indicative of the conservatism of scholarship that a whole

new publication has to be launched to give new approaches a hearing.

In the foreword to Issue No. 8 of *Semeia* the editor, Robert W. Funk, makes the following critical/prophetic remark: "It will take time for biblical scholars to grow familiar with forgotten ways."[37] There is something highly suggestive about the phrase "forgotten ways." In the context of Funk's foreword, it refers primarily to methods of literary criticism such as are employed in the articles in the issue, e.g., an analysis of the biblical presentation of David's kingship in comparison to Shakespeare's portrayal of Henry V. The reference of Funk's remark can be extended, however, to include the recovery of ancient ways of biblical interpretation—not all the ancient ways, of course, and not necessarily in exactly the same form. But as modern analysts come to appreciate the comprehensiveness of the world of the biblical text, they may find more guidance than they would expect in the interpretations put forth in ages when the world was not parceled out into academic departments, and when the identity of the Bible as a text with a communal world, and belonging to a community, was simply assumed.

There is no small irony in the emergence of a journal designed to familiarize biblical scholars with "forgotten ways" from the University of Montana, which has developed a major and quite thoroughly "secularized" program in the study of religion. Montana might be thought an unlikely place to find confirmation of one of the theses of this book: that the shift of a great deal of biblical study to colleges and universities will, in the long run, be of benefit to the churches. But it is just such unlikelihoods that constitute the history of the relationship between the academy and the church.

CHAPTER
FOUR

THE JEWISH MATRIX

The second chapter of Samuel Sandmel's book on the first century
A.D. is titled "Palestinian Judaisms." At first glance the reader
might think a typographical error has slipped past the proofreader,
but Sandmel is giving a signal by means of the plural, and that letter
"s" is a clue to what might be called, quite soberly, a revolution in
the study of Christian origins.

As we noted in the previous chapter, the question of the relationship of Christianity to Judaism is built into the very nature of
Christianity; even those, such as Marcion, who rejected the connection completely had to account for the apparent connection. In the
first part of the twentieth century George Foot Moore surveyed the
development of Christian attitudes toward Judaism, and concluded
that until the nineteenth century the opinion that Jesus and his
earliest followers were integrally part of the Judaism of their time
was dominant in the Christian churches. It was in the nineteenth
century that, for a variety of reasons (including Hegel's notion that
history moves forward by the dynamic of a thesis, e.g., Judaism,
generating an antithesis, e.g., Christianity), a sharp contrast was
drawn, and Jesus was portrayed as directly opposing the whole
Jewish religious system.

In order to heighten Jesus' attractiveness, the Judaism of his time
was "reconstructed" as a rigid, narrow, stifling "legalism"; and
even some twentieth-century scholars, though conscious of the
spiritual depth and value of Jewish writings of the third century
A.D. and later, maintained the nineteenth-century prejudice by assuming that the first century was a "convenient low point" in the
history of Jewish religion. A whole tradition of scholarship was
built up around the assumption, not as thoroughgoing as Marcion

70

but sharing in his spirit, that Christianity was a great leap forward religiously because it had repudiated Judaism.

Moore attacked this tradition, and did so in the only way that could have been effective: he worked patiently through the sources. What he perceived in a bewildering variety of kinds of texts was something he called "normative Judaism," a central tradition which was carried on by the rabbis following the Roman destruction of the Temple in A.D. 70, and which Moore believed could be traced back into the period before 70—that is, into the formative Christian generation. This "normative Judaism" was a very different phenomenon from the "legalistic" system set forth by earlier generations of scholars. It was characterized by devotion to sacred texts, fervent prayer, ethical concerns. There was room for diversity within the norm, and of course existence of a norm makes possible rejection of the norm (there were likely plenty of rigid legalists around), but Moore's major point was that the norm, and not the exceptions, should be at the heart of our overall understanding of first-century Judaism.[1]

Moore was arguing not only against the tradition of scholarship that belittled Judaism in general but also against another tendency, one that had come to public attention in the writings of Albert Schweitzer: the effort to show that first-century Judaism was shaped not so much by the rabbinic interpretation of the Hebrew Scriptures as by apocalyptic expectation. Apocalyptic literature, which vividly describes the imminent end of the world, has survived in some abundance from the period, so while it was never accepted as authoritative by the rabbis, the apocalyptic point of view clearly had a following. Schweitzer had placed Jesus squarely in this tradition, and thus, while not abstracting him from the Judaism of his time, had nevertheless found another way of portraying Jesus' direct conflict with what Moore was to call "normative Judaism."

Moore's point was timely, and he had to make it as forcefully and uncompromisingly as he did in order to reverse what had become by his time virtually an unquestioned premise of New Testament study. The full effect of his effort has been a long time in coming, and it still has a way to go, but Moore is clearly one of those scholars of an earlier generation to whom scholars of the coming generation are increasingly turning for guidance. And yet, rather ironically, just as Moore's insistence that Christian origins are intricately and positively linked to Judaism is finally being appreciated, his reconstruction of a "normative Judaism," or more precisely, his claim that normative Judaism was "the norm" in the formative Christian period, has been seriously challenged. Judaisms is a shorthand way of indicating what scholarship has found in recent decades.

I. THE PROBLEM OF THE SOURCES

Historians are accustomed to dealing with sources that do not tell them what they really want to know, or tell them things that are quite inconvenient for the story they want to tell. It is not simply an insider's frustration, however, that finds the sources for Judaism and Christianity in the first century particularly difficult to deal with. Rabbinic texts are even harder to date than New Testament ones, and virtually all the literature we have, both Christian and Jewish, comes from a period when schism between the two communities was an accomplished fact. That is not to say that everything in the texts is to be chalked up to polemics, but it is to say that we have to be very, very careful in telling our story. And, as Sandmel has warned, we have to guard constantly against the assumption that a document, or our analysis of it, gives us more precise knowledge than it does.

A. The Sects

Toward the end of the first century A.D. the Jewish historian Flavius Josephus, writing in Rome and attempting to make sense of the divisions within the Jewish community for his Gentile readers, presented the three major groups—Sadducees, Pharisees, Essenes —in the guise of philosophical schools, as if they corresponded to, for example, Platonists, Stoics, Epicureans, and so on. This had certain advantages as a way of making contact with Josephus' readers, and it was more than a clever device, since Greek philosophical schools did have more of a religious orientation than do most groups of philosophers today. But it is true that Josephus distorts the evidence by implying that Jewish sects were more centrally concerned with intellectual matters than they actually were.[2]

Josephus does have one lesson to teach us, however, that is often overlooked: by suggesting that the sects are philosophical schools, he is implying that they exist in a somewhat rarefied atmosphere, that they are elitist, and hence when we know what the sects thought and did, we may still be far from knowing what the majority of the population thought and did. The suspicion in which the Jerusalem Christian community held Paul may have been suspicion not simply of Paul the former persecutor but also of Paul the highly educated Pharisee, who said he became all things to all persons in order that he might by all means save some (1 Cor. 9:22).

Some scholars have argued that since the sects do not get us to the heart of the Judaism in which the Christian events happened, we must look to the mass of the population, called in the sources 'am ha'aretz ("people of the land"). Scholars often make a rather quick leap to identify the 'am ha'aretz with the social outcasts with whom Jesus is reported to have consorted, and thus a convenient direct opposition is set up between the followers of Jesus and the religious "establishment." Or, other scholars assume that the 'am ha'aretz were the fertile ground in which "apocalyptic Judaism" took root; but this presupposes that apocalyptic had an appeal limited to a particular class, and careful studies of rabbinic literature have demonstrated that that simply is not so.

To both "leaps" (the 'am ha'aretz are the socially and religiously dispossessed to whom Jesus primarily appealed, or they are the heart of the apocalyptic movement) Sandmel replies that we simply do not have adequate information to make such identifications. In rabbinic sources the 'am ha'aretz are treated as lacking piety, and this has been used to characterize the Pharisees, whose tradition was carried on by the rabbis, as arrogant. But as Sandmel suggests, in a religion as devoted to a Book as Judaism had already become, inability to read and study the sacred text could be seen, without undue arrogance, as a hindrance to piety. We cannot dismiss the possibility that persons considered to be lacking in piety by the religious authorities found new and satisfying status in the company of Jesus or in the Christian community, but we are simply not in a position to make a decisive judgment on the matter.[3]

While we cannot assume that the sects tell us all we need to know, we cannot do without knowledge of the sects. For the Pharisees we are well supplied with source material—except that almost all the written sources date from A.D. 200 and later. Like the Gospels and Acts, the rabbinic texts purport to record statements of religious leaders of the past, and there are problems involved in the quest for the historical Hillel or the historical Shammai, two leading Pharisaic teachers about a generation prior to Jesus, not unlike those involved in the quest for the historical Jesus. The tradition has been shaped by subsequent concerns.

The rabbinic materials, reflecting the Pharisaic viewpoint, were recorded after several generations during which the Pharisaic position had established itself as "normative" for Judaism. Sandmel has briefly—and for that reason, all the more strikingly—listed the momentous changes that came over Judaism in consequence of the Roman demolition of Jerusalem: "the Temple destroyed, priesthood unnecessary, the synagogue vital, the rabbi essential, animal sacrifice gone, and prayer a surrogate for it."[4] Synagogue, rabbi, prayer—these, along with ever more intense devotion to the study of the Book, were the new heart of Judaism, and to a large extent it was the Pharisaic tradition which was the link between pre-70 and post-70 Judaism. But the drastic changes that Sandmel catalogs do create a presumption that Pharisaism itself must have undergone some alterations too, and it is not easy to determine how much, for example, of the sayings of Hillel had passed authentically from a time when Pharisaism was one sect competing with others to a time when the Pharisaic tradition was in practical terms virtually unchallenged. In Paul's time, as Richard Rubenstein has recently remarked, "rejection of Pharisaism was not equivalent to rejection of Judaism."[5]

For the Sadducees, at least in the period we are considering, we have no direct firsthand evidence. However, their disappearance from view following the destruction of the Temple makes plausible the records we do have, that they were tied both religiously and economically to the Temple and its sacrificial worship. They were a conservative group, with a kind of "fundamentalist" commitment to "the simple gospel" of Moses. The only religious text they acknowledged was the Torah (the five books of Moses), and they refused to admit the authority either of the prophets or of the immense store of oral tradition by which the Torah had been interpreted and adapted for changing historical and social conditions. It was this dispute over "Scripture and tradition" which most sharply divided the Sadducees and the Pharisees. When the book of Acts (23:6–10) tells of Paul's getting himself out of a scrape by inciting

Sadducees and Pharisees to argue about resurrection, it is reflecting that fundamental distinction: the Sadducees could find nothing about resurrection in the Torah, while the Pharisees found it suggested in some of the prophets and stated directly in the oral tradition.

The third of Josephus' sects, the Essenes, lived a shadowy scholarly existence until the documents of the Qumran community were discovered and brought out of the caves three decades ago. There are still scholars who are not persuaded that the Qumran sectarians were actually Essenes, but they are a small minority, and their arguments depend on a few discrepancies between Josephus' description and the content of the documents. The Dead Sea Scrolls are of sufficient importance to deserve a special section of their own; for the moment it is enough to say that at Qumran we find an attitude of opposition to the Sadducean party analogous to the Christian opposition to the Pharisees described in the New Testament.

Just as Jesus is reported to have denounced the Pharisees for substituting human commands for the commands of God (Mark 7:8–9)—a denunciation which, incidentally, the Sadducees would have heartily endorsed—so the Qumran covenanters denounced the proprietors of the Temple in Jerusalem as guilty of apostasy from the genuine traditions of Israel. Indeed, the Qumran group was more disaffected from the religious "establishment" than was the Christian church, if Acts 5:42 is basically accurate when it portrays the apostles after Easter continuing to worship daily in the Temple. At the very least, we can say that the author of Acts thought it proper for them to have done so.

B. The New Testament

A drastically schematized view of Judaism is one of the unfortunate legacies bequeathed to the Christian community by John's Gospel. In that Gospel virtually all distinctions are eliminated as "the Jews" are presented over and over again as a monolithic mass of unrelieved hostility to Jesus. This reflects to a large extent the theological viewpoint of the Evangelist: "the Jews" are a category, not a historical entity, for the author. John believes that God the Father has chosen those who belong to the Son from before the foundation of the world, and one of the functions of the incarnation is to serve as a catalyst for precipitating out those who demonstrate, by responding to Jesus' call, that they are his sheep. "The Jews" is simply John's shorthand expression for those who do not respond.[6]

That may well be what John meant, but his choice of terminology has had very deplorable consequences, and even if there is no reference intended to the Jews as a historical people, it is likely that the historical circumstances of his own time influenced John's choice of their name for those who reject Jesus. By the time the Fourth Gospel was written, it was clear that very few Jews had responded favorably to the Christian message, and it may have looked as if it was part of the divine plan that the Jews were not of the Son's sheepfold.

The Synoptic Gospels (Matthew, Mark, Luke—so called because of the basic pattern they share) present a somewhat more differentiated picture, although patient attention to the details of the Parallels reveals clear biases in certain directions. Matthew turns Mark's scribes into Pharisees, while Luke tends to avoid the Jewish sectarian labels and uses indefinite pronouns instead, perhaps so that those in his Gentile audience could more readily identify with what they were reading. It is notoriously difficult to outline, on the basis of the Synoptic Gospels, Jesus' attitude toward the law. Many scholars are persuaded that the words concerning the law attributed to Jesus must be seen as reflecting the needs and convictions of the early church as it attempted both to hold on to the Jewish heritage and to sever itself from the Jewish community. Do we, then, know about the attitude of Christians toward the law, while the attitude of Jesus eludes us? Are Jesus' attacks on the Pharisees accurate reflections of his polemic, or are they filtered through the particular theological viewpoint of Matthew or of the church for which he was writing? As we have already seen, these questions are further complicated by our uncertainty concerning the range of attitudes toward the law that were represented by and within the various sectarian groups.

The question of the relationship of Christianity to Judaism was, for the apostle Paul, the central question of his own identity; there are no more poignant passages in the New Testament than those in Romans 9–11, where Paul tries to make sense for his readers, and even more for himself, of the resistance of the Jews to the Christian preaching. Paul boasts of his Jewish heritage, and claims to be a Pharisee (Phil. 3:5; Rom. 11:1). We might assume that such information would help us a great deal in understanding Paul; but, as Sandmel has pointed out, apart from Paul's evidence we know absolutely nothing about the character of Pharisaism in the Jewish Diaspora ("Dispersion," referring to Jews living outside Palestine; for many in Paul's time Diaspora ancestry would stretch back many generations), and it was from there that Paul came.[7] Paul's deeply felt conviction that by becoming a Christian he had become a complete Jew proved to have little appeal to his fellow Jews, but until we reach the point of understanding how he could *plausibly* believe what he did about Christian and Jewish identity we will not have a full historical grasp of the situation in which Christianity emerged.

There are in the New Testament two documents that have often been singled out as having, on the surface at least, an easily recognizable "Jewish" character: the Letter of James and the book of Revelation. Indeed, they have both sometimes been described as Jewish treatises to which a few sentences have been added to give them a Christian coloring. However, to single out books in this way begs two fundamental questions.

First is the question about the *process* by which Christianity and Judaism became separate entities. To say, for instance, that Revelation is a Jewish work with a few Christian additions is to assume that "Jewish" and "Christian" elements in a text can be neatly parceled out into clear and distinct categories. Jaroslav Pelikan makes an observation that highlights the precariousness of such a neat division:

> According to tradition, only one of the writers of the New Testament, Luke, was not a Jew. As far as we know, none of the church fathers was a Jew, although both Hermas and Hegesippus, for example, may have been; Justin Martyr was born in Samaria but was a Gentile. The transition represented by this contrast had the most far-reaching of consequences for the entire development of Christian doctrine.[8]

Pelikan has chosen his terms carefully: "according to tradition." It is possible that one or another, or all, of the Gospels besides Luke was written by a Gentile, and the same may be true of some other New Testament books as well. But there is also a good chance that the tradition preserves an accurate memory, at least to the extent of recognizing the thoroughly Jewish matrix of Christian origins. Evidence of bitterness, of strain, and even of schism between Judaism and Christianity can be found on nearly every page of the New Testament, but that evidence is itself a testimony to the intimate relationship of the two traditions. It was a fight over the rights to an ancient inheritance.

The second question begged by the designation of certain New Testament books as particularly "Jewish" is that of the nature of first-century Judaism itself. As we have already seen, there were significant sectarian divisions, but scholarship has recently become aware of variety far more extensive than had previously been recognized. The discovery of the Dead Sea Scrolls has given momentum to this new portrayal of first-century Judaism, but the reevaluation of old evidence is perhaps even more fundamentally significant. It is to these developments that we now turn.

C. The Dead Sea Scrolls

In 1955 a mild sensation was caused by Edmund Wilson's book, *The Scrolls from the Dead Sea.* [9] With the social and cultural critic's instinct for the popular mood, Wilson suggested that the Qumran documents finally provided the answers to the main unanswered questions about Christian origins: the whole Christian pattern of belief about Jesus, of community organization, of eschatological expectation could be found at Qumran, and there was nothing left over that Christianity could claim as its own.

A flood of technical and popular literature since then has made Wilson's book appear shallow, but his effort was symptomatic of a more general weakness that afflicted scholarship itself for a time: the fervent desire to find in totally unanticipated source material the answers to questions that have remained unsolved for generations. When the scholarly dust settles, it usually turns out that if there are some new certainties, there are probably just as many new uncertainties. And this happens in the doing of history generally. An eminent historian of sixteenth-century England has noted that, for his period, "it has to be confessed that what the picture has gained in truthfulness, it has lost in simplicity; and that each fresh contribution makes it more instead of less difficult to generalize with any confidence upon the subject."[10] Qumran, like agrarian changes in Tudor England, is now being assessed in more sober perspective.

For an understanding of the thought world of the early Christians, the overriding fact about Qumran is its concern with eschatology, with the expectation that the last days are at hand, when God will bring to completion his plan for Israel and the world. The Covenanters, as they called themselves, had withdrawn to the shores of the Dead Sea, and had created a community in isolation from the rest of the Jewish people, to await the final battle between the forces of light, with which they were in league, and the forces of darkness, with which they believed the corrupt priesthood in Jerusalem was allied. Their interpretation of the Scriptures tended to find eschatological prediction everywhere, and they assumed that the organizational pattern established in Israel at the beginning by Moses was the appropriate pattern for the end; hence their use of the arrangements in the Torah as a model for their own structure. They called themselves the Community of the New Covenant, but much more than the Christians, they saw the New Covenant as a restoration, in detail, of the original one.

Two aspects of the Qumran community that derive directly from the eschatological emphasis are also of special significance for studies of the New Testament. First is the community organization itself, which was centered on priesthood, required common ownership of goods, and involved a strong sense of separation from the rest of Israel. Second is the messianic expectation, which takes the peculiar form of waiting for two Messiahs, the priestly Messiah of Aaron and the kingly Messiah of Israel, with the priestly Messiah clearly being preeminent. The sect looked back to a somewhat shadowy figure, the Teacher of Righteousness, who they believed had received from God special powers of interpretation of Scripture, and whose presence among them had given warrant for their claim to be the heirs of the covenant that God had made with Israel. The Teacher had been persecuted by an unidentified "wicked priest," and indeed had apparently been killed. It is no longer thought by scholars that the Qumran sect viewed the Teacher as one or other of the Messiahs, and it is unclear whether the sect thought him in a technical sense even to be a forerunner of the Messiahs.

The early assumption among critics that the parallels with Christian interpretations of Jesus were compelling has given way to recognition that there are striking differences. In any case, too, it should not surprise us that religious movements nearly contemporary with one another and in the same general context should have some similarities in the pattern of their founding and development. The same holds true in the matter of organization. The withdrawal of the Qumran Covenanters from all daily contact with society, and their strict asceticism, contrast markedly with the picture we get of the early Christians in Paul's letters and in Acts, even though community of goods (in the Acts picture) and self-designation as the people of the new covenant are noticeable similarities.

The problem posed by the Dead Sea Scrolls for interpreters of the New Testament is a conceptual one: how are we to conceive of the *historical* relationship? Only when we have some notion of that are we in a position to interpret the similarities and the differences. Do we imagine, for instance, that some of Jesus' earliest followers were apostates from Qumran? Was Jesus competing with the Qumran community for followers? Was Jesus himself at one time a member of an Essene community (as many scholars and novelists have speculated)? What was the connection, if any, between John the Baptist and Qumran? John's activity is reported to have been in that region, but his once-for-all baptism of repentance was a very different rite from the frequent purification washings that were part of the daily routine at Qumran. If there was, however, some close connection between John the Baptist and Qumran, then the conflict between the followers of John and those of Jesus, which can be detected beneath the surface in Acts and in the Gospel of John, becomes indirect evidence of a struggle for adherents between the Qumran tradition and the Christian tradition.

The Christians claimed that the Messiah had come. Most Jews rejected the claim, and we might suspect that the Qumran community would have rejected it more decisively than any others, since they were the ones, so far as our evidence goes, with the most clearly articulated messianic theory. One can imagine a Qumran leader telling his community, as Jesus is reported to have told his disciples (Mark 13:21–23; Matt. 24:23–25), that there would come many false claimants to the messianic title. But Qumran might well have designated Jesus one of these false messiahs. Might Qumran have seen Jesus and his movement initially as a kind of ally, and then

come to sense in them a dangerous rival? Or were the two groups
appealing to basically different social classes?

The questions multiply, and most of them are unanswerable—
but they are important to ask anyway, because they alert us to the
fact that every time we propose an interpretation of the similarities
and differences between Qumran and the church, between the
Teacher of Righteousness and Jesus, between the social isolationism of the Dead Sea sect and the social involvement of the Christian
sect, we are operating with an implied theory of historical interaction that may or may not be plausible. We ought at least to be
self-consciously critical of our own assumptions about the way
movements influence one another, and even more, about the way
those influences are reflected in the documents, which is all that is
left for us to work with.

It is instructive to think of the way the catchall term "the movement" is used by various radical spokespersons today. Even in the
late 1960's there was more diversity than that term would have
implied, but there was some sense of common purpose. Many
different groups were motivated by a kind of human perfectionist
apocalypticism, a mood captured succinctly in the title of the autobi-
ographical memoir by my former student Mark Vonnegut, *The
Eden Express.* [11] Groups in "the movement," and members of particular groups, fell out with one another over all sorts of issues, both
ideological and organizational, and yet in certain contexts people
are still willing to talk about "the movement" as a continuing
reality.

We must be wary of reading too much of the present into the
past, but we must be equally wary of assuming too much difference
between antiquity and the present, and if things can have changed
within our society as much as they have in a decade (it comes as a
shock at the end of *The Eden Express* to realize that the entire story
recounted there covers a period of only about three years), we
would be rash to assume that relationships between groups like the
Qumran community and the Christians could not undergo deep
changes in the course of a generation. Qumran and the church were
not abstract entities. They were people in a highly charged atmosphere trying to bring complex traditions and decisive events into
phase, and the possibilities—indeed probabilities—of many permu-
tations and combinations are clear.

II. The Search for a Dynamic Model

A. Unlocking Categorical Boxes

Underlying the problem of sources is a conceptual problem, already referred to briefly, which must be confronted in any attempt to present an adequate reconstruction of the Judaism in which Christianity appeared. There is a strong tendency, even among professional scholars, to assume that influences and attitudes existed in sealed environments.

The most striking instance of this in New Testament study is the long dispute over the origins of the Gospel of John. Opinion has ranged all the way from Ephesus in Asia Minor to Alexandria in Egypt, and all the way from classifying John as the epitome of Hellenistic Christianity to declaring it the most Jewish of the Gospels.[12] The variety of opinion suggests not that one must surely be right and the others wrong, but rather that we must take the implications of variety within Judaism seriously.

Why could a Christian text not include elements from both Qumran and Philo of Alexandria? What was to prevent a Jew from traveling to Alexandria to study with Philo and then returning to join the Qumran sect and eventually coming into contact with Christians? Or what was to prevent a Palestinian Jew from staying home and reading the works of Philo? There was much cultural coming and going in the Roman world; indeed, only in recent times has there been as much.

> It is the simple truth that travelling, whether for business or for pleasure, was contemplated and performed under the [Roman] empire with an indifference, confidence, and, above all, certainty which were unknown in after centuries until the introduction of steamers and the consequent increase in ease and sureness of communication.[13]

Everyone knows persons (perhaps it even applies to oneself) who tend to be profoundly influenced by the last book they have read, and whose conversation, if it does not become identical with the style and vocabulary of that book, nevertheless does take on that coloring, at least for a while. John's Gospel is usually treated as though it were self-evidently the product of a lifetime's profound meditation. Why could it not be a more nearly spontaneous reaction of a Christian to the reading of some Philo, or to a series of conversations with a student of Philo, for example? The New Testament has suffered from being looked at too microscopically, and from being taken too deadly seriously. Many scholars who have rejected a dogmatically defined inspiration have substituted for it an assumption of deliberateness on the part of the New Testament authors that is a functional equivalent of such a dogma.

The point is this: just as many modern Christians, if asked to talk about their faith, may sound more like Dietrich Bonhoeffer or Daniel Berrigan or Rosemary Ruether or Billy Graham or Norman Vincent Peale or Jonathan Livingston Seagull than like the official formulas of the particular denominational traditions to which they belong, so many a Jew of the time of the apostles would likely have put together a personal belief system not necessarily congruent with one or another official line—without, however, feeling unfaithful to one or another official line. It is a narrow academic prejudice to assume that someone had to fit a sectarian category.

W. D. Davies showed, thirty years ago, that it is inaccurate to draw a sharp line between Pharisaism and apocalypticism; the rabbinic texts themselves show a positive appropriation of several key apocalyptic motifs.[14] But it takes a long time for this kind of fresh insight to weave its way into the texture of scholarship. It seems to me we are justified in speculating even a bit beyond the sources themselves, to consider the possibility that not only did Pharisees (and maybe even Sadducees) read, mark, and at least partially digest apocalyptic treatises but also that there were people who changed their allegiances and yet retained some of the habits of thought and images from their previous belief system.

B. The Hellenistic Umbrella

The reevaluation of evidence that has been known for a long time, even more than the appearance of the Dead Sea Scrolls, has provided the challenge for a dynamic conceptual model, and at least some of the materials for its construction.

The nature of this development can be highlighted by citing

passages from two books published within a year of each other. In 1969, Samuel Sandmel wrote:

> When I speak of Sadducees, Pharisees, Essenes, Therapeutae [an Egyptian Jewish "monastic" group described by Philo], and the like, and, in this context, Christians also for at least part of the century, I find it essential to keep reminding myself that all these groups or sectaries or sectarians were Jewish. Granted that they differed from each other in certain ways, and that some of the ways can be classified as antithetical, as for example, the Pharisees and the Sadducees on the oral law, still it is essential to note that, since they were all Jews, what they had in common was overwhelmingly greater than what it was that separated them.[15]

In 1968, Martin Hengel introduced his book *Judaism and Hellenism: Studies in Their Encounter in Palestine During the Early Hellenistic Period* with the following challenge:

> One fundamental presupposition of historical work on the New Testament which seems to be taken for granted is the differentiation, in terms of tradition, between "Judaism" on the one hand and "Hellenism" on the other. Distinctions are made between "Jewish apocalyptic" and "Hellenistic mysticism," between the "Jewish, rabbinic tradition" and "Hellenistic, oriental gnosticism," between "Palestinian" and "Hellenistic" Judaism, between a "Palestinian" and a "Hellenistic" community. Investigations of particular concepts, above all, usually result in a separation of these two "lines of tradition," which are often traced back into the Old Testament or to classical Greece. This unavoidable distinction does, of course, pass too lightly over the fact that by the time of Jesus, Palestine had already been under "Hellenistic" rule and its resultant cultural influence for some 360 years. Thus, even in Jewish Palestine, in the New Testament period Hellenistic civilization had a long and eventful history behind it. If New Testament scholars are to apply these unavoidable differentiations properly, and not just schematically, they must take account of the result of this history.[16]

What Hengel has demonstrated, with immense learning, is that "what the sects had in common as Jews" was far more extensively shaped by the "world culture" growing out of the conquests of Alexander the Great in the fourth century B.C. than scholarship in general has noticed. Hengel's thesis does not leap out of the blue; there was a flurry of interest in the whole question in the early

nineteenth century, and articles dealing with various limited aspects
of the question have appeared in great numbers in recent years. But
Hengel is honestly able to say, "No 'history of scholarship' can be
offered here, as this treatment of the theme in its complex multiplic-
ity is a first attempt; it is only possible to enter discussion with the
flood of secondary literature in connection with particular problems." He says that the " 'atomizing' of individual pieces of scholarship was a stimulus to bring a comprehensive synthesis to some sort
of meaningful conclusion."[17]

With an almost uncanny convergence, Hengel's book appeared
at just the right time to substantiate a suspicion that Sandmel had
expressed, on the basis, surely, of acquaintance with some of the
"atomized" literature, but also on the basis of his own general
experience as a historian:

> Jews inherited from the third, second, and first pre-Christian centu-
> ries aspects of Hellenized Judaism which by the first Christian century
> they took to be normal Judaism. . . .
>   If only we knew more about the kind of communication that went
> on between Dispersion Jews and the religious leadership in Judea, we
> would be able to see more clearly to what extent there was a substan-
> tial difference in the acuteness and extent of Hellenization in Judea
> and the Dispersion. . . . We should . . . avoid some of the modern
> anachronistic preconceptions which would dictate that Jewish Pales-
> tine rejected every kind of Hellenization and that Dispersion Judaism
> accepted it only in externals.[18]

What does all this amount to for study of the New Testament?
In order to make an estimate, it is necessary initially to indicate the
limits of the theory. First, Hengel himself does not dissolve all
distinctions in a sea of Hellenism. In his opening passage, quoted
above, he calls the distinction between "Jewish" and "Hellenistic"
"unavoidable," and says its use by New Testament scholars is
equally "unavoidable." Second, Hengel's detailed study covers the
period only to the middle of the second century B.C., though he
makes frequent forays into the time of Christian origins (he
promises another volume, to bring the full story up into the time
of the New Testament). Third, while the critical reaction to Hengel's book has been generally enthusiastic, some questions have
been raised about the reading he gives to some of the evidence; the
sharpest questions have been asked by Arnaldo Momigliano, an

ancient historian who has himself recently published a book with the rather pointed title, *Alien Wisdom: The Limits of Hellenization.* [19]

Even when these limitations are taken into account, the potential impact on New Testament study of the tradition of scholarship synthesized and carried forward by Hengel is immense. Hengel's work calls into question so many long-held assumptions about the nature of Judaism in the period of Christian origins that it is quite impossible to predict with confidence the overall shape the Jewish matrix will come to have in New Testament study over the next several decades, but a few elements can be suggested.

1. It will likely be accepted as plausible, even probable, that Jesus or at least several of his apostles were bilingual—that is, they spoke Greek as well as Aramaic (the language related to Hebrew that had become the common tongue of the Semitic world several centuries before the Christian era). If language is anywhere near as important in constituting human experience, and even human "nature," as many psychologists, linguists, philosophers, and theologians today think it is, it would be of signal importance if Christianity *at its origins* was shaped, at least in part, by the Greek language. Hengel reminds us that "Andrew" and "Philip" are Greek names, and that "Simon Cephas-Peter, Andrew's brother, later undertook extensive missionary journeys among the Jewish Diaspora of the West, which spoke only Greek." [20] If the apostles either heard Jesus speak Greek or were able through their own fluency in two languages to make the first translation from his Aramaic words into Greek, the whole matter of the "cultural translation" of the gospel for the Hellenistic world becomes a very different question from what it formerly was. There is nothing by way of certainty here, and it is hard to imagine how one might "prove" that Jesus and/or the apostles knew Greek. But Hengel and others have raised to at least the same level of uncertainty the frequently unchallenged assumption that turning the gospel into Greek was the work of persons several degrees removed from the original events. As Wayne Meeks has said, "The standard rule of thumb about the Jesus traditions, 'Semitic early; Greek late,' looks more and more dubious." [21]

2. We have to reckon with the possibility that the Jews in Palestine as well as those in the Diaspora came under the influence of Greek educational practices. The evidence here is scanty in the extreme; we really know next to nothing about how education was

carried on, or how extensively it was available. Yet we in our own
time are acutely aware of the power of education to shape an entire
society: parents fight for control of schools because they believe
(whether rightly or wrongly) that the schools have an almost creative power over their children. Hengel suggests that the proliferation of Palestinian Jewish literature in Greek, modeled on Greek
literary forms, is evidence of the spread of Greek education in the
Jewish homeland,[22] and while this is a slim reed on which to hang
a theory, the suggestion is timely, and may make scholars sensitive
to nuances in the documents that have hitherto escaped their notice.

3. Certain key terms may come to be seen in a new light. The
main example Hengel gives is "Torah," which became the watch-
word of Judaism following the Maccabees' stunning victory over
those who attempted to carry through a thorough Hellenization
between 168 and 165 B.C. Scholars are now generally agreed that
it was Jewish aristocrats, who themselves had become thoroughly
enamored of Greek culture and of the social advantages it gave
them, who instigated the "reform" actions of the ruler Antiochus
IV Epiphanes. Thus the Maccabean revolt was directed against
apostate Jews, who were considered to have sold out the charter of
Jewish existence, the Torah with its regulations for a distinctive
form of life.

Subsequent to 165 B.C. the Torah enjoyed a new pride of place
—and yet, Hengel has argued, the various ways in which the Torah
was interpreted all show unmistakable signs of the influence of
Greek philosophy and/or Hellenistic religion.[23] In the nearly two
and a half centuries between the Maccabees and the fall of Jerusalem in A.D. 70, then, we have to take into account a wide range of
interpretations of key matters in Judaism, and yet the range itself
appears nowhere to have escaped beyond the bounds of Hellenistic
influence. There are degrees of influence, of course; but from now
on anyone who wishes to assert that a particular point of view is
"Palestinian Jewish" in clear distinction from "Hellenistic Jewish"
will have to argue the case.

4. Apocalyptic literature will come to be seen as evidence for the
overall Hellenistic influence. Hengel's argument here is particularly subtle, and will require careful testing by scholars who are
intimately acquainted with what is usually called "intertestamental
literature" (that is, writings that fall chronologically between Dan-

iel, the latest book in the Old Testament, and the writings of the New Testament, though some of the writings usually included in the class are later, and in numerous cases dating is almost hopeless guesswork). But for now it can be said that Hengel's evidence, from the pre-Christian period, coincides with Davies' conclusion about later rabbinic literature: that apocalyptic ideas, terms, and even patterns of thought were part of the intellectual and spiritual equipment of all sorts and conditions of Jews in the period of Christian origins.

Hengel also insists on the rich variety of imagery and speculation included within apocalyptic thought, and after he has laid out the full range of what Judaism shared in the religious realm with its "Hellenistic Oriental environment"—

> the idea of a "natural revelation" which appears even before wisdom, the knowledge of God from the purposefulness and perfection of the natural order, and especially the stars; . . . the idea of divine providence and retribution in the life of the individual and above all after his death, the expectation of a future realm of peace, the existence of heavenly hypostases [personified divine attributes, such as the figure of Wisdom or the Logos] and redeemer figures, angels, demons and spirits of the dead, the significance of astrology, manticism and magic, the forms of supernatural revelation of divine wisdom through dreams, visions, journeys through heaven and the underworld, ecstatic or inspired discourse or holy scriptures given by God[24]—

it becomes easier to see that elements of the New Testament which were once thought to reflect a specifically Greek and not Jewish (and hence not "original") context now can be called quite unmistakably Jewish.

The Diaspora Judaism from which Paul came and the Palestinian Judaism from which Jesus and his first followers came were, as Sandmel noted, united in their identity as Judaism. What Hengel has shown is that they were united, in many more ways than has previously been realized, by their common heritage of nearly four centuries of Hellenistic influence. "Strictly speaking, for the Hellenistic-Roman period the Judaism of the mother country must just as much be included under the heading 'Hellenistic Judaism' as that of the Western Diaspora."[25]

C. Apostolic Baggage

Hengel's case may be too tight. He indicates that in an area as broad and difficult as the one he has studied, it is impossible to come up with a neat, succinct synthesis, but he does make some very sweeping claims, and at points it is difficult to see what is left under the heading of "unavoidable use" of the terms "Jewish" and "Hellenistic." In order to highlight the dynamic relationship between Judaism and Hellenism, Hengel may have extricated the subject from one trap only to catch it in another: that is, Judaism and Hellenism come out of their boxes to interact furiously, and then we reach a stage where everything is Hellenistic Judaism, which itself runs the risk of becoming a fixed point of reference, of becoming a locked (although very large) box.

Nevertheless, whatever modification Hengel's theories are found to require, the way is open for new ways of thinking about the dynamics of Christian origins. We shall deal in Chapter 6 with some of the implications for the "locating" of Jesus in his historical context. There is another question, equally important for understanding the formation of the Christian tradition, but a question that has not received adequate attention: What cultural baggage did the apostles bring with them? There is no way of giving a clear or precise answer, but the new understanding of first-century Judaism provides some hints of ways in which we might think about the question.

The apostle Paul was deeply aware of the continuities of individual life, but he said that the only thing that matters is a new creation, and that all old distinctions are dissolved (Gal. 6:15; 3:28). Still, people were conscious of connections between what they had been and what they had become. We are sometimes oversold by Paul's dramatic conversion, and think it was normative for Christians to look upon the past as dead and gone. A good case can be made that Judaism and Christianity contributed the notion of conversion, and hence of religious exclusiveness, to the world, and the Christian claim on the whole of a person's life did appear strange in the ancient world.[26] But dramatic reversals of the sort Paul reports are probably always rare, and most Christians, then as now, are more deeply creatures of cultural habit than they theologically suppose.

In the light of current study, it appears likely that the first follow-ers of Jesus would have been possessed of a bewildering variety of cultural habits—the apostolic baggage would have been anything but a "matched set." The romantic picture of simple fishermen in a cultural backwater, with perhaps more or less defined grievances against the religious and political authorities, seeing in Jesus' es-chatological message a ray of hope for a hopeless situation, simply will not mesh with the Palestinian environment.

Hellenistic influence had helped to multiply distinctions and divi-sions, and at the same time to blur them, so it is likely that if twelve persons heard Jesus say something, each of them, having come with a special configuration of questions, hopes, fears, ambitions, would thus have "heard" Jesus in a unique way. Furthermore, we cannot say that "a Pharisee" would have reacted thus and so to Jesus; we would have to know what a particular Pharisee's attitude toward apocalyptic was—even more, we would need to know how Jesus would formulate his speech in terms of his knowledge of, or as-sumptions about, that Pharisee's attitude toward apocalyptic.

It begins to appear that what Bindoff said about Tudor English history definitely applies to our understanding of the Jewish matrix of Christian origins: "What the picture has gained in truthfulness, it has lost in simplicity." But if our ability to describe with confi-dence the precise relationships within the first century A.D. has been diminished, that very diminution may help confirm an expla-nation of the eventual decisive break between Christianity and Judaism.

The capacity of Judaism to include within its bounds a wide variety of belief at the time of Christian origins has long been recognized, and that recognition has been immensely broadened by the discovery of the Dead Sea Scrolls and the detection of the pervasive Hellenistic influence. Now more than ever, there are strong reasons to avoid saying that there was a specific item of belief at the root of the Jewish/Christian schism.

Paul said that a crucified Messiah was a stumbling block to Jews as well as foolishness to Greeks (1 Cor. 1:23), and of course Paul was in a position to know what he was talking about. But the crucified Messiah was not initially a stumbling block to all Jews, and it is not self-evidently true that the Christian assertion, "The Mes-siah has already come," was the heart of the controversy. Josephus

suggests that James, the brother of Jesus and head of the Jerusalem
church, was held in high regard in the city.[27] This suggests that you
could believe that Jesus was the Messiah and still be a pillar of the
Jewish community in Jerusalem.

More important than the messianic claim in leading to schism was
the mission to the Gentiles. We know of course that there was a
Jewish proselytizing effort, but its aim was to make of Gentiles full
members of the covenant community, which meant adhering to
those laws and customs which distinguished Jews from everyone
else. Acts presents Peter as the initiator of the Gentile mission,
while Paul claims credit for its inauguration himself, and since both
reports are polemical, it is difficult to sort them out. There was a
kind of anticipatory friction within the very earliest Christian community; at least that is one way of reading the report in Acts (6:1–6)
of conflict between groups in the Jerusalem church called "Hebrews" and "Hellenists." The latter are apparently Diaspora Jews
who had become Christians, but had brought with them into the
Christian community their traditions—developed in some cases
through centuries—of living a fully satisfactory Jewish life without
direct involvement in Temple and sacrifice. With them, there was
already a precedent for elimination of certain religious requirements that had been central in earlier generations of Judaism.

Thus there may have been some Jews for whom the opening up
of the Christian (sectarian Jewish) community to individuals who
did not undergo circumcision or obey the food laws would not have
appeared so momentous a step after all. As Roman pressure against
the Jewish community mounted, however, the dangers of assimilation would have become ever more apparent, and perhaps Jews
who would initially have been annoyed, but not to the point of
action, with the easy opening that the Christian sect provided for
the Gentiles, would have come increasingly to resent and resist such
action. There is an analogy in the rapidly growing sense of the need
to preserve identity among Jews today. Many Jews who twenty
years ago were cool toward Zionism fervently support it now.

In a characteristically wry observation, Jaroslav Pelikan has suggested that "for Jewish Christians, the question of [the] continuity
[between Judaism and Christianity] was the question of their relation to their mother; for Gentile Christians, it was the question of
their relation to their mother-in-law."[28] The value of the remark is

that it directs attention to the intensely *personal* quality of the question. By the middle of the second century, debates between Jews and Christians were becoming a literary convention, but prior to that time the question was one of personal identity.

D. A Question of Identity

In the attempt to work through the first-century sources, including the New Testament, it is important not to lose sight of the dynamic power of this question of identity. There were many ideological and social tensions within the Jewish community: looking for God's new action in the world while holding on to a tradition developed through more than a millennium; the conflict between the priestly and prophetic traditions still unresolved; all the opportunities for dissension created by an oppressive occupying imperial power; the diversity of habits fixed through generations of living either in proximity to Jerusalem or at great distances from it; the circulation of literatures that blurred sectarian distinctions; the cultural richness, and confusion, of speaking at least two tongues. All these tensions, and many more besides, made up the world in which Jesus and his followers lived, and the tensions are enough to make us suspicious of any easy identification of this or that as a specific influence on that or this aspect of Christianity.

A thorough study of the Jewish matrix of the New Testament, which is now under way and gaining momentum, is of importance for New Testament interpretation not primarily as providing sources for particular passages, but rather as making clear the rich, complex human reality out of which Christianity, which eventually defined itself in opposition to a newly restricted Judaism, emerged. It has been said, in connection with the schism between the Greek and the Latin churches, that schism is a reality when it is felt by average people to be so.[29] To make this specific, we might say that schism occurs when two groups no longer pray for one another as a matter of course. Official pronouncements are not religious reality; what a community prays for is. Perhaps the question about the relationship of Judaism and Christianity is the question about the gradual shortening of the radius of the circle of people included in the prayers of two communities.

CHAPTER FIVE

THE GNOSTIC CHALLENGE

In 1945, two years before the first of the Dead Sea Scrolls was brought to light, an ancient library was unearthed at Nag Hammadi, a town on the Nile in Egypt. Many persons, if asked to name a recent manuscript discovery with major implications for New Testament study, would be able to respond, "The Dead Sea Scrolls from Qumran." Very few persons, if asked to indicate the importance of "The Coptic Gnostic Library from Nag Hammadi," would have any idea what the question was referring to. And yet, many New Testament scholars would argue that in terms of overall impact on our understanding of the New Testament, the Nag Hammadi documents will prove more decisive than those from Qumran.[1]

Gnosticism is unfamiliar to most people, so it is not immediately apparent why New Testament study should be preoccupied with the subject. The issue is, however, fundamental: Does a religious attitude that severs redemption completely from creation, that makes a sharp distinction between the God who made us and the God who saves us, have any basis in original Christianity? Is the New Testament, which appears to block such a view, in fact a smokescreen?

Before we consider the historical questions, we can begin to get some sense of the nature of Gnosticism by means of a brief period of personal reflection. Recall the period in your life when you felt most alienated from the world around you. Family, friends, politics, religion—all your surroundings were conspiring against you. Your sense of identity was threatened. It was as if you were some virus, and the world's "immune system" had been activated to drive you out. Perhaps the word of salvation which came to you in one way

93

or another was the assurance that you are, after all, at home in the world; that forgiveness and grace are real; that the universe is, despite appearances, hospitable to human beings.

There is another, very different word of salvation that may have come to you, and it is one that had enormous appeal in early Christian times. This word was the assurance that your profound sense of alienation from the world is a vital step on the way to true self-understanding; that the universe is indeed inhospitable to human beings because the world is a ghastly, catastrophic mistake. The appeal of Gnosticism—and it is an appeal that did not die with the second or third century—is the appeal to a person's sense of superiority to the world. It is not I who am the victim of the Fall, of original sin, but the world itself. We come trailing clouds of glory—into a polluted atmosphere.

Just as Gnosticism presented a formidable spiritual challenge to the early church, it presents a formidable intellectual challenge to modern scholars. The baffling complexity of the subject is reflected in a flood of specialized studies and the occasional brave effort at synthesis. This chapter will be neither a specialized study nor a synthesis; it is, rather, an effort both to alert the reader to some of the main features of Gnosticism and to indicate where research into Gnosticism appears to be carrying the New Testament.

After a brief outline of some central theological and ethical points in Gnosticism, we will get to the matter of our primary concern: the relationship of Gnosticism to the New Testament and Christian origins more generally. There we shall have to confront the following question: If we acknowledge the authority of the New Testament, do we thereby inadvertently acknowledge some of the claims of Gnosticism? Or, to put it another way: Does the contention of the church fathers Irenaeus and Tertullian that the Gnostics have no claim whatever on the Scriptures stand up under close analysis? And finally, we shall see that the study of Gnosticism has raised for many persons in an acute way the question of whether the New Testament is a reliable guide to original Christianity.

I. THEOLOGY: GOD AND THE WORLD

As far as we know, there was no central Gnostic "creed," and the diversity of Gnostic sectarian beliefs and practices makes a succinct characterization of "Gnosticism as such" impossible. Irenaeus names a score of Gnostic groups known to him around A.D. 170, and we know that they often hated each other more than they hated their common orthodox opponents (this use of "orthodox" is subject to much debate, as we shall see later in this chapter). Despite all the variety, however, there are some characteristic beliefs and attitudes which the groups share.[2]

A. Creation

In chapter 1 of Genesis, God looks at the world he has created and says that it is very good. The Gnostic looks at the world and says that it is very bad. It follows either that God was mistaken in thinking it good, or that God did not know any better. If he did not know any better, that must be because he is not really God. He had done the best he could, and his best fell far short of what the Gnostics themselves would consider a good world—one in which there would be no noxious insects, no disease, in which the righteous would be rewarded and the wicked punished.

If Gnostics could imagine something better than this world, if they could, in short, pass an adverse judgment on the creator of this world, then they must in some essential way be superior to the creator. And this superiority of the Gnostic to the creator must be grounded in the Gnostic's affinity with a divine being superior to the creator—with a divine being who is *really* God.

With numerous variations, this is the basic pattern of Gnostic logic. It provides an explanation for an individual's sense of radical alienation from the world, and justifies that individual's adverse judgment on the world. The Gnostic is not burdened, as is the orthodox, with explaining how the fall of human beings involved the fall of the whole creation. The "problem of evil" is solved by locating the fall not in post-creation humanity, but in pre-creation divinity. Through processes conceived in different ways by the various sects, the originally single divine being spills over into a steadily descending series of levels, which eventually become so far removed from the source that they lose all knowledge of where they came from and what they are, and they begin to think they are supreme.

It is one of these subordinate powers, often called the Demiurge, who rashly undertakes to create a world. He is so grossly ignorant of the true structure of reality that he uses matter and fashions a world of corruption and mortality. The imperfection of the world is a symptom of a catastrophe in the divine world, and the root cause of that catastrophe is ignorance. The Demiurge is not really malevolent; he simply did not know the limits of his derived power. According to one of the major Gnostic teachers, Basilides, "he [the Great Archon, the name Basilides gives to the Demiurge] soared aloft as far as the firmament, which blocked his course, but he believed that nothing lay beyond, and that he himself was the sole god; he therefore began to create the cosmos." And he created from the outer edges in toward the center, as far as the sphere of the moon. Then an even less competent Second Archon took over for the creation of our earth.[3] Throughout all the Gnostic systems, the enemy to be overcome is not sin or death, but ignorance.

How does it come about that human beings, in this world, can judge this world an inappropriate place for them to be? It is because human beings (some of them, at least) are more than they appear to be. The God who is really God has emitted sparks of his true divinity, and these sparks, whether unwittingly or because of scheming by lower divine beings, have been trapped in human, material bodies. Not everyone contains a spark of divinity, but some do—and yet even they are so weighed down with the shroud of flesh that they have forgotten their true nature or, as Theodotus said in the passage with which this book began, "who we were, and what we have become, where we were, where we were placed, whither we hasten, from what we are redeemed, what birth is, what rebirth."[4]

The knowledge (Greek *gnōsis*) of which Gnosticism speaks is not a conclusion reached at the end of a process of reasoning; human reasoning itself is tangled with the imperfect world in which it functions. The knowledge that brings salvation must be *revealed* knowledge, carried into the world by an ambassador of the genuine God. And the ambassador's task is to call back out of the Demiurge's prison of a world those parts of the true God which have been captured and incarcerated. As Hans Jonas has put it, Gnosticism is concerned with God's salvation of himself.[5]

B. The Incarnation

If God's chief concern is not to redeem human beings, or rather if his concern to redeem them is mainly to get himself put back together again, it becomes difficult to see what role an incarnation might serve in the process. Irenaeus, in his treatise *Against Heresies,* gave succinct expression to the purpose of the incarnation: God the Son became what we are in order that we might become what he is.[6] To a Gnostic, that would seem absurd. We and God are already essentially the same, and God would not accomplish anything except further confusion by getting himself in the same fix we are in.

It would not do any good for God to become human, but it was necessary that he send a messenger who would remind those persons with divine sparks in them who they really were. There was some procedural advantage to be gained by the messenger's having at least the appearance of being human, and in one way or another most of the Gnostic systems have what is known as a "docetic" view of Jesus (from Greek *dokeō,* "to appear" or "to seem"). This gives rise to a certain picturesque quality. In one treatise we are told that after Jesus gave the cross to Simon of Cyrene he did not take it back again, and stood on the sidelines at Calvary laughing while Simon was crucified—laughing not at what was happening to Simon, but at the ignorance of the onlookers (including his own disciples) who were so deluded that they thought the revealer could suffer and die.[7]

Gnostics did not believe that the messenger of the true God could truly die; neither did they believe that he could really have any intimate connection with the material world, as the following passage about Jesus' manner of digestion makes clear:

> Having endured everything he was continent; thus Jesus exercised his divinity. He ate and drank in a peculiar manner, not evacuating his food. So much power of continence was in him that in him food was not corrupted, since he himself had no corruptibility.[8]

To put it crudely but accurately, the Gnostic found the notion of the Son of God defecating too distasteful even to contemplate. And such fastidiousness may linger even today. How many Christians, viewing a creche at Christmas, suspect that the swaddling clothes might need changing?

For the Gnostic, the incarnation (such as it was) serves two main purposes. First, the divine messenger is able to call the Demiurge himself to repentance. "The Archon, then, being orally instructed, and taught, and being thereby filled with fear, proceeded to make confession concerning the sin which he had committed in magnifying himself."[9]

Second, Jesus was able to gather around himself followers, some of whom were genuine Gnostics (that is, possessors of the divine spark), and to these he committed secret teachings that were to be handed down in a tradition separate from whatever public traditions might develop. The Gospel of Thomas begins: "These are the secret words which the living Jesus spake, and Didymus Judas Thomas wrote them down." One of the sayings in the Gospel clarifies the distinction between Thomas, who truly comprehends the meaning of Jesus, and the other apostles, whose understanding is limited:

> Jesus said to his disciples: Make a comparison to me, and tell me whom I am like. Simon Peter said to him: Thou art like a righteous angel. Matthew said to him: Thou art like a wise man of understanding. Thomas said to him: Master, my mouth will in no wise suffer that I say whom thou art like. . . . And [Jesus] took him, went aside, and spoke to him three words. Now when Thomas came to his companions, they asked him: What did Jesus say unto thee? Thomas said to them: If I tell you one of the words which he said to me, you will take up stones and throw them at me; and a fire will come out of the stones and burn you up.[10]

According to the Gnostic, the public tradition about Jesus was corrupt and was all you could expect from people so coarse as to believe that the Son of God would really become flesh. If he became what we are, then all would be lost.

C. Redemption

For the Gnostic, knowledge was not a cultural ornament or an instrument for mastery of people and things in this world. It was the key to escape, the "Open Sesame" into the world of pure spirit where the Gnostic really belonged. And the knowledge *was* the redemption—to learn your true identity from the Revealer was to be sprung free from the trap of this world and its incompetent (but possessive) creator. The only mechanism holding the trap shut is one's own ignorance. There is no need for a redeemer who is tempted in all things as we are, who carries our griefs, who is bruised for our iniquities, by whose stripes we are healed. The problem is not sin requiring forgiveness, but ignorance requiring knowledge.

There are as many schemes of revealed knowledge as there are Gnostic sects, and the very emphasis on secrecy must mean that many details are forever hidden from us. But much did find its way into texts, and a few examples may help convey a sense of the varieties of redemptive knowledge that were available.

A scheme that must have had a special appeal to the ancient love of the hidden and the mysterious—an ancient love that has appeared anew among many persons in our own day—was the set of passwords the initiate learned in order to get past the guards of the various levels of spiritual being between this world and the true God. Some Gnostic groups conceived of seven gates, some of thirty, and at least one of three hundred and sixty-five. However many there were, the gatekeeper at each level was there to keep out those who did not, by knowing the password, demonstrate that they actually belonged at a higher level.[11]

The Gospel of Thomas has none of this complicated cosmology, but seems rather to teach a kind of pantheism (God is all things). The Gospel of Thomas is notoriously difficult to systematize, but something of its notion of redemption can be glimpsed in the following passage: "Jesus said: I am the light that is over them all. I am the All; the All has come forth from me, and the All has attained unto me. Cleave a (piece of) wood: I am there. Raise up the stone, and ye shall find me there."[12] In this instance knowledge is not so much the key to future bliss as it is the source of insight into the true nature of things now; it amounts to achieving a proper perspective.

In one particularly subtle Gnostic system the dynamic of redemption from one level to another depends on the confusion of levels. Lying beneath the scheme, probably several layers of cultural tradition deep, is the notion of ancient Greek physics, according to which motion in the world is caused, at least in part, by the "desire" of the basic elements to return to their "proper" place (fire wants to move up, for instance, and earth down). The Gnostic Basilides held that spirits of varying degrees of purity are trapped at various levels of impurity, and as they come to have knowledge of their true nature, they seek to move upward. The end of the age will arrive when everything is at the level appropriate to its nature, and

> when this takes place, God will bring upon the whole cosmos enormous ignorance, that all things may continue according to their nature, and that nothing may desire anything of the things that are contrary to its nature. . . . And there will not prevail any rumor or knowledge in regions below concerning superior regions, lest subjacent souls should be wrung with torture from longing after impossibilities.[13]

When everything gets sorted out, but only then, it is ignorance that is bliss.

II. ETHICS: HUMAN RELATIONS

When we read the scandalous things the church fathers say about the behavior of Gnostics, it is worth remembering what pagans said about the behavior of Christians: that they ate children and engaged in incest. Groups that are seen as threats to stability and order, which is how the Christians were seen by the Romans and how the Gnostics were seen by the orthodox, tend to become projection screens for fertile imaginations, and we must always treat such reports with severe skepticism.

Origen claims that the pagan opinion of Christian behavior results from the pagans' failure to make necessary distinctions between Gnostics and real Christians: many groups are calling themselves Christian, Origen points out, and opponents of Christianity conveniently characterize the whole movement by referring to the most despicable people who claim its name.[14] This is one of Origen's strongest motives for his dogged effort to differentiate orthodoxy from Gnosticism. But we must wonder to what extent he is himself overplaying both the vice of the Gnostics and the virtue of the orthodox.

Before we consider the criticism of Gnostic behavior by their

opponents, however, we need to look at what the Gnostics themselves say about the proper relations among persons. Here, as
elsewhere in this brief survey of Gnosticism, we have to oversim-
plify a wide variety of beliefs in order to get a grip on the fundamental scheme. Our attention will focus primarily on the Valentinians, who seem to have been particularly concerned to construct a
church organization that would reflect Gnostic ethical principles—
and many of whose newly available writings have been extensively
studied.

A. Spirituals, Psychics, Somatics

The Valentinians used a ready-to-hand terminology, that of
spirit, soul, and body (Greek *pneuma, psychē, soma*) to designate
three different classes of Christians. The somatics were made of
earthy stuff, and had in them nothing capable of redemption. They
were prisoners of the creator of the world, and were inextricably
locked in the illusion that Jesus was the Messiah expected by the
Jews. The pneumatics, at the other end of the spectrum, were those
whose essential being was divine stuff, and in whom the spark of
divinity had been blown into full heat by the breath of the Revealer.
The psychics were those in the middle, capable of being pulled up
toward the level of the pneumatics, capable also of sinking down
to the level of the somatics. The missionary impulse of the Valentinian pneumatics was directed toward the psychics; the somatics
were a waste of time.

The Valentinians found evidence of this threefold division
mainly in the way sacred texts were interpreted. The somatics, they
said, were those who simply read the Gospel accounts of Jesus as
a biographical story. The psychics believed that the story was about
divine activity, but they assumed that the active involvement of
God in history was an essential element of the revelation. The
pneumatic was the one who recognized that *all* the terms of the
Gospel, even "God" and "Christ" and "resurrection" and "incarnation," were merely images of the truly redemptive reality, which
was a set of events and activities in the spiritual world, far, far
removed from this earthly scene.

Pneumatic conversion was the liberating experience of seeing
clearly *through* the images of the biblical tradition, and realizing that

it is not time which must be redeemed from futility, but that it is the futility of time from which we must be redeemed. On occasion a psychic may undergo this conversion experience, but prior to that time the psychic thinks the order of nature and the order of law established by nature's creator are the standard to which human beings should aspire. The pneumatics, and the psychics who make the quantum jump to the pneumatic level, are beyond all that.[15]

We shall discuss a bit later the relation of all this to the New Testament, but at this point it is interesting to note the way in which Paul provides both support for and refutation of this theory of a class system in the church. Paul makes much of the distinction between those who are spiritually mature, to whom he can convey the full meaning of Christ, and those who are still spiritually infants, to whom he must administer spiritual milk. Gnostics, among whom we can at least provisionally count Marcion (although for him the creator was guilty of vindictiveness more than of ignorance), seized on this distinction of Paul's, and tied it to his antithesis of law and gospel, saying that Paul clearly understood the difference between the creator and the Father of All.

Counter to this, however, Paul insists throughout his correspondence that there are no second-class Christians, that all are one in Christ—and that, indeed, if there are any who will enter the kingdom of God ahead of others, it is the Jews themselves. We could say that while for the Valentinians there are classes according to nature (that is, according to the condition in which one is born), for Paul there are classes according to nurture (that is, according to stages of growth and development), and the nurture itself has to do, not with redemption (Christ has accomplished that already), but with the Christian's process of sanctification in this world. All have fallen short, Paul declares, all are sinners, no one can claim to have reached already the prize of the high calling in Christ. Everyone is still to press on, and will have to press on throughout life.

Most important of all, in Paul's scheme, is the actual historical event of the life, death, and resurrection of Jesus of Nazareth; the history of Jesus, not just the things he taught, has changed the situation in which persons live and move and have their being. Paul does say that once we knew Christ after the flesh, but now we know him so no longer (2 Cor. 5:16), and it is well known that Paul's letters give almost no information about the career of Jesus. But a

Gnostic could find comfort in Paul's statement in 2 Corinthians only by entirely disregarding the first clause. For Paul, we can know Christ according to the spirit only because we first knew him according to the flesh.

B. Ascetics and Libertines

The logical, or perhaps better, psychological implications of the Gnostic class system, when coupled with the radical devaluation of the material world, are not difficult to figure out, and according to the church fathers it was characteristic of Gnostics to move to one extreme or the other. If my true being is not of this world, if matter is a prison and what I want is that this too too solid flesh would melt, then I can demonstrate my superiority to my physical bondage in either of two ways. I can treat my body with contempt in rigorous ascetic exercises, or I can treat my body with contempt in wild orgies of sensual excess. In the first case I am showing that the spirit is willing *and able,* while the flesh is weak *and powerless:* I pay no attention to the desires of the flesh. Those needs—food, sleep, warmth—which loom large for others are negligible for me. In the second case I am expressing my conviction that there is no intimate connection between spirit and flesh, that whatever excesses I allow to my flesh, my spirit is untouched.

In either form of excessive behavior, whether ascetic or libertine, the Gnostic is grounding action in a radically dualistic view of human nature: spirit is spirit and flesh is flesh, and never in any significant sense shall the twain meet. It is this, more than anything else, which makes the Old Testament distasteful to the Gnostic, for a dualistic view of human beings as spirit trapped in matter is entirely foreign to the religious tradition of Israel, which thought of the human being as an integral being, a body which God breathed into life.

As suggested earlier, we have to be wary of assuming that most Gnostics behaved in one or another extreme way. The church fathers were right in their analysis of the behavioral conclusions that could follow from Gnostic presuppositions, but people do not often operate according to the full logical implications of their basic beliefs. Paul himself was accused of advocating what some took to be the logical outcome of his doctrine of grace: "Let us sin all the more, that grace may abound all the more." His reply was, "God forbid!" So, too, we must take equally seriously Marcion's disclaimer when he was confronted with the ethics that he "should" favor, given his basic beliefs: like Paul, he said "God forbid!"[16] It is likely that most Gnostics in their overt behavior were not much different from their neighbors. What really distinguished the Gnostics was not what they did, but what they knew.

C. Individualism

The chief ethical danger of Gnosticism was not asceticism or libertinism, but a thoroughgoing individualism. If the apostolic story was not significant in historical terms, then the church itself was *only* an image of some genuine spiritual reality, and there was nothing about the community of believers that was essential to redemption. For the Gnostic, the only thing that really mattered was the relationship of the spark in himself or herself (and the Gospel of Thomas, at least, suggests that the "herselves" were in a decidedly lower class than the "himselves") to the divinity of which that spark was a part. To the extent that there was mutual upbuilding in the church, it was the effort of the pneumatics to make the psychics like themselves. There could be no meaningful sense given to the image of the church as a body, with various members serving particular functions for the benefit of all.

Gnostic individualism in the earthly sphere has as its counterpart a dissolution of individuality in the spiritual sphere: the sparks of divinity are all essentially the same. That which makes me what I really am is not the creator's endowing me with certain unique traits, but rather is that in me which has nothing to do with the creator. What I really am is pure spirit, identical with the pure spirit that is in all others who are actually or potentially pneumatics, and are therefore capable of redemption through knowledge of who they really are. The dissolution of individuality fosters individualism, since the *apparent* differences between my neighbors and me are not hard realities with which I must come to terms, to which I must adjust. If my neighbors are somatics, they are beyond help; if they are capable of salvation, they are fundamentally just like me. Individualism of this sort tends to eliminate ethical ambiguity, but the price paid may be ethical insensitivity.

III. Gnosticism and the New Testament

What do these rather esoteric second-century sects have to do with the New Testament? Attempts to answer that question are filling journals and publishers' lists. The basic problem of historical reconstruction is that of moving back from second-century materials, which we have in abundance, to the first-century situation, where the materials are extremely scanty, and where, in fact, the issue revolves around the nature of the sources themselves.

A. Gnosticism at the End of the First Century

"O Timothy, guard what has been entrusted to you. Avoid the godless chatter and contradictions of what is falsely called knowledge (*gnōsis*), for by professing it some have missed the mark as regards the faith" (1 Tim. 6:20). This summary admonition raises in the most direct way the question about the particular character of Gnosticism in the first century—except that the argument can quickly become circular, since the dating of the pastoral letters (1 and 2 Timothy and Titus) is itself subject to much dispute. If the pastorals are first century, then "Gnosticism" was by that time sufficiently developed to be pointed at as a danger; if "Gnosticism" developed only later, then the pastorals, which refer to it, must be dated in the second century.

Assuming for the moment, however, that 1 Timothy is evidence for the end of the first century, we still have many questions to ask. Is the reference here to an organized movement, perhaps already divided into a number of sects? Was Gnosticism something that people already had, and brought with them into the Christian community, working the Christian ideas and symbols into their preexisting framework, or did it originate within the Christian community? Is the *gnosis* referred to in this passage simply the improper conclusion drawn by some Christians from the Pauline distinction between the spiritually mature and the spiritually immature? Questions such as these are even more characteristic of study of "the Gnostic challenge" than of study of "the Jewish matrix," but in both cases there is simply no shortcut past the questions.

It is important to remember that *gnosis* is simply the regular

Greek word for "knowledge," and we must not assume that whenever it appears in a religious context it carries overtones of the
esoteric and the elitist. And whatever we decide about the nature
of the *gnōsis* that is denounced in 1 Timothy, we have to ask how
much we can legitimately read back from the situation described
there to the earlier apostolic period. Moreover, we always have to
consider whether what is reflected by a particular writing is a general situation in the church, or tells us only about a particular
geographical region.

Earlier in 1 Timothy we are given some indication of the kinds
of things that must be countered: teachings that "occupy themselves
with myths and endless genealogies which promote speculations
rather than the divine training that is in faith" (1:4). We are warned
against asceticisms that are challenges to the goodness of the world:
exponents of these practices "forbid marriage and enjoin absti-
nence from foods which God created to be received with thanksgiving by those who believe and know the truth. For everything
created by God is good, and nothing is to be rejected if it is received
with thanksgiving; for then it is consecrated by the word of God
and prayer" (4:3–4).

The Letters of John warn their readers to beware of those who
deny the reality of the incarnation: "Many deceivers have gone out
into the world, men who will not acknowledge the coming of Jesus
Christ in the flesh; such a one is the deceiver and the antichrist" (2
John 7). And a primary concern of the letters of Bishop Ignatius of
Antioch, written on his way to martyrdom in Rome about A.D. 110
(that is, in the general time period to which the pastoral and Johannine letters are usually assigned), is the spread of docetism:

> Be deaf, then, to any talk that ignores Jesus Christ, of David's lineage,
> of Mary; who was really born, ate, and drank; was really persecuted
> under Pontius Pilate; was really crucified and died, in the sight of
> heaven and earth and the underworld. He was really raised from the
> dead, for his Father raised him, just as his Father will raise us, who
> believe on him, through Christ Jesus, apart from whom we have no
> genuine life.[17]

All these references point to the presence on the Christian scene
by the early second century of movements with tendencies we have
come to recognize as Gnostic. Whether there are as yet Gnostic

churches it is impossible to say with certainty, but clearly the threat from these tendencies is taking on a definite shape.

What are we to say about the earlier period, from Paul's first letters to the writing of the Gospels? Were the apostles having to deal with Gnostics? Were some of the apostles Gnostics?

B. Paul and John

Walter Schmithals, in a provocative book called *Paul and the Gnostics,* has undertaken to reorient the study of Paul's opponents. His conclusion is unflinching: one

> would no longer need to contend about the question whether Christian Gnosticism is a *product* or *manifestation* of primitive Christianity. It would then be demonstrated at least to be contemporary with Hellenistic Christianity. Of course here is the tender spot of our inquiry. The reluctance, which though unfounded is nevertheless understandable, to admit Christian Gnosticism into the beginnings of Christianity is the strongest retarding factor.[18]

Schmithals theorizes that the opponents Paul is fighting in Galatia, in Corinth, and in Philippi are all Jewish-Christian Gnostics. The implications of this for our understanding of Paul in his relations with the Jerusalem church were mentioned in Chapter 3, and will concern us at length in Chapter 7. For now we should note that if Schmithals is right, Paul's theology is shaped not so much in opposition to those who would tie Christianity to the old Law as in opposition to those who would transmute the whole historical emphasis of the biblical tradition into a myth about heavenly, precosmic happenings. In short, Paul is fighting not against an attack from "right-wing conservatives," but against an attack from "left-wing radicals." He becomes not the corrupter of a simple ethical gospel into a Hellenistic mystery religion, but the major force against the absorption of Christianity into the Gnostic melting pot. If Paul is attacking Gnostics, and we are then mystified at the use second-century Gnostics made of Paul's letters to buttress their positions, we should simply remember that Christian theologians in our time frequently make favorable references to and citations of Marx, Nietzsche, and Freud. Once something is written, as Ricoeur reminds us, it becomes subject to interpretation.

We have already seen how there are elements of Paul's teaching about the nature of the church that run directly counter to the central claims of the Gnostics; and when Paul's writings are taken as a whole, he does come across as a firm barrier against the main contentions of Gnosticism. It might have been an intellectual relief to Paul to sever the connections between the God of Israel and the God of Jesus Christ, but that would have been to shatter his own identity. Paul's teaching about the two covenants is through and through rooted in history, and it is the historical process that is moving on toward God's intended conclusion.

The central question about Gnosticism for interpreters of the New Testament is the question of the Gospel of John. It is undeniable that there is much in John's Gospel that fits neatly into a basic Gnostic pattern—the heavenly redeemer who descends into the world and ascends again to the heavenly realm; who identifies his purpose as that of calling his own who will hear his voice and respond automatically, while those who are not his own will not respond and will indeed reject him; who characterizes the world as the arena for the struggle of antithetical forces (light and darkness, the Prince of this world and God).

As was noted earlier, the first known commentary on any New Testament book is the Commentary on John by Heracleon, a Valentinian, writing around A.D. 170. Heracleon is able to present a quite plausible reading of the Gospel in terms of the Valentinian distinction among the three grades of persons (pneumatics, psychics, somatics). Indeed, Heracleon's pattern of exegesis has about it a comprehensiveness that many subsequent commentaries on John lack, and if the ability to make a text fit together is a criterion for a valid interpretation, then the Valentinian exegesis of John has a great deal to commend it.

One reason the Gnostic interpretation can be coherent is that the Gnostic has different categories to which to assign various discordant pieces of the writing being interpreted. For example, when in John we are told that Jesus said he was thirsty or hungry, this does not mean he really was undergoing those human experiences, but only that he was temporarily adapting his speech to the level of those who were hearing him at the time, either psychics or somatics. It is thus impossible for a text to refute a Gnostic position; and as we noted earlier, Tertullian at the end of the second century said that there was simply no use arguing on the ground of Scripture, since there is always some method of interpretation by which a text can be made to yield up the meaning one wants.

Tertullian insists that the only criterion can be the whole general tenor of Scripture, and he claims that a reading of the Bible which makes of the world a ghastly mistake and of the incarnation a shadow play simply will not do. But there is, finally, no compelling argument, other than one's sense of plausibility, against the assertion that Jesus kept his real message for private sessions with a few of his special apostles, who were instructed to pass the tradition down secretly through oral teaching. In those terms, the authentic interpretation of even the public tradition must be sought among those who know the secret tradition. The public tradition publicly interpreted is a snare and a delusion.

The chief question about John's Gospel and Gnosticism is the weight, or one might even say the gravity, that is to be assigned to John 1:14: "And the Word became flesh and dwelt among us." A Gnostic could agree about the "dwelling among us," but the "becoming flesh" would be beyond the bounds of what the Gnostic could affirm. And with the incarnation standing thus squarely athwart the whole Johannine Gospel, all the apparently Gnostic-sounding terms and attitudes and events must be seen as direct challenges to the Gnostic position: that is, everything the Gnostic claimed for the heavenly redeemer could in fact be claimed for the fully human Jesus, a Jesus who was an integral part of the tradition of Israel.

C. Dynamic Models and Historical Understanding

If Paul is fighting Gnostics, if John is doing with Gnosticism what Marx claimed he was doing with Hegel's philosophy—finding it standing on its head, and setting it on its feet—then we must squarely face the implication that Gnosticism in one way or another (or, more likely, in several ways) was present in the formative stages of the Christian tradition.

Helmut Koester and James Robinson have suggested that we shift the images we use for thinking about the relationships of apostolic Christianity and Gnosticism from "backgrounds" to "trajectories." According to these scholars, ideological tendencies and psychological states have a kind of independent life which can be plotted along historical graphs. A particular text is then located not against some particular background, but rather by its point on the trajectory. Its place is defined as much in terms of what comes after it as in terms of what comes before it. The imagery of trajectories also permits the interpreter, using a great deal of caution, to trace a curve back beyond the point at which the earliest documentary evidence begins, and hence to speculate about the state of a particular tendency where the evidence is lacking but the questions are insistent.[19]

Any application of models from one realm of discourse to another presents problems as well as new opportunities, and missiles and spaceships moving through their trajectories are not the same thing as ideas and persons moving through history. But Koester and Robinson have made an important suggestion about new ways of thinking, and they have, perhaps inadvertently, reactivated some insights of the church fathers. They have recognized, as Tertullian did, that contexts are the key to meaning, that "orthodoxy" and "heresy" are directions of movement, not fixed positions. They have recognized, as Origen knew, that Christianity moved through a series of language worlds, not just languages, and that with each "translation" it underwent subtle but pervasive changes.[20]

Koester and Robinson adopt as a principle the statement that "for historical inquiry the New Testament itself has no special claim to have made the correct and orthodox use of the criterion of true faith."[21] Like many interpreters of Christian origins today, they consider the "triumph of orthodoxy," with the consequent designation of Gnosticism as "heresy," to be the outcome of political power struggles within the Christian community, not a result of the "essence" of Christianity asserting itself against an alien threat. The New Testament, in this view, is not the charter of Christianity, but is the expression of the prejudices of the bishops who were victorious at the end of the second century and who admitted as authoritative only those writings which had proved useful in their polemical fight against Gnosticism.

Koester, indeed, carries his analysis along the "Gnosticizing trajectory" back through the New Testament documents, and makes the following revolutionary suggestion: perhaps a *"gnosticizing Christianity" predates* an "apocalyptic Christianity."[22] It has been almost universally accepted by scholars for at least a hundred years that the one thing we know *for sure* about Christian origins is that Jesus' message was at its core apocalyptic; various modifications of his apocalyptic predictions were forced upon the church as historical circumstances changed, but these were *modifications*. Koester's theory calls this assumption into question, and would require a thorough recasting of the story of Christian origins.

No longer could we say that the earliest Christians expected the end of the world soon. Treatises such as the Gospel of Thomas would be our best sources for the nature of the teaching of Jesus, and the New Testament, with its pervasive apocalyptic coloring, would be seen as reflecting a later development. Apocalyptic thinking, which of course had been around for a long time, would have made its way into the Christian community as a challenge to the original belief that this world cannot be redeemed. The apocalyptic Christian would agree with the Gnostic that this world is a mess, but the apocalyptist would insist that the God who created the world was fully capable of redeeming it and would do so soon. If Koester's theory were to be worked through to its full implications, the title of this chapter would not be "The Gnostic Challenge," but "The Apocalyptic Challenge."

Schmithals has made an even deeper challenge to traditional ways of interpreting Christian origins, though his approach and technique have much in common with Koester and Robinson's.

Of course one may not even expect that documents of a "pure" pre-Christian Gnosticism will ever come to light, thus that a "pure" Gnostic sect ever existed. Indeed there was also never a "pure" Christianity, but only a Hellenistic Christianity, a Jewish Christianity, a gnosticizing Christianity, thus a Christianity which from time to time made use of the forms of existing manifestations of religion for the expression of its own religious understanding.

He then goes on to say that Gnosticism likewise existed only in concrete forms (Jewish, Christian, various pagan sects).

Therefore Christian Gnosticism is just as legitimate a form of this religious movement as, say, the Jewish Gnosticism of the pre-Christian era—as indeed also a gnosticizing Christianity no less than the Hellenistic one is a proper Christianity if it maintains the genuinely Christian understanding of existence.[23]

There are many assumptions tucked away in these lines from Schmithals. For example, "the Jewish Gnosticism of the pre-Christian era" is a supposition, not a demonstrated fact. To speak of a "pre-Christian Jewish Gnosticism" at all requires a working definition of Gnosticism as "an attitude with certain characteristic main features and without any necessary organizational consequences."

Another assumption, and one far more momentous than that of a pre-Christian Jewish Gnosticism, is conveyed in the phrase "the genuinely Christian understanding of existence." As we have seen in various references to Bultmann and in the discussion of "the new hermeneutic," this phrase has become a fixed point in much New Testament study. The "genuinely Christian understanding of existence" turns out to be almost the same as that of modern existentialist philosophy. And not only does "the genuinely Christian understanding of existence" become the criterion for determining what in early Christian texts is authoritative, it also becomes a device for neatly extricating Christianity as such from the category of "religion." Schmithals indicates this when, having declared that there never was a "pure" Christianity, he goes on to speak of "a Christianity which from time to time made use of the forms of existing manifestations of religion." "Essential Christianity" has been ushered out the front door, only to be readmitted at the rear. Christianity is an understanding of existence, which goes about seeking a religious house to inhabit, and can be accommodated anywhere.

Some recent scholars, theologically more conservative than Schmithals, have been historically more daring, and have called into question the reconstruction of a single early Christian preaching (kērygma). The apostolic faith becomes not a fixed point, but rather the sense of common purpose and fellowship of persons who responded in a variety of ways, in terms of their own language and previous experience, to Jesus. Very quickly, almost immediately, the process of elaboration and development became more complex, as people began responding not to Jesus directly, but to the various reports about him and the interpretations of his significance by those who had known him.

All was not arbitrary. It was generally recognized that some people were in a better position than others to speak authoritatively about Jesus. Virtually every viewpoint claimed some sort of apostolic origin, so even if many of the claims were fabricated, nearly everyone agreed that the apostles had a preeminent right to declare what the faith was. However, despite our growing recognition of the wide base of agreement in the apostolic generation, it remains true that there were several "apostolic understandings of existence," and it is historically unjustified to say that only one (and the one that corresponds to a major philosophical position today) is the "genuinely Christian" one. The image of the body with many members, none self-sufficient and none expendable, is useful as a model for original Christian belief as well as for the church as an institution. The Gospels can be seen not as variations on the theme of the single *kērygma,* but rather as expressions of diverse and authentic *kērygmata.* [24]

All of this puts the problem of Gnosticism and the New Testament in a different perspective. The question becomes not whether Gnosticism maintains the genuinely Christian understanding of existence, but whether Gnostics, hearing and seeing Jesus, could make coherent sense of what they saw and heard.

The key term here is "coherent." In one sense, as we have seen, the Gnostic is a master of coherence. Literally every detail of a text, of group life, of individual experience could be fitted into a comprehensive scheme. Moreover, an anti-Gnostic argument framed in terms of the public traditions about Jesus can *always* be countered by appeal to an alleged secret tradition. And some modern scholars want to say that we are in no position to judge among the responses to Jesus: if a Gnostic found meaning in Jesus in terms of a Gnostic pattern of understanding, then there is no reason, historically or theologically, to deny that such an apprehension of Jesus is "authentically Christian."

As a historian, I have some sympathy with those who do not want to rule out of definitional bounds any group in the ancient world that considered itself Christian. We certainly must be on guard against too easy an acceptance of the judgments made later by the "orthodox." However, also as a historian, I am by instinct, training, and professional experience suspicious of any view of reality that fits everything into a formula with no inconvenient remainders. Gnostic coherence is bought at the price of another sort of incoherence: the Gnostic makes coherent sense of Jesus by disregarding, indeed by dissolving, the ambiguities of history. As a historian I find it implausible—not impossible, but implausible—that the meaning of a historical occurrence can be totally at variance with the nature of history itself.

We here touch on an issue of much concern in Christian theology today—the question of the relationship of history and revelation. We shall have to deal further with the issue in the final chapter of this book, but as a foretaste of that discussion it should be noted now that my view has much in common with that of the late H. Richard Niebuhr, who argues that revelation in history serves to illuminate—not to explain, but to illuminate—history as a whole.

Revelation in history does not, as the Gnostic would have it, serve to expose the meaninglessness of history as such. Just as certain key passages of Scripture have traditionally been seen as useful clues to the meaning of other passages, so the revelatory events of history serve to clarify the meaning of other events. But the interpretation of Scripture has elements of art as well as of science—and the same is true for the interpretation of history. And just as the key passages of Scripture are themselves not beyond the scope of investigation and reflection applicable to all of Scripture, so the revelatory events of history are not sealed off from the uncertainties and lingering incoherence characteristic of all history. The Gnostic could make completely coherent sense—but it was not really sense of what was seen and heard, for seeing and hearing are apprehensions of historical reality, and historical reality does not come in a neatly tied package.

IV. THE PERENNIAL TEMPTATION

Some years ago I read aloud to a class of undergraduates a portion of Irenaeus' description of the Valentinian system, with its thirty Aeons of strange-sounding names, its universe crowded with rank upon rank of spiritual beings separating our world from the God who is really God. I expected them to find it amusing, even grotesque, and I waited for the laughter. It did not come. They said they found the whole scheme very interesting, and not entirely implausible. I date from that moment my own growing understanding of the intellectual seriousness and psychological appeal of the Gnostic challenge.

There is much that is attractive about Gnosticism. A recent article by Richard H. Drummond has called for a far more positive evaluation of Gnosticism than has been customary in New Testament study. He considers that

> the problem was and is a familial one, an issue within the family of Christian faith. In this context of understanding, then, we may cite the names of Basilides, Valentinus, Ptolemy, Heracleon, Marcus, and Theodotus both as Gnostics and also as among the most spiritually perceptive and intellectually capable Christians of the second century.[25]

Drummond reminds us of the wide scope of the term *gnōsis,* and sees those known as Gnostics simply carrying out the implications of *knowledge* as a trait of the mature Christian in the theology of Paul. The Gnostic understanding of religious life, especially in the writings of Valentinus, is portrayed by Drummond as emphasizing growth and avoiding reliance upon events external to one's own existence: the Gnostics "were evidently concerned to affirm salvation as a repeatable 'now,' as a meaningful process of spiritual and moral growth both on earth and in the unseen realms beyond." The heart of Gnosticism, then, according to Drummond, is its analysis of the growth process; the Gnostic imagery is, as the psychologist C. G. Jung recognized, a profound depiction of deep psychological processes, and the Gnostic approach to Scripture permits the ancient text to serve as a guide for persons on a spiritual journey. Gnosticism is, in short, an early and positively instructive example of a way to make Christianity relevant to everyday life.[26]

One can grant many of Drummond's points, especially his call for an awareness of the wide range of Gnosticisms and of the theological moderation of one of the most important of the Nag Hammadi texts, the Gospel of Truth, a work in all likelihood from the pen of Valentinus himself. Nevertheless, Drummond's argument is reminiscent of the conclusions to which interpreters jumped soon after the discovery of the Dead Sea Scrolls. Just as in that case it was exciting to see the prospect of a total rethinking of Christian origins, so with the Nag Hammadi discovery, there is the excitement of discovering the prejudices in the church fathers' treatment of the Gnostics. To a large degree, of course, it is simply a truism that the bulk of records from the past are those of the victors, and when documents of those who were eventually defeated happen to survive, they can serve as a valuable corrective to the "official record."

But our time is inordinately suspicious of authority, and we are strongly tempted to go too far in heralding as evidence of "the truth" whatever runs directly counter to "the line" put forth by those who come out on top.

The second century was, to be sure, a time of fierce struggle, and in polemical battles of the sort fought then, dispassionate appraisals of what one's opponents were saying were unlikely to be made. Valentinus and others must be heard speaking for themselves. But Drummond does have to qualify his overall contention that Valentinus was teaching a message fundamentally in line with the New Testament. First, he notes that Gnostics had a negative view of the material world. Second, he skirts rather quickly around the problem of "creation through mediation" in the Gnostic texts. The Gnostics speak of creation by the agency of a being or beings subordinate to the true God, and John's Gospel and the Letter to the Colossians also distinguish the agent of creation from God the Father; but the New Testament documents make the Word, the "Firstborn," through whom creation occurs, the one through whom redemption also occurs.

To insist that creation and redemption have the same agent amounts to a good deal more than simply an alternative view of mediation. It literally makes all the difference in the world. Nag Hammadi certainly makes the old hard-and-fast lines between Gnostic and orthodox impossible to maintain, but the church fathers were right that there were fundamental issues at stake. And as I shall argue, it was not simply a quarrel within the family.

V. Is Gnosticism Christian?

Just as Drummond's article is a corrective which needs correcting, so is Koester's suggestion about the gnosticizing tendency preceding the apocalyptic. Koester has opened wide the question of how the Christian message was first formulated, and has, in effect, asked scholars to consider fully the implications of the time lag between the Gospel events and the composition of Paul's letters. Could it have been that in that period of about a decade and a half an originally Gnostic movement, with a founder who preached a Gnostic message, was taken over by apocalyptists, who purged the community's memory of much of its original material?

When the question is posed this starkly, the answer appears to be a certain "No," and yet we have seen movements undergo extraordinary changes in a very short time in our own revolutionary age, and the argument against Koester's theory cannot rest simply on our imagination's unwillingness to stretch as far as Koester would have it stretch.

There are at least three specific arguments that weigh against the notion that Christianity was at its origins Gnostic (this is not to be confused with the notion that there were among the original followers of Jesus some who heard him "gnostically," a notion that has a fair degree of plausibility).

First, Koester has to depend too much on reading between the lines of the sources. He could respond, of course, that the sources all reflect the influence of the apocalyptic tendency which supplanted the original Gnostic one. Still, arguments of this sort have something of the insubstantiality of allegorical interpretations of texts.

Second, the New Testament sources are themselves extraordinarily complex, and it is hard to see in them a kind of deliberate purging of one or another line of tradition. The very fact that a good deal of the New Testament can be read as reflecting Gnostic tendencies suggests that if apocalyptists took over, they did a singularly inept job of recording their victory in the texts they eventually adopted as authoritative.

Third, as far as we know, the Gnostics did not themselves turn the tables of the argument the church fathers used against them: that they had appeared late on the scene. The Gnostics certainly claimed to have a tradition going back to Jesus, but they did not claim that the "public tradition," that is, the basically apocalyptic tradition, did not originate in the time of Jesus. If the apocalyptists had in fact moved in and taken over, the Gnostics would likely have complained about it.

Clearly, the debates about Christian origins—indeed, about the definition of Christianity itself—that have been generated by the Nag Hammadi library and the consequent reevaluation of the New Testament evidence and the writings of the church fathers (not to mention Qumran and the extensive intertestamental literature) will continue long into the future, and will probably recur again and again after each provisional "settlement," as fresh ways of thinking about the dynamics of history send scholars back again to sources they thought they already knew thoroughly.

When everything is in flux, as it appears to be in Gnostic studies, caution would dictate ending this chapter with the paragraph immediately above. However, I have already indicated that my assessment of Gnosticism is much less favorable than Drummond's, and I should conclude with some account of my reason for thinking that despite the attractive qualities of Gnosticism, and despite the real possibility that there were Gnostic understandings of existence at the very beginning of the Christian movement, Gnosticism is, at its heart, not Christian.

We know from Hengel and others that Judaism was pervasively Hellenized, and that in the time of Jesus the Hebrew Scriptures were already subject to a wide range of interpretation. We know, further, that all varieties of the Christian movement considered the Hebrew Scriptures to be a sacred text; even Marcion treated it as an authentic record of divine activity, but of a deity he could not stand. We know that subsequent to A.D. 70 there developed recognizably Gnostic tendencies among some Jews in their interpretation of Scripture, but we have no unequivocal evidence that prior to that time any of the wide range of interpretations clamoring for attention proposed a clean break between the God spoken of in the Hebrew Scriptures—that is, the God who created the world and called the people of Israel to a special mission—and the God who was worthy of human worship. Some speculation, particularly in Alexandria, came close to crossing the line, but it stopped short.

Therefore it is historically implausible that Jesus and his earliest followers severed the connection between the God of Israel and the God who is really God. There was much despair of the world in the Judaism of the first century A.D., but its characteristic expression was apocalyptic, which insists, in the face of what look like overwhelming odds, that the God who created the world is quite capable of rescuing it: the apocalyptist has not yet given up on the creator.

I contend, therefore, that the defeat of Marcion was not simply a victory of bishops who played their political trump cards but was also a victory for the original status of Christianity. Even Origen, who felt a strong pull toward Gnosticism, was held in check by the church's retention of the Old Testament, and he found a place for

the world in his cosmic scheme which made of the world an educational device, not a trap or prison. Drummond suggests that there
is not much difference between Origen and the Gnostics in the
evaluation of the world, and Origen does not sound much like the
"orthodox"; but on the main issue he is on the orthodox side—
creation and redemption work together, not at cross-purposes.[27]

Gnosticism can be viewed positively, as promoting spiritual
growth. But to say that such growth requires prying Christianity
loose from its grounding in history is to shortchange historical
understanding, and is to overlook the capacity of sacramental and
communal life to give meaning to historical reminiscence. Gnosticism's individualism, and exaltation of "the spiritual," run counter
to the heritage of Israel built into Christianity at its origin, and
retained in Christianity through the church's insistence that the
Hebrew Scriptures are an integral part of the Christian charter.
Every time we dismiss the "God of wrath" of the Old Testament
as unworthy to stand alongside the "God of love" of the New
Testament, and every time we say that Christianity has to do with
individual spiritual growth and has nothing to do with the world
of the flesh—society, politics, economics, business, and all the rest
—we are succumbing to the perennial temptation of Gnosticism.

The world evoked by T. S. Eliot in "East Coker":

> The time of the seasons and the constellations
> The time of milking and the time of harvest
> The time of the coupling of man and woman
> And that of beasts. Feet rising and falling;
> Eating and drinking. Dung and death[28]

is the world for which the Gnostic feels revulsion, in which the
Gnostic experiences total alienation, out of which the Revealer calls
the Gnostic. If Gnostics could get up beyond dung and death,
beyond the coupling of man and woman and of beasts, to the
heavenly realm of the constellations, then they would feel less ill
at ease. What the Gnostic cannot bear is the claim that the constellations and intercourse and dung and death are all part of the *same*
system. A world that appears to be going to hell does not provide
the most pleasant voyage imaginable. But the call to abandon ship
is Gnostic, and not Christian.

CHAPTER
SIX

JESUS: HOW MUCH HISTORY
IS ENOUGH?

Is Jesus essential to Christianity? Most people would never think of asking the question, since the connection between Jesus and Christianity appears self-evident. Christians treat as divine revelation a book that talks a great deal about Jesus, and Christian worship is full of references to him.

One of the earliest Christian creeds was the simple declaration "Jesus is Lord," and in recent years the name of Jesus has become a cultural cliché in America, from "Jesus Christ Superstar" to bumper stickers with the assurance that "Jesus Loves You" and with instructions to "Honk If You Love Jesus."

The connection between Jesus and Christianity cannot be taken for granted, however. For more than a century the question about the historical Jesus has exercised learned and discriminating minds. Many a serious student of the New Testament might want to attach to the car a bumper sticker imploring, "Honk If You Know for Sure What Jesus Said and Did."

Of course, anyone who is content to say that it is all a matter of faith, and that God reveals the truth about Jesus to whomever he pleases, will judge those who are bothered by historical difficulties to be weak in faith, or will treat them with a kind of pity, saying as Festus did to Paul (Acts 26:24), "Much learning has made you mad." But the questions the scholar asks are not idle pastimes. An underlying assumption of the Bible is that God has chosen to reveal himself in history. It would be much more convenient if the revelation were made directly to our intellects, but the Bible will not let it be that easy. Our attention is directed not to abstractions, but to history, and the historical questions are a Christian response to the biblical text.

As we saw in Chapter 3, the differences among the Gospels present an initial problem about the historical Jesus, and while Irenaeus offered a rather sophisticated explanation for the differences in terms of the purposes motivating each Evangelist, many Christians through the ages have functioned with some sort of practical "harmonization" of the Gospels. Another way to solve the initial problem was that of Marcion, who made Jesus logically consistent by treating only one Gospel as authoritative, and by eliminating from that one (Luke) all passages incompatible with what he conceived Jesus to be. Other Gnostics sorted out conflicting passages according to a theory about the variety of audiences to which Jesus was addressing himself.

Debates about the identity of the historical Jesus—that is, disputes about what he really said (and what it meant), what he really did, what was really done to him—are thus as old as the church itself, and in that sense the quest of the historical Jesus is not new. But until the beginning of the nineteenth century all participants in these debates, no matter which side they were on, assumed that we have the materials necessary for reaching firm conclusions about Jesus: *your* trouble is that you do not use *my* method of interpretation, which gets at the truth. What the nineteenth century added to the ancient quest was an inquiry into the assumption. Scholars began to suspect that the materials themselves are not the sort that will sustain firm conclusions.

It was in biblical scholarship, and particularly in the study of the life of Jesus, that the intellectual obsession and tension of the nineteenth century first became apparent: the aim of the historian was conceived to be an account of the past as it actually was, and yet the practical experience of working with the relics of the past made the achievement of that aim increasingly improbable. The result by the end of the nineteenth century was despair of ever knowing much about Jesus, coupled with a confidence that most of what the Gospels claim to know about him cannot be trusted.

It has now been three quarters of a century since Albert Schweitzer declared that the possibilities in the quest of the historical Jesus had been exhausted, and that the enterprise must be abandoned. The whole issue remained very much in the background for several decades, but the question of the historical Jesus has come back to life. Christianity seems unable to rest content with Bultmann's dictum that the message of Jesus is a "presupposition of the theology of the New Testament" but not a part of that theology, and historical study itself cannot rest content with a story of the rise of Christianity that seals Jesus off from Christianity's beginnings.

I. FIRST CHAPTER OR LAST?

The issue is very far from being resolved. The current debate is being carried on in articles and books that deal directly with questions of historical theory and method in their relation to theology, but the nature of the debate, and its depth, are made clearest by the contrast between two excellent introductory textbooks for New Testament study. In such books, the question of the historical Jesus is first of all a thoroughly practical one: where does the chapter about him go? The answer given in any particular case is of more than practical significance.

One of the books, *Understanding the New Testament,* by Howard Kee, Franklin Young, and Karlfried Froehlich, is now in its third revised edition (1973), and has been widely used since it was first published in 1957. The other book, *The New Testament: An Introduction,* by the late Norman Perrin, was published recently (1974), and is sure to become influential. In both cases the authors are committed to the most up-to-date analytical techniques in their treatment of the textual materials, and yet they deal with the question of Jesus in strikingly different ways.[1]

Kee, Young, and Froehlich begin their book with a section on "Community and Identity," which has subsections on the Roman Empire and Judaism. Then they launch into the study of the New Testament itself with a section on "The Community of the New Covenant," subtitled "Jesus and the Gospel." In this section, after a chapter on the relationship of "the gospel" to "the four Gospels," they devote an entire chapter of twenty pages to "Jesus, Prophet of the New Age." From there the authors move on to discuss the developments, including the activity of Paul, by which the church became an "inclusive community" which took definite shape as it "confronted the world."

Perrin, after two preliminary chapters about the nature of the New Testament documents and New Testament ways of speaking, devotes his third chapter to "A Theological History of New Testament Christianity," the first part of which considers the Roman conquest of Jerusalem in A.D. 70 and the delay of the return of Christ. Analysis of Paul's writings and of those which go under his name precedes Perrin's treatment of the Gospels, and the final chapter of the book is entitled "The Presupposition of the New Testament: Jesus." Material with which Kee, Young, and Froehlich begin—a description of the Hellenistic world and the historical situation of the Jewish people in New Testament times—appears as the first two appendixes to Perrin's book.

Each of these introductory textbooks is implying that the other book is organized improperly. Perrin would appear to say that if you are going to use *Understanding the New Testament,* you should read it from back to front, and Kee, Young, and Froehlich would appear to say the same thing about *The New Testament: An Introduction.* The two books are almost exact mirror images of each other.

Perrin recognizes that his ordering of the material is not what most people would expect, and he explains how he came to put things together as he has. He says that for twenty-five years he struggled with Bultmann's contention about the message of Jesus —that it is a presupposition of New Testament theology but not a part of it—and he has finally become persuaded that Bultmann is right. Presuppositions are of course involved in our thinking about anything, whether theology or science or politics or family, but seldom can we get at them directly. Perrin, following Bultmann, believes that we must first figure out what the New Testament is about, and then we may be able to infer a few things about the New Testament's "presupposition," the message of Jesus (where "message" is understood to be both words and deeds). The shape and tenor of Perrin's book are eloquent testimony to the thoroughness of his scholarly conversion to Bultmann's way of thinking.[2]

Kee, Young, and Froehlich do not explain directly how they arrived at their organization of the material. Their presentation is closer to what most people would expect to find, although in the view of many scholars the shape of *Understanding the New Testament,* even in its recent third edition, would appear somewhat out of date and in need of justification.

Kee, Young, and Froehlich do provide an implicit argument in favor of their enterprise. The very terminology of their book, with its concentration on categories of community, is a challenge to the existentialist approach of Bultmann and his followers, who see the meaning of the New Testament as centrally concerned with the individual and the authenticity of the individual's existence. Kee, Young, and Froehlich, precisely because for them community is a fundamental category, find possibilities of establishing continuity between the activity and teaching of Jesus and that of the early Christian church. They place Jesus himself in community. They do not set Jesus off against a community that presupposes him; on the contrary, Jesus himself presupposes community.

Somewhat ironically, it is those who pay more attention to the Jewish, Hellenistic, and early Christian quests for community who are more sanguine than those of existentialist (and hence individualistic) sympathies about the prospects for a successful quest of the individual Jesus. *Understanding the New Testament* provides a better way of approach to the New Testament than does *The New Testament: An Introduction*—better because the understanding of history with which it operates is more comprehensive and less strained; better because the understanding of religion with which it operates corresponds more closely to the life and thought of the religious community that is recorded in the New Testament.

II. History as Enterprise and Concept

In what follows we shall have to review briefly some of the points that were made in Chapter 2. There the matter of "thinking historically" was dealt with in fairly general terms, while here the questions are related directly to the investigation of Jesus.

When Ranke's ideal—an account of the past "as it actually was" —was set beside the Gospels as the standard to which they must be made to answer, the suspicion quickly arose that by the time the Gospels were written the church itself had lost touch with the facts of forty or fifty or sixty years earlier, and that the most the historian could recount with any confidence was the beliefs, including the beliefs about Jesus, of the Christian church toward the end of the first century. The idea was seriously entertained in the nineteenth century that "Jesus" was a construct of the church, a figure purely of legend invented to account for the beliefs which the Christians found themselves holding in common. Such views appear quaint today, when even the most radical historical critics consider the existence of Jesus scarcely more open to doubt than that of Pontius Pilate, but nineteenth-century suspicions that there was no historical Jesus were the logical extension of new and serious attempts to determine what we can claim to *know* about the past.

Much modern interpretation of the New Testament has been content with salvaging only the bare minimum from the nineteenth century's demolition of the traditional picture of Jesus. Bultmann has insisted that nothing matters about Jesus except *that* he existed; if Jesus was made up, the Christian gospel's claim would be fraudulent, but the existence of Jesus in history is all the contribution Jesus need make to the authentication of the gospel. Whether Jesus did this or that, whether he said one thing or another: all such questions we can take or leave, calmly giving up all concern about the details of the life of Jesus.

A reaction against Bultmann's reduction of the "Jesus question" to the bedrock matter of factuality—*that* Jesus lived—has developed in recent years among some of Bultmann's pupils. They have recognized that the early Christian preaching appeals to Jesus in ways that are compelling only if some things and not others about Jesus are true. To put it in more technical terms: they now insist that the early Christian preaching must have some integral *and historically detectable* connection with the "presupposition" of that preaching—the presupposition must be historical as well as logical and psychological.

The "new quest of the historical Jesus" among the new generation of Bultmannians is one of several ways in which the question for which Schweitzer wrote the obituary in 1899 has come alive again in our own time.[3] In order to understand this revival, we have to consider in general terms issues left over from the nineteenth century, and some of the practical, procedural matters that every historian has to deal with.

A. Historical Investigation

Up to a certain point, the historian must adhere strictly to Ranke's ideal: distinctions must be made between fact and fantasy. For instance, many medieval texts justify papal claims to temporal sovereignty over the Roman Empire by reference to the "Donation of Constantine," by which the first Christian emperor, in the fourth century, willed the Empire to the bishop of Rome in gratitude for curing him of leprosy. A scholar in the fifteenth century proved that the Donation was a forgery of the seventh or eighth century. Anyone who would today undertake to write a history of the fourth century with a reference to the Donation of Constantine as a fact of the fourth century would be treated with deserved contempt.

The Donation of Constantine is a useful example, but it is an easy one. Very often scholars have to deal with problems that are much less clear, where the distinction between fact and fantasy is blurred, and where the answer you get depends to a large, and sometimes disconcerting, extent on the way in which you put the question. As we shall see, one of the more vexed questions about the historical Jesus—whether or not he claimed to be the Messiah—is formally similar to the question about the Donation of Constantine, but a clear answer is harder to come by.

Ranke's ideal itself becomes a problem, and not simply the solution to a problem, when it tricks us into thinking that the past can be separated neatly into two baskets, one labeled "fact" and the other labeled "fantasy." The notion of "fact" is not as simple as many people think it is. The reader of a history book is entitled to expect a report of facts, but the book is written on the basis of documents, and every document records an event from a particular point of view. The document itself might be called a "bare fact," but usually what is interesting about the document is not its own existence, but the occurrence or thought or situation to which it refers, and whatever it refers to is not a "bare fact," but is necessarily subject to interpretation and evaluation.

A recent occurrence will make the point clearer. No one would contest the statement that in August of 1974 Richard Nixon resigned the presidency of the United States. That is a historical fact, but by itself it is not very interesting. The fact becomes of interest when we start talking about whether the resignation was a "hounding out of office" by Mr. Nixon's political opponents, or an act of self-sacrifice to spare the nation the agony of a long trial in the Senate, or a calculated, self-serving evasion of prosecution in order to assure a substantial pension, or simply a recognition that "the game was up." We debate whether President Ford's pardon was part of a tacit deal made earlier or was the generous gesture of a guileless man. We wonder whether Richard Nixon will be remembered primarily as the first president to resign or as the president who opened the way for the establishment of relations with China. In each of these questions, the answer we come to will depend partly on other "facts" that are beyond dispute; the answer will depend significantly on what we take to be plausible about human nature, about politics, about collective memory. And the fact that the Nixon resignation is recent helps to drive home the point: events to which we are close, at least to the extent of living contemporaneously with them, are subject *necessarily* to our exercise of judgment.

If we cannot arrive at a generally agreed upon explanation of Richard Nixon's resignation, why should we hope ever to be able to explain completely the conversion of the Emperor Constantine, or the schism between Judaism and Christianity—or the reasons for the crucifixion of Jesus? It is often said that the historian has the advantage of perspective, that the past is "closed off" and therefore one can see it whole and with an objectivity that cannot be managed for contemporary affairs. But the past is subject to uncertainty and interpretation just as the present is. As objects of inquiry and reflection, two thousand years ago and yesterday are in the same general category.

The problem of the historical Jesus is a problem, to be sure; but it ought not to be thought of as a unique problem. Even more important, the difficulties of historical investigation and judgment ought not to be thought of as the special province of scholars. The historian requires training aimed at sharpening of analytical techniques and refinement of critical judgment, but as was suggested in Chapter 2, historical thinking is something everybody does.

The problem is not unique, and the way of thinking about it is not esoteric. But the problem is complex, and the thinking about it must be careful. We have to be prepared for a wide range of answers. For instance, we might want to know, Did *x* happen? On some such questions, we can be almost certain of the answer: either the crucifixion of Jesus took place or it did not. Virtually every historian today considers the evidence for this event to be substantial and convincing. On a related question, the answer is much less clear: Was Jesus crucified on the Passover, as John's Gospel reports, or on the day after the Passover, as the Synoptic Gospels report? In each case a specifically theological interpretation of the significance of Jesus' death is being put forth: the Synoptics present the Last Supper as the new Passover, John presents Jesus on the cross as the new Passover Lamb. And given the theological intention of both traditions, one may venture to wonder whether the crucifixion took place in the Passover season at all. On another related question, the answer is unclear, but not for internal theological reasons: What does the fact of Jesus' death at the hands of the Romans mean for our understanding of the opposition to Jesus, and hence for our understanding of the nature of Jesus' teaching and activity? The answer to such a question cannot finally be dictated by the concerns of today's renewed dialogue between Jews and Christians, but the way in which the question is put is bound to be influenced by current issues.

The historical fact of the crucifixion of Jesus, about which there is no serious doubt, poses its own set of difficult questions. There are other matters of great importance about the historical Jesus for which the determination of the "fact" itself is a problem. For example, either Jesus claimed to be the Messiah or he did not. Many, probably most, New Testament scholars today are persuaded that Jesus did not make such a claim for himself. On some questions, the very possibility of arriving at a historical answer depends on the particular aspect of the question we single out for emphasis. For example, the statement "Either Jesus rose from the dead or he did not" cannot be dealt with without first asking whether we are talking about the experience of many early Christians that Jesus was alive again with them. If that is what we are talking about, we are clearly dealing with historical "fact," although we need to differentiate among a variety of ways in which the presence of Jesus was experienced and reported. If the statement is concerned with an empty tomb and a resuscitated corpse, the question becomes extraordinarily ambiguous, not only because of our modern difficulties with such an account but also because the New Testament itself offers other ways of talking about Easter morning. Finally, there are New Testament declarations about Jesus that are totally beyond the reach of historical assessment. For example, the declaration that "the Word became flesh and dwelt among us" cannot be judged by the historian as historian to be either fact or fantasy.

Distinguishing the historical from the unhistorical—that is, things that happened from things that did not happen—is only part of the historian's task, but it is a much more complex part than is popularly supposed. There is no neat formula that can be applied to the assessment of documents, whether they be gospels two millennia old or newspapers one day old. Each assertion about an occurrence has to be dealt with individually. The establishment of what is historical is not a single enterprise, but is a variety of critical exercises applied to a wide spectrum of kinds of statements.

B. Historical Judgment

The historian has to determine as carefully as possible what is historical, but that is only the beginning. The chief aim of the historian is not to compile a catalog of indisputable facts, but to tell a story, using what is historical as the material. The historian is constantly making judgments about what is *historic* within the *historical.*

Nearly everybody knows, at the level of personal experience, something of the distinction between the historical and the historic. An activity, an encounter, a decision which at the time seemed trivial and inconsequential proves in retrospect to have been pivotal, and to be that in terms of which what came afterward (and perhaps also what came before) makes coherent sense. There are also occurrences which at the time seem momentous and later can hardly be remembered at all. As was suggested in Chapter 2, the historian is engaged in an extension of the human activity of remembering, which is simply another way of saying that the historian is attempting to tell a story about what is historic.

At one level, the decision about what is historic depends on an evaluation of the evidence: Did x in fact have long-range consequence y? There is yet another level of the enterprise and concept of history, however, and concern with this level has been the leading characteristic of recent work on the question of the historical Jesus.

Our century, more than any previous one, defines persons as historical beings. Whatever possibilities for growth I have are both given by and bounded by my location in history. As we saw in the discussion of "the new hermeneutic" in Chapter 3, the term that has come to characterize this understanding of the human situation is *historicity.* Historicity as a characteristic of our total life is reflected in the tension within our intellectual activity between uncertainty about what is historical and the necessity for judgment about what is historic.

Depending on how you order and evaluate the facts, the story can add up as it does in Ecclesiastes, to "All is vanity . . . and there is nothing new under the sun," or as it does in *Macbeth,* to "a tale told by an idiot, full of sound and fury, signifying nothing," or as it does in *Peanuts,* to Lucy Van Pelt's diagnosis of Linus' problem as "pantophobia—the fear of everything," or as it does in Shelley, to "a dome of many-colored glass, staining the white radiance of Eternity," or as it does in Paul, to "a new creation" in the midst of the old.[4] And just as there are many different ways the story can be told, all appealing to the same set of "facts," so in our own life: the facts about us are limited (for example, we cannot live in a world that does not yet know how to unleash nuclear power, or in an America that has not yet been confronted with forceful demands for black liberation and women's liberation), but our judgments about the facts, what they mean in general and what they mean for us in particular, are enormously varied.

The historicity of human existence has been the starting point for existentialist, or "encounter," theology. The existentialist interpreter of the New Testament says first of all that the word of God speaks to us through the text by confronting us with the challenge to decide for faith against unfaith in every moment of decision (which can amount to virtually every waking moment). But the interpreter goes farther than that, and says that the existentialist understanding of the human situation was itself already grasped by the early Christians, or at least by the most perceptive of them. The early Christian preaching was not simply a challenge to decision but also, at least implicitly, an analysis of the human condition; and, as we have seen previously, it turns out to be an analysis corresponding in its main points to modern existentialist conclusions. Historicity, then, becomes in this view the link between the New Testament documents and us. We come to know ourselves and to discover that the New Testament caught on to who we are long ago. The New Testament describes our predicament, and points the way out of it.

There is a scent of Gnosticism about this existentialist interpretation of the New Testament. Historicity becomes an avenue of

escape from history, for when attention focuses exclusively on isolated moments of decision, attention is necessarily diverted from
the patient discipline of a religious life, life with coherence and
continuity not only in itself but also with the life, both historical and
contemporary, of a religious community.

The existentialist might suggest that if the New Testament were
to be set to music, the music should be written by a practitioner of
a modern form known as "aleatory music," that is, compositions
that require the exercise of choice on the part of performers. There
are many degrees of options, from the modest—where the duration
of pitches is dictated by the throwing of coins—to the ultimate—
where the instructions read, "The player may mimic his part or
rebel against it entirely."[5] I would suggest that disciplined
Gregorian chant, sung by monks in a monastery church, remains a
more appropriate setting for the New Testament, a setting that is
true both to the sustained community life that produced the New
Testament, and to the quest for persistence in community of persons who continue to look to that same New Testament for guidance.

The flaw in the existentialist tradition of interpretation is not
directly in the emphasis on historicity; it would be pointless to deny
that human beings are fundamentally defined by their existence in
history. But, as Howard Kee has pointed out, the attention paid to
a particular view of historicity has kept scholars from noticing several other New Testament assessments of the significance of the
historical Jesus, assessments that would help us enrich and deepen
our own perception of the possible meanings for ourselves in the
documents.[6] Kee's point is very important, and comes down to this:
historicity is itself a complex concept; part of one's *historicity* is the
variety of ways of thinking about the world and one's place in it to
which one opens oneself up. The existentialist interpreters of the
New Testament have opened the door to relevance, and then they
have shut it as soon as the first candidate has come through.

Later in this chapter we shall look briefly at some of the new
possibilities that Kee and others are discovering in the New Testament, but prior to that we must consider developments in method-
ology that have undergirded the existentialist approach and, more
recently, an approach that is challenging the adequacy of the existentialist interpretation of the New Testament.

III. From Event to Tradition to Gospel

Albert Schweitzer was skeptical that a "Life of Jesus" could be written, but he did accept as basically valid the structure of Mark's Gospel, according to which Jesus claimed to be the Messiah but instructed those who found this out to keep it a secret. Schweitzer therefore concluded that Jesus not only proclaimed the imminent end of the world and the bringing in of God's kingdom but also identified himself with the Messiah expected by the people of Israel. Schweitzer's assumption was to be challenged head on almost immediately by Wilhelm Wrede, who developed powerful arguments that the messianic secret motif in Mark is editorial—that is, the messianic secret is a theological device of the Evangelist, and cannot be attributed to Jesus.[7]

Scholarship at the beginning of this century was thus left in a quandary. Everyone was convinced of one historical fact: Jesus had preached an apocalyptic message. But the connection between that message and the central New Testament conviction that the career of Jesus himself was integrally part of the whole divine drama and not just the announcement of it seemed to have been broken. The question was posed squarely: Is the account of Jesus in the Gospels the result of the complete transfiguration of the Jesus of history by the Christ of faith? Is there any way of detecting what is *historical* in the materials we have about Jesus?

New Testament scholarship in this century has been dominated by the development and refinement of an analytical technique known in German as *Formgeschichte*, "form history," usually translated into English as "form criticism." In one way or another every serious New Testament scholar has had to come to terms with the method and its results. Only recently, in the last decade or so, an important corrective to the excesses of form criticism has come into prominence, known as *Redaktionsgeschichte*, or "redaction criticism." This approach pays particular attention to each of the Gospels as a theological treatise, and attempts to discern each Evangelist's overall view of the Christian message from his selection and ordering of the material. This new analytical method does nothing by itself to get us back closer to the "historical" in connection with Jesus, but it clarifies the intention of the various Evangelists as form criticism, by its very nature, cannot do, and it brings to light early Christian ways of thinking and preaching that do not fit the existentialist model.

A. Form Criticism

Once scholars had stopped looking for the skeleton of a biography in the Gospels, even in the Gospel of Mark, they began to notice the literary artificiality of the structure of the gospel story. Indications of place are often vague, and indications of time even vaguer. Sayings of Jesus are frequently strung together according to one or two key terms they have in common. It began to be apparent that the Gospels have a mosaic quality: they are built up out of many individual, discrete pieces held together with various sorts of verbal mortar. Attention turned from the mosaic to the pieces, and form criticism was born.[8]

Form criticism concerns itself primarily with what happened in the interim of forty years or more between the events of the life of Jesus and the composition of the Gospels. We know that during the time before the Gospels were written the Christian missionary enterprise went far and wide, and the schism between Judaism and Christianity was well on the way to definition by the time of the fall of Jerusalem. In general, one can say that the Christian movement encountered all sorts of situations and conditions very different from those in which Jesus and his immediate followers lived and moved and had their being (although, as we have seen, new studies of the Hellenistic influence in Judaism tend to reduce the contrast). The historicity of Jesus and the historicity of the early church were decidedly distinct from one another.

The form critic believes that new occasions not only teach new duties, but also require new teaching, and that the traditions about Jesus, passed down orally in the missionary preaching and in the forms of training for new converts, were shaped by the requirements of new social and institutional patterns. The form critic reconstructs the life of the early Christian church in order to provide contexts, or "settings in life" (*Sitzen im Leben* is the technical German phrase), in which the various kinds of units of tradition can be placed.

Christians were involved in debates with Jews, hence the traditions about Jesus' confrontations with his contemporaries would be shaped to fit the practical needs of the church's debates. The church would have to make decisions about appropriate behavior for its members: for example, marriage and divorce issues would certainly arise, and for Gentile Christians, who were most of the Christians, the operative question would be about Roman law, not Jewish, so a tradition developed in which Jesus pronounced on matters of marriage and divorce with reference to Roman legal practice (Mark 10:12, which presupposes a woman's right to divorce her husband, permissible under Roman but not under Jewish law). The Hellenistic world was unacquainted with the parable as a form of teaching, but was thoroughly familiar with the allegorical story, so as the parables of Jesus (such as the sower) were transmitted, their original form and intention was forgotten as they came to be shaped and interpreted as allegories. We know that one of the activities of the early Christians was prophesying, often in the name of the Lord; prophecies that proved beneficial to the community's survival and development would naturally be attributed to Jesus, and would eventually become part of the common tradition of the things he had said.

This is only a small sample of the kinds of "setting in life" that the form critics have reconstructed. There is certainly much to be said for the view that material was shaped by ecclesiastical concerns, although I find the form critics' assurances about the details of early church life in curious contrast to their skepticism about the details of Jesus' life and teachings, and I can echo Sandmel's words: "They seem to be certain—where I find myself tantalized by uncertainties." To take one case: on the question of Jesus' pronouncements on marriage and divorce, why could he not have spoken in terms of Roman law? After all, the Romans were the overlord, the occupying imperial power, and if, as seems not unlikely, Jesus may have known Greek as well as Aramaic, why might he not have been knowledgeable about Roman law and concerned about its implications? Would we consider it a "later development of the tradition" about Gandhi if we came across some statement of his that presupposed a concern with British law?

Some people have argued, against the form critics, that eyewitnesses must have been a check on the free development of the traditions about Jesus; there were almost certainly original followers of Jesus who survived to the time of the writing of the Gospels, or very near to it, and they would have kept the oral tradition within bounds. However, an appeal to supposed eyewitnesses is itself highly problematical, since recent research has raised very serious doubts about the reliability of eyewitness testimony.

The research has dealt primarily with criminal investigation and courtroom situations, but the findings are applicable in a much broader field, since they are rooted in human perception.

> Human perception and memory function effectively by being selective and constructive. . . . Perception and memory are decision-making processes affected by the totality of a person's abilities, background, attitudes, motives and beliefs, by the environment and by the way his recollection is eventually tested. The observer is an active rather than a passive perceiver and recorder; he reaches conclusions on what has been seen by evaluating fragments of information and reconstructing them. He is motivated by a desire to be accurate as he imposes meaning on the overabundance of information that impinges on his senses, but also by a desire to live up to the expectations of other people and to stay in their good graces. The eye, the ear and other sense organs are therefore social organs as well as physical ones.[9]

The important point here is that *perception,* as well as memory, is selective and constructive. "Expectancy" helps the observer be more efficient, but it also warps testimony; the observer may "report facts or events that were not present but that he thinks should have been present." If you asked Peter and John what Jesus said yesterday, you would get two different reports. We could go even further: if you asked Jesus what he said yesterday, it likely would not correspond exactly to a tape recording of what he had said yesterday. The compounded difficulty of eyewitness testimony is put succinctly by Buckhout: "Unreliability stemming from the original situation and from the observer's fallibility is redoubled by the circumstances attending the eventual attempt at information retrieval," and there is a tendency "for people to 'improve' their recollection by making it seem more logical." In summary, eyewitness testimony is "based on a theory, constructed by a human being (often with help from others), about what reality was like in the past."[10]

This understanding of the selective and constructive activity of eyewitnessing corresponds closely to what we have said earlier about the nature of historical thinking, and its further implications for the quest of the historical Jesus will concern us shortly. For the present, it is enough to point out how little comfort the thought that "there were eyewitnesses to control the tradition" can legitimately provide for someone who is made uneasy by form criticism.

At this point, the argument abruptly reverses field. I am strongly persuaded of the unreliability of eyewitness testimony, both because of the accumulated evidence of psychological and legal research and because of my own experience of perceiving and remembering. Nonetheless, I am called up rather short by the following account of a recent luncheon gathering of seven men who had served at various times as legal secretary to Supreme Court Justice Oliver Wendell Holmes. The occasion was the fortieth anniversary of Holmes's death, a figure that itself suggests interesting parallels with the composition of the Gospels.

> The secretaries worked hard for Holmes and had little time for girls or parties. They made some money, but not very much. And for the rest of their lives they probably all looked back on the year with the old man who called them "sonny" and "idiot boy" as the most important thing that ever happened to them. . . .
> There is a Hindi word, *darshan,* which is taken these days to mean "sitting at the feet of a master." It really means "breathing the same air." All seven of the secretaries who turned up for lunch—the oldest was eighty-three and the youngest sixty-eight—spoke of "the Justice" as if he were in the next room and they had just finished talking to him, or being bawled out by him. They all remembered exactly what he had said to them, how he had stood when he said it, his pink-and-white complexion, his suit, his tone of voice, his bristling white cavalry mustachios, and what he had had for breakfast that morning. . . .
> "I once asked Holmes [said Harvard Law professor emeritus Austin Wakeman Scott], when he was in his nineties, and apropos of what I do not know [notice the recall of the interchange, without recollection of the *Sitz im Leben*], 'Mr. Justice, how old a man do you conceive God the Father to be?' 'About seventy,' he said. 'Young enough to be vigorous but old enough to be wise.' "
> "When I was with him," said Alger Hiss, "he was reading Thucydides in the original, and I asked him why. 'When I appear before *le Bon Dieu* [God],' he said, 'He may say to me, "Holmes, can you recite on Thucydides?" If I have to say, "No, Sire," think what a fool I'd feel.' ". . .

We [the anonymous *New Yorker* reporter—another interesting parallel with the Gospels, all of which are in fact anonymous] asked the secretaries if they had ever guessed they would be chosen by Holmes.

"Hell, no," said Chapman Rose.

"I've been trying to figure out for forty years why *I* got picked," said Donald Hiss.

"The first I knew about it," said his brother Alger, "was when he wrote me telling me I had the job. The letter said, 'You realize at my age I must reserve the right to die or resign.' He had just turned eighty-eight."

"Oh," said Chauncey Belknap, who had clerked for Holmes when the Justice was only seventy-four, "he started putting that sentence in the letter when he was sixty."

During the luncheon, "stories poured out." The secretaries remembered in detail the accounts Holmes had given of his experiences in the Civil War, and how he told of his grandmother's having seen, as a little girl, the British march into Boston. "We all imbibed that tremendous sense of the continuity of history," said Laurence Curtis, former congressman from Massachusetts, "that we were all part of one woven strip."[11]

I do not suggest that the Gospels were written by the apostles over lunch, and I do not basically question the premise of the form critics, that the tradition was shaped in the course of oral transmission. But this account of the Holmes reminiscences should make us wary of discounting the possible check on the arbitrary development of the gospel tradition exercised by eyewitnesses, who perhaps had had the indelible experience of "sitting at the feet of a master," or of "breathing the same air" with him.

If a modern illustration has been injected into the argument to raise a question about form criticism, it is only fair to conclude our discussion of the method with another modern illustration, one that demonstrates rather graphically the kind of development the form critics say took place in the past. It is a story from *The New York Times* for Nov. 8, 1971 (p. 3), telling about the way in which the small French village of Colombey-les-Deux-Églises had become a place of pilgrimage in the year since Charles de Gaulle had been buried there.

A national committee, with the blessing of President Pompidou, has collected more than $1-million for a lasting memorial: A 130-foot

Cross of Lorraine, to be built next year on the hill where today's procession was held.

A leaflet published by the Committee quotes the general as having said, pointing to the hill from his study: "A Cross of Lorraine will be erected there when I am dead, and one will be able to see it from anywhere."

The remark is rendered rather differently by André Malraux, in his book "Fallen Oaks": "Everybody will be able to see it, and since there isn't anybody [around], nobody will see it. It will incite the rabbits to resistance."

B. Redaction Criticism

If form criticism concerns itself with what happened in the forty-year interval before the Gospels were written, redaction criticism concerns itself with what happened in the mind of the Evangelist himself. The form critics had left the impression that the Gospel writers were not much more than collectors, who were motivated chiefly by a desire to gather in and record the memories of Jesus' activities and teachings as it became increasingly clear that the end of the world was unlikely to come any time soon. The activity of Gospel writing was, in short, a response to the delay of the return of Christ.

It is only in the past decade that the appreciation of the Evangelists as creative theologians has come to prominence in the field of New Testament study. The redaction critic looks at what the Evangelist did with the material that was available to him, and discovers that each Gospel presents a comprehensive interpretation of the significance of Jesus, an interpretation that may reflect not simply the idiosyncratic view of the Evangelist but more generally the understanding of the gospel shared by the Christian community of which the Evangelist was a part and in which he had been nurtured. What the redaction critic insists is that the early church was characterized not only by liturgical, missionary, and organizational concerns (those *Sitzen im Leben* to which the form critic calls attention) but also by a specifically intellectual concern, and that the Gospels —all of them, not just John's—testify to a highly developed theological activity that has been at work on the tradition.

The full implications of redaction criticism for the interpretation of the New Testament are peculiarly difficult to predict, for to a surprising degree it really is a new way of approach. One might have assumed that prior to the rise of form criticism the Gospels would have been treated as literary units, but either consciously or unconsciously most reading of the Gospels prior to the nineteenth century was governed by the tradition of "harmonization." It may be that just as form criticism and the existentialist approach suited each other admirably, redaction criticism and the interpretation theory of Paul Ricoeur will reinforce each other, for Ricoeur insists above all else that the integrity of the text be respected. The redaction critic, dealing with one of the Gospels, is attempting to describe and interpret "the world of that text" in a way that corresponds closely to Ricoeur's account of the activity of interpretation.

As has been mentioned already, redaction criticism does not directly affect the question about the historical Jesus; the redaction critic is making no claim that Mark's interpretation of the significance of Jesus gets us closer to Jesus than does form criticism. But for the interpretation of the New Testament more generally, redaction criticism is of enormous significance. It calls directly into question one of the major assumptions of much New Testament study in this century—the assumption that there was a single original kerygma, of which the various specific patterns in the New Testament are variations (and, by implication, corruptions). As Howard Kee has said,

> Failing to take with full theological seriousness the diverse pictures of Jesus represented in the biblical tradition, the theologian must either settle for a monochrome portrait, painted by conscious or unconscious harmonization of the tradition, or adopt one perspective —usually that of the Pauline kerygma—and force the gospel tradition to conform to that view of Jesus.[12]

Kee's book *Jesus in History: An Approach to the Study of the Gospels* is an impressive initial attempt to discern the particular theological bent of each Evangelist. He begins his analysis with the reconstructed "Sayings Source," Q, which comprises the material Matthew and Luke have in common but which is not in Mark. Not every New Testament scholar would share Kee's confidence in our ability to put Q together, and many would deny that Q was ever a written document, but there seems to be increasing willingness to treat the material included in Q as evidence for a stage of the traditions about Jesus prior to the writing of the Gospels. Kee concludes:

> The tradition embodied in Q is more concerned with presenting Jesus as bearer of the eschatological message than as someone whose primary function is to perform deeds that effect salvation. Jesus brings salvation by evoking the response of faith to the word from God that he offers, not by virtue of his saving actions.[13]

Of course this initial concentration on a "document" that must be reconstructed from other texts is not, strictly speaking, redaction criticism. And the conclusion to which Kee comes would appear to support strongly the existentialists' description of the original nature of the Christian message: Jesus' primary function is to evoke the response of faith to the word from God. But when Kee goes on to consider the portrayal of Jesus in the Gospels, the thrust even of the Q material is seen to be quite different from what the Bultmann tradition has claimed.

Mark, Matthew, and Luke all have as their primary focus the existence of the eschatological *community,* the church. And in this they are not reflecting a later corruption, by which Jesus' radical message was domesticated into the structured (and self-enhancing and self-preserving) life of an institution. Rather, they are transmitting one of the essential features of Jesus' original eschatological message, a feature embodied in the apocalyptic view of the world and of history: the apocalyptist is concerned above all else with how God deals with peoples, with groups, with communities.

Existentialist interpreters of the New Testament have "demythologized" early Christian apocalyptic, but in addition to eliminating the dramatic trappings (angelic trumpets, going to meet the Lord in the air, blood flowing up to the bridles of the horses in the Valley of Jehoshaphat), they have also eliminated the fundamental communal emphasis in favor of an emphasis upon the individual as the one in whom alone the question of faith comes to focus. Kee admits that this view can point with considerable confidence to John's Gospel; the role of the Christian in history and of the church in the world is minimal in John's scheme, although the mutual love of Christians for one another, presented in that Gospel (13:34–35) as the sign to the world that Jesus' followers belong to him, has an irreducibly communal dimension. Paul, too, in at least some passages, can be read as having transformed the apocalyptic history of a people into the eschatological existence of the individual.

Kee's chief argument against the existentialists' interpretation is this: the apocalyptic message of Jesus in Mark simply does not correspond to their rendition of the "true meaning" of early Christian apocalyptic. The Bultmann tradition has assumed that Mark's Gospel can be treated as a source for their account of the basic Christian message, and Kee argues that to use Mark as such a source is to misconstrue that Gospel almost entirely.

> What was Mark's historical aim? What historical value does his book have? In juxtaposing these questions, we must recognize that in the first we are asking about Mark's own understanding of history; in the second, about history in terms of modern historiography. Some scholars have attempted to merge these two issues by theorizing that there is identity between a modern conception of historicity as a mode of man's self-understanding and Jesus' summons to man to find his true life (or self) by deciding for the will of God and against the world (Mark 8:35). This view implies that by turning away from being obsessed with facts and toward helping man gain self-understanding, the historian is heading toward the same goal as that to which Jesus invited men in his gospel preaching: the achievement of a true understanding of human existence. The existentialist approach, however, is a distortion of modern historical work, with its attention to factual evidence and its attempt to reconstruct the past, just as the exclusive concentration on self-understanding in the message of Jesus is inadequate for dealing with the wider range of the gospel tradition. . . .
>
> The kind of "history" that Mark knew was the apocalyptic variety as it has been preserved for us in such works as the Book of Enoch, the Book of Jubilees, and the Book of Daniel. These works deal with actual events of the past (or events believed to have occurred, such as the experiences of the patriarchs); they set them in a framework of divine purpose, in the light of which the meaning of the present is grasped and illumined and the hope for the future is specified. . . .
>
> Mark took the synoptic tradition as he found it, largely in scattered units, and worked it into a consecutive account of "history" in which past, present, and future are viewed apocalyptically. He did not have to do violence to his material to set it in this mold, since the basic outlook of Jesus and what seems to have been his understanding of his own exorcisms and healings were also apocalyptically oriented.[14]

The crucial statement here is this: *He did not have to do violence to his material*—that is, the earliest traditions about the teaching and

activity of Jesus, as extracted through analysis of Q and more generally through application of form-critical method to the Gospel
materials, present to us a message which has to do not with the
future as a characteristic of each individual's existence, but with the
future as what is yet to come in world history. As J. D. G. Dunn
has noted:

> The apocalyptic hope brings the believer *a new sense of responsibility
> towards the world.* He ceases to be dependent on the world for value
> and hope, but he becomes more responsible for it—to live and work
> *in* the world for the hastening of God's purposed End. Notice that
> the apocalyptic hope as such is *not* one which ignores or turns its back
> on the world.[15]

And Kee is able to show how Matthew and Luke gave further
expression to that *original* intention of the preaching and activity of
Jesus: in summary, after many pages of detailed argument, he concludes: "Whereas Matthew placed Jesus in the history of the
church, Luke placed the church and Jesus in the history of the
world."[16]

To make the point as precise as possible: the redaction critic does
not say that "the world of the text" of any of the Gospels is identical
with the "world" of Jesus' activity and preaching. The redaction
critic does conclude that there is more overlap between the Gospels' "worlds" and the "world" of Jesus than between the "world"
of Jesus and the "world" that modern New Testament study has
abstracted from the records, precisely because the Evangelists have
maintained essential features of Jesus' understanding of existence:
namely, that our existence is communal, and that God deals with
history as a whole, as well as with each individual. The historical
Jesus presents a challenge to, not a confirmation of, the existentialist
understanding of human existence.

IV. Jesus

Frequently students say to me that they find this or that statement
in the Gospels "out of character with Jesus." When I ask them why
they think that, it usually turns out that the statement is something
they do not like, and they would rather Jesus had not said it. Some
want him to have been concerned with each unique individual, and

they are upset when he lumps whole groups of people together in a comprehensive denunciation. Others wish he had had an acute understanding of the class basis of human society, and are hence upset by evidences of his concern to deal with individuals instead of with systemic evil. Once in a while students will say to me that this or that statement in the Gospels confirms what they have suspected about Jesus, that he was a charlatan.

It is virtually inevitable that people will pick and choose from the New Testament material those pieces they need to construct the picture they want for reasons quite other than those of historical curiosity. Such selectivity has characterized the quest of the historical Jesus since the nineteenth century; as Fuller remarks, "The chief motivation . . . was to get back behind the orthodoxy of the church to the original teaching of Jesus and thus acquire a corrective to the Church's version of Christianity."[17] And in our own century this motivation has been even more pronounced. The attempt to get back to Jesus is not simply an end run around the orthodoxy of our own day, but around that of the first-century church as well, for the New Testament itself is seen as representing "the church's version" of Christianity.

Virtually all the questing appears to be in pursuit of a figure who can be neatly classified, whether the Jesus be a liberal humanist in the nineteenth-century mold, a radical existentialist in the Bultmann tradition, a "super-salesman" as Bruce Barton portrayed him in the 1920's, a political revolutionary with unmistakable (if not entirely clear) ties to the Zealot party, or an absolutely consistent pacifist (as two recent studies have argued).[18]

Leander Keck, in *A Future for the Historical Jesus,* has insisted that Jesus was more Jewish than Lutheran, and that by looking for the *distinctive* Jesus—that is, the Jesus who can be differentiated from the Jewish milieu out of which he came and from the early church in which memory of him was distorted by concerns of faith—we are bound to find a caricature. The Jesus to whom the New Testament materials direct us is the *characteristic* Jesus, who is presented in great complexity, and a complexity that can be reduced to a formula only by discarding large chunks of evidence. Jesus holds different motifs in tension, and it is precisely the complexity of Jesus that calls for reflection, both theologically and historically. Keck takes with full seriousness the identity of the God of Jesus and the God of the

Jews, and is thus able to appreciate the full historical dimension of Jesus' preaching.[19]

Keck judges that existentialist, "kerygmatic" theology distorts the New Testament not only because it has a faulty sense of history but also because it is based on too narrow an understanding of religious life. The conception is too narrow to do justice to the Bible (a conclusion to which, as we have seen, redaction criticism comes): "When one comes to the New Testament evidence for earliest Christian preaching, such as it is, from a reading of Bultmann, one is struck by the overall absence of interest in 'encounter.'" It is also too narrow to do justice to human experience: "Faith as persistence, as loyalty, as trust in the face of ambiguity, scarcely receives adequate attention." Elsewhere Keck speaks of the lifelong process of repentance as the practical meaning of the Christian life, and that is something very different from a disjointed series of existential decisions.[20]

It is important to understand that Keck is not doing theology in disregard of questions of history. He is arguing that a particular view of theology, and even more, a particular view of the religious life, has so dominated the recent quest for the historical Jesus that that quest has, like earlier ones, found a Jesus in the image of the questers. Of course Keck and Kee and everybody have presuppositions, and it could be argued that Keck is projecting his own desires onto Jesus. But Keck's approach has the merit of making more historical sense of Jesus, who was, after all, a first-century Jew. That could mean many things, as we have seen. Keck suggests that in the case of Jesus it likely meant many things, and not just one of the many things it might have meant.

A. Career

There is general agreement, even among scholars most committed to a radical use of form criticism, that some elements of the tradition about Jesus can be traced back to historical facts of his career. For instance, the later conflict between the followers of Jesus and those of John the Baptist suggests that the careers of the two men were intertwined. Jewish tradition as well as Christian attests to Jesus' reputation as an exorcist, and however one wants to explain such activity, that Jesus did engage in it and was considered by his contemporaries to be good at it appears to be something that can safely be included in history books. The importance of table fellowship in the early Christian community can most easily be accounted for as the continuation of the habits of Jesus and his close followers. Jesus' death by crucifixion is probably no more to be doubted than Julius Caesar's death by assassination.

A succinct summary of this consensus on the accessible historical facts about the career of Jesus is provided by Perrin, and it is worth quoting as the conclusion of his quarter century of careful reflection.

We are now in a position to make a general statement about the life of Jesus. He was baptized by John the Baptist, and the beginning of his ministry was in some way linked with that of the Baptist. In his own ministry Jesus was above all the one who proclaimed the Kingdom of God and who challenged his hearers to respond to the reality he was proclaiming. The authority and effectiveness of Jesus as proclaimer of the Kingdom of God was reinforced by an apparently deserved reputation as an exorcist. In a world that believed in gods, in powers of good and evil, and in demons, he was able, in the name of God and his Kingdom, to help those who believed themselves to be possessed by demons.

A fundamental concern of Jesus was to bring together into a unified group those who responded to his proclamation of the Kingdom of God irrespective of their sex, previous background or history. A central feature of the life of this group was eating together, sharing a common meal that celebrated their unity in the new relationship with God, which they enjoyed on the basis of their response to Jesus' proclamation of the Kingdom. In this concern for the unity of the group of those who responded to the proclamation, Jesus challenged the tendency of the Jewish community of his day to fragment itself and in the name of God to reject certain of its own members. This aroused a deep-rooted opposition to him, which reached a climax during a Passover celebration in Jerusalem when he was arrested, tried by the Jewish authorities on a charge of blasphemy and by the Romans on a charge of sedition, and crucified. During his lifetime he had chosen from among his followers a small group of disciples who had exhibited in their work in his name something of his power and authority.

That, or something very like it, is all that we can know; it is enough.[21]

B. Message

Perrin's summary includes the central element of Jesus' teaching, the proclamation of the coming and of the availability of the kingdom of God. As we have seen, this central element can be read through a filter that eliminates several of its features, and Perrin's extremely cautious presentation of what we can *know* about the teaching leaves the way wide open for the existentialist interpretation. Moreover, Perrin's overt reference to Judaism in the summary amounts simply to saying that Jesus opposed a widespread tendency in the Judaism of his day. Still, the fact that Perrin can say as much as he does is remarkable, in view of the skepticism at the beginning of this century as to whether one could say anything at all as a historian about Jesus.

Perrin and others have developed four "tests" by which to determine what in the accounts of the teaching of Jesus can be safely attributed to Jesus himself.

1. Dissimilarity from both Jewish and Hellenistic usage; for example, to address God directly as "Father" appears not to have been characteristic either of Jews or of Greeks, so this is likely to have been an innovation of Jesus, not something attributed to him as the tradition developed.

2. Multiple attestation—themes or concerns are authentic if they occur in different literary forms within the tradition (that is, they can be traced form-critically to different "settings in life," which would have been unlikely to produce the same results); "So, for example, the concern for 'tax collectors and sinners' is authentic because it is attested in sayings, parables, and controversy stories, and that Jesus had a distinctive eschatology is evident from the fact that a particular view of the End Time is stamped on Kingdom sayings, proverbial sayings, and parables."

3. Coherence—"Material may be accepted as authentic if it coheres with, or is consistent with, material established as authentic by other criteria. The validity of this criterion is self-evident."

4. Linguistic and environmental tests—the results here are only negative, that is, the test determines only that something is not authentic; Perrin notes, by way of example, that the interpretation of the parable of the sower in Mark 4:13–20 uses the technical

vocabulary of the early church, and is therefore not to be attributed to Jesus.

Using these criteria, many scholars have concluded that there are four components of the teaching of Jesus recorded in the Synoptic Gospels that are authentic reflections of what Jesus actually said: (1) proclamations of the kingdom of God; (2) parables (minus their explanatory contexts) which have some striking, unexpected point (for example, the good Samaritan challenges the hearer to think the unthinkable thought that a hated Samaritan could be close to the kingdom of God; the unjust steward challenges the hearer to applaud that which must not be applauded); (3) proverbial sayings, particularly those, such as "Leave the dead to bury their own dead," which would necessitate a reversal of long-accepted practice; (4) the Lord's Prayer (probably in the shorter form, found in Luke's Gospel).[22]

The first criterion, dissimilarity, is a particularly ruthless critical weapon. If one's intention is to determine what can be treated without question (or with minimum question) as authentically going back to Jesus, then the criterion has to be used, since anything that can be demonstrated to correspond to Jewish tradition or to a particular concern of the early church *may* have intruded itself into the tradition about Jesus. But, as Keck has warned, if the further step is taken—which can very easily, even unconsciously, be done —and "these are the only teachings we can be sure are authentic" becomes "these are the only authentic teachings of Jesus," we are in imminent danger of having a Jesus who is consistent with himself at the expense of total abstraction from history.[23] By methodologically ruling out the connection of Jesus with what came before him and what came after him, we conveniently create for ourselves a Jesus who can be our contemporary because he had no contemporaries of his own.

C. Jesus' Teaching About Himself

The question about the historical Jesus that poses the most serious issue for theology is the question of Jesus' teaching about the future, which is a form of the question about the claims, if any, he made about himself. Perrin states his position squarely: "I am convinced that all sayings or teachings ascribed to Jesus in the gospels that give a definite form to a future expectation—for example, a future coming of the Son of Man—fail the test of the criteria for authenticity." Perrin is persuaded that there was a future thrust to Jesus' teaching—the parables of growth (sower, mustard seed, leaven, seed growing of itself) strongly suggest such an emphasis —but he believes that when the early Christians gave to this hint of future things a definite form, they were mistaken.[24]

One subject of much interest at the end of the last century, the "messianic self-consciousness" of Jesus, has been effectively dismissed as beyond the reach of meaningful investigation (although some practitioners of "the new quest of the historical Jesus" have claimed the ability to get at something similar, Jesus' understanding of existence). We cannot get inside Jesus' head, and to this extent I am entirely persuaded by the form critics' refusal even to imagine that we might know "Jesus' self-consciousness." Furthermore, I find it very difficult to say with assurance that Jesus identified himself as the Messiah, but I find it equally difficult to go along with the assurance of the form critics that Jesus did not make such a self-designation.

It could be that the tests for authenticity constitute too narrow a mesh, through which some elements of the tradition that do go back to Jesus in their basic assertion, even if they have been significantly shaped in transmission, cannot pass. The confidence of Perrin's statement seems to me overextended: "The explicit claims [to Messiahship] in the gospels reflect the piety and understanding of the early church, not historical data about Jesus of Nazareth."[25]

I find myself wondering what, in the view of the form critics, would count as evidence that Jesus had made such claims. Why must we make a sharp distinction between the needs of the early church to identify the role of Jesus and the needs of the first followers of Jesus? Why does the question, "Who do men say that I am?" not fit into the context of the life and activity of Jesus and his closest followers? One year in my introductory Hebrew Scriptures course I received two term essays on Martin Luther King, Jr., and the analogy between the movement he led and the exodus of the Israelites from Egypt. Both students made reference to King's frequent citation of passages about Moses, and one claimed that King clearly identified himself with Moses and saw the whole contemporary historical drama as a replay of the ancient situation, while the other student argued just as strongly that King was not claiming a connection. I can well imagine that Jesus claimed to be the Messiah, but in many different ways—some of them explicit, some of them indirect—which would give rise to various lines of tradition. Also, while the messianic self-consciousness eludes us, I can imagine that in the course of Jesus' career he made different claims for himself, claims which would not easily cohere, and which might even contradict one another. If Jesus was fully human, we have to grant him the right we all claim for ourselves—the right to change our minds. And as a classical historian has reminded us: "In his ministry, Jesus surely repeated himself far more often than the individual gospels indicate, but not necessarily in exactly the same words. This would hold also of the preaching of the Apostles, just as of modern preachers and candidates for office."[26]

I would, indeed, suggest that we might push Howard Kee's argument one step further back: might it not be that the variety of early Christian interpretations of the identity and significance of Jesus goes back to Jesus himself—that is, the historical fact of the career and teaching of Jesus includes a collection of differing judgments by himself on his own historic significance? Jeremiah, we know, had deep doubts about his own prophetic call, and thought God was playing tricks on him. Why should the Messiah be exempt from such experiences, and why should the traditions about him not be highly ambivalent on just the central point of his claims about himself? Why, in short, must the historical Jesus have been consistent? or, to put it another way, Why should he be forced to meet our criteria for consistency? Why cannot differing, even contradictory, traditions be authentic?

V. How Much History Is Enough?

At the conclusion of his summary of the career of Jesus quoted earlier, Perrin says, "That, or something very like it, is all that we can know; it is enough." He does not say what it is enough for, and it is unclear whether he means that it suffices for Christian faith, or that it is enough for an understanding of the early Christian church's developing ideas about the significance of Jesus. He has begun his book disclaiming a concern to pass judgment on what the New Testament says; he wants rather to place the New Testament in the context of the general history of religion. "The aim is to help the student understand the New Testament, nothing more, nothing less."[27]

I think the statement "It is enough" is more than a historian's declaration that enough evidence has been assembled to make a convincing story; it sounds to me like a late twentieth-century equivalent to the more romantic conclusion of Schweitzer's *The Quest of the Historical Jesus* at the beginning of the century:

> He comes to us as One unknown, without a name, as of old, by the lake-side, He came to those men who knew Him not. He speaks to us the same word: "Follow thou me!" and sets us to the tasks which He has to fulfill for our time. He commands. And to those who obey Him, whether they be wise or simple, He will reveal himself in the toils, the conflicts, the sufferings which they shall pass through in His fellowship, and, as an ineffable mystery, they shall learn in their own experience Who He is.[28]

If Perrin is, for one brief moment, identifying himself as professor in a Divinity School as well as in the University of Chicago, I think he is basically right: that the recoverable data about the career and teaching of Jesus provide the necessary historical grounding for the Christian faith. Even Origen, who was prepared to "spiritualize" anything, insisted that while it was not essential to faith that everything recorded in the New Testament had actually happened, it is necessary to the faith that the whole thing not have been made up. Origen believed it crucial that Jesus actually lived a couple of hundred years ago, that the basic outline of the history (perhaps corresponding fairly closely to Perrin's "enough") is accurate. And the reason Origen insists on the historicity of Jesus is that it alone serves as a guarantee that Christian faith is not arbitrary.[29]

Origen was well acquainted with the staggering variety of gods and goddesses available to the religiously-minded citizen of the Roman Empire. He knew that anyone could construct a story. In one of the most thoroughgoing reversals in the history of thought, the nineteenth century wanted to free Christian faith from its ties to the Jesus of history, on the grounds that historical knowledge is necessarily tentative, uncertain—and faith has to have a sure foundation. For Origen it worked just the other way: that the story of

Jesus was a fundamentally historical story was its only sure guarantee against arbitrariness.

To say that the recoverable historical data are necessary is not to say that they are sufficient grounding for the Christian faith. One can certainly admit everything in Perrin's summary without in any sense being a Christian. Identity as a Christian requires judgments about the significance of the historical data, judgments that must have some connection with the judgments made about Jesus by the apostles. It is clear that those early judgments were extraordinarily various, and nobody can claim *historical* justification for a narrow definition of Christianity.

Research into the historical Jesus is beginning to show, however, that not all the claims made about Jesus in the first two centuries are continuous with his historical life and teaching. It is increasingly apparent that there is a discernible continuity between the life and activity of Jesus and that of the community which produced and canonized the New Testament. Even in his sharpest attacks on the Jewish religious establishment of his time and in his most vivid apocalyptic predictions, Jesus remained committed to the basic affirmation of the Hebrew Scriptures: that the God who created the world is the only God there is, that history and not just historicity is the arena of divine activity, that God deals with communities as well as with individuals. The early church's determination to hold on to the Hebrew Scriptures was thus a form of homage to the historical Jesus. Moreover, as Dunn has shown, there are continuities of religious experience between Jesus, the apostles, and the later first-century church, and analysis of religious experience can help reduce apparent discontinuities in language and doctrine.[30]

This is why I consider the ordering of material in Kee, Young, and Froehlich's *Understanding the New Testament,* with community and background first, to be more congruent with the message of the New Testament itself than is the order of Perrin's *The New Testament: An Introduction.* The identity of Jesus and his significance are inextricably woven into the story of divine activity in the world centered in the history of the Israelite community. This is not to overlook the extraordinary variety of Judaism in the time of Jesus, or the major differences between the religious ideas and practices recorded in the Hebrew Scriptures and the religious ideas and practices of those who treated those Scriptures as authoritative. But the differences should not blind us to the deep continuities, and all efforts, both ancient and modern, to disentangle Jesus from the community of Israel and the community of the church simply do not make historical sense.

CHAPTER SEVEN

PAUL: ENIGMA VARIATIONS

Paul succeeded in stealing the image of Christ crucified for the figurehead of his Salvationist vessel, with its Adam posing as the natural
man, its doctrine of original sin, and its damnation avoidable only by
faith in the sacrifice of the cross. In fact, no sooner had Jesus knocked
over the dragon of superstition than Paul boldly set it on its legs again
in the name of Jesus. . . . There is not one word of Pauline Christianity
in the characteristic utterances of Jesus. . . . There has really never
been a more monstrous imposition perpetrated than the imposition
of the limitations of Paul's soul upon the soul of Jesus.

—George Bernard Shaw

It was [Paul] who placed the Gospel in the great scheme of spirit and
flesh, inner and outer existence, death and life; he, born a Jew and
educated a Pharisee, gave it a *language,* so that it became intelligible,
not only to the Greeks but to all men generally, and united with the
whole of the intellectual capital which had been amassed in previous
ages.

—Adolf Harnack

With judgments such as these to start it off (Shaw wrote in 1913,
Harnack in 1900), the twentieth century has had its work of Pauline interpretation cut out for it.[1] What Shaw saw as an unmitigated
disaster, Harnack saw as the sublimest transformation in the history
of religion. Paul has a way of generating such passionate responses,
and despite the enormous weight of the scholarship of the past two
generations, which has undermined the basic assumptions of both
Shaw's and Harnack's judgments, there remains in the popular
mind a strong suspicion either that Paul corrupted Christianity (or
even founded a different religion) or that his understanding of the
nature of the gospel is the only one that can speak to persons today.

153

Such a view is hard to eliminate, because the alternative to either extreme is a complex analysis in which Paul turns out to be elusive, to be fundamentally, irreducibly enigmatic, and we are reluctant to look to an enigmatic figure for guidance in our own enigmatic experience.

I. THE ENIGMA OF PAUL IN ANTIQUITY

Paul has always been difficult to understand. Sharply negative judgments—judgments as negative as that of Shaw—have been made from the very beginning. Paul's letters are often prompted by misunderstandings of what he had said to the churches he had founded ("Is that what I meant? God forbid!"). He had bitter enemies, and he could on occasion treat them sarcastically. As we have seen previously, the New Testament book called 2 Peter suggests that Paul's letters are already being treated as authoritative, but it also admits that some of what Paul says is obscure, and people are interpreting it in many different ways; and Marcion, the ruthlessly consistent champion of gospel against law, considered Paul to be the fountainhead of true understanding of Jesus, but yet, in a famous epigram of Harnack's, "Marcion was the only Gentile Christian who understood Paul, and even he misunderstood him."[2]

Paul's favorable remarks about Israel posed a problem for Marcion, and Marcion simply excised those passages as though they were interpolations injected into the manuscript tradition by Paul's enemies. From the other side, the Ebionites, a group who held to the Jewish law as binding on Christians, dealt with Paul's unkind remarks about the law by subjecting him to slander:

> They declare that he was a Greek, child of a Greek mother and a Greek father. He went up to Jerusalem, they say, and when he had spent some time there, he was seized with a passion to marry the daughter of the priest. For this reason he became a proselyte and was circumcised. Then, when he failed to get the girl, he flew into a rage and wrote against circumcision and against Sabbath and Law.[3]

The Ebionite story is pure historical fabrication, and yet it provides an interesting clue to dynamic factors in early Christian life that we often overlook as we theorize about the adventures of ideas and the development of doctrines. For the Ebionites, the only way to account for Paul's derailing of the movement begun by Jesus was to suppose that Paul's actions and teaching were grounded in a national-racial identity crisis brought on by passion and intensified by the thwarting of that passion. As far as the Ebionites were concerned, religious revolution presupposed a deep emotional catastrophe, and while their account of Paul is in no sense to be taken seriously, their underlying assumption can remind us that too "spiritual" a conception of conversion may prevent our full understanding of Christian origins (or of virtually any significant religious development).

Concern about Paul's attitude toward women, a topic of lively interest today, was evident in antiquity also, and not only among the polemically inclined Ebionites. A popular romance of the end of the second century, the Acts of Paul and Thecla, tells of Paul's mesmerizing effect on a young lady of Iconium, who is influenced by his preaching to renounce her impending marriage.

> Thamyris [her fiancé] rose up early in the morning full of jealousy and wrath and went to the house of Onesiphorus [Paul's host] with the rulers and officers and a great crowd with cudgels, and said to Paul: "Thou hast destroyed the city of the Iconians, and my betrothed, so that she will not have me. Let us go to the governor Castellius!" And the whole crowd shouted: "Away with the sorcerer! For he has corrupted all our wives."

Judgment is passed, Paul is imprisoned, Thecla bribes the jailer to let her into his cell. Her own mother, angry that her daughter has rejected the chance for a good marriage, calls on the governor to burn Thecla as a warning, so that "all the women who have been taught by this man may be afraid." Thecla escapes death as a thunderstorm puts out the flames, and she then lives a life of adventure as she follows Paul from place to place.[4]

These are only the most dramatic and picturesque of the transformations Paul underwent in the early church, and they suggest that we need not wait for the twentieth century to find radical judgments on the apostle to the Gentiles.

The most influential of the Pauline "transformations," however, and one of which we are often oblivious, is that of the book of Acts. Just as many people operate with a kind of unconsciously harmonized picture of Jesus, made up of blended elements of all four

Gospels, so most people would be hard pressed to say what parts of their impression of Paul come from his letters and what parts from the portrayal of him in Acts (for example, Acts recounts the Damascus road conversion experience three different times, while Paul says only, 1 Cor. 15:8, that the risen Lord appeared to him).

Scholars have been vindicating what had been previously chalked up to bias in Acts—the conviction that Paul and the Jerusalem church had got on relatively well together.[5] To establish the basic reliability of Acts is of enormous importance for the historian, since if Acts cannot be trusted, we really know next to nothing about the earliest development of Christianity. However, the current positive reassessment of Acts cannot mask the fact that the author of Acts appears not to have understood some of the major themes in Paul's preaching and missionary activity. The "domestication" of Paul is already at work in the writing of the first history of the church.

The bewildering variety of assessments of Paul in generations close to his own should make us skeptical of there being some neat, all-inclusive solution to the problem of his enigma.

One might argue that Paul is elusive because we have so little to go on, and there is uncertainty about the proportion of the little we do have that we can properly use in the attempt to understand him. There are thirteen letters in the New Testament attributed to Paul (the letter to the Hebrews was not attributed to him in the ancient church, and, as Origen said, "Only God knows who wrote the letter to the Hebrews"; no serious scholar would claim it for Paul or for anyone who had been significantly influenced by Paul). With a near unanimity that is rare in New Testament study, scholars across a whole range of the theological and historical spectrum are agreed that at least seven of the letters are undoubtedly genuine: 1 Thessalonians, Galatians, 1 Corinthians, 2 Corinthians (which may be two or more letters put together), Romans, Philippians, and Philemon. For various reasons, some more compelling than others, 2 Thessalonians, Colossians, and Ephesians are subject to divided opinion among the scholars, although there seems to be a trend in the direction of admitting their genuineness—partly, at least, as the result of a new willingness among historians to allow persons in the past to move about more freely than they could in the straitjackets of "consistency" in which they used to be bound.

The pastoral letters (1 and 2 Timothy, Titus) are regarded by a large majority of scholars as coming from a time considerably later than that of Paul; their themes, and particularly the pattern of church organization they describe, are so different from what we encounter in the undoubtedly genuine letters, that even loosened-up historical imaginations balk at stretching so far as to say Paul is the author of those letters. But more and more frequently in the scholarly literature, one comes across references to "the Pauline school," and there is a growing appreciation for the continuation of the apostle's tradition by his followers in succeeding stages of the church's development. In other words, Paul did not write the pastoral letters, but they were written by persons who had some authority for saying that in their situation, very different from Paul's, this is something like what Paul would have said. Perhaps a useful model for such a "school" would be the traditions of a court of law, where a judge today may wonder what this or that judge of the past would have said in this new situation.

For a man as wide-ranging in his activity as Paul, these letters, coupled with a few extracts from the travel diary of a companion of his on the journey to Paul's trial in Rome (the so-called "We sections" of Acts), are not very much by way of primary evidence, but as evidence from antiquity goes, it is quite a lot. The enigma of Paul is not primarily a result of the volume of our sources, or even of their nature, although it can be argued that letters written in the heat of controversy, which is what most of his writings are, make a balanced judgment especially hard to achieve.

To a certain extent, being enigmatic is simply a function of being human; no person is ever a completely "open book" to another person. Yet Paul seems especially hard to get hold of. Shaw and Harnack illustrate two reasons for the difficulty—we assume either that Jesus is easily accessible to us, so Paul becomes distant, or that Paul's language has a kind of timeless, universal, and immediate applicability that liberates it from the uncertainty which inheres in all other language. A central feature of the enigma of Paul is his driving so many people to insist that he is not enigmatic; many cannot rest until they have demonstrated that Paul is either *the* villain or *the* hero of the Christian story.

The Pauline enigma is built into his thought and activity itself, and it is recognition of this structural enigma that makes it possible to understand Harnack's remark: "Paulinism has proved to be a ferment in the history of dogma, a basis it has never been."[6] There is no complete resolution of the enigma, and there will continue to be revolutions in the understanding of Paul; or, to put it another way, there will be enigma variations until we see face to face—and maybe even then.

II. VARIATION I: ALL THINGS TO ALL PERSONS

Paul invites misapprehension when, in 1 Cor. 9:22–23, he declares a form of inconsistency to be his consistent practice: "I have become all things to all [persons], that I might by all means save some. I do it all for the sake of the gospel, that I may share in its blessings." Numerous commentators have pointed out that this does not amount to Paul's admitting that he is a chameleon; what he expresses here in vigorous language is simply a well-recognized technique of argument and persuasion, in which you make as much contact as you can with the position of the person to whom you are addressing yourself. But even with that modification, the passage should still make us wary of deriving a whole theological structure from isolated parts of Paul's letters, or even from a collection of parts, for it is always possible that he is being something to somebody he would not be to somebody else (us, for instance).

A. The Jews

We tend to assume that Paul is the great barrier between Jews and Christians; that Jesus can be, without too much distortion, made over into a teacher in the mainstream of Jewish prophetic piety (especially if, as many modern scholars believe, Jesus never claimed for himself the privileged title of Messiah), while Paul, despite his claims of Pharisaic upbringing and loyalty to Israel, takes the irrevocable step away from Judaism of rejecting the law, treating it as a temporary expedient in God's overall plan for the world. Because Paul's role in the Jewish/Christian schism appears so clear to us, it comes as a surprise to learn that until modern times he has played little role in debate and discussion.

There is not a single reference to Paul in the chief monument of Jewish/Christian discussion in the second century, Justin Martyr's *Dialogue with Trypho,* and through the Middle Ages, Paul's role in dispute is minimal.[7] The accusation of deicide ("The Jews killed God") had more elemental popular appeal than did intricate arguments about the relationship of two covenants. In the church of the early centuries it was understood that Paul's arguments had been mainly with Christians over the proper role of law within Christianity; in the medieval world it was Christianity as a social and political force that Judaism had to face, and the Gospels, with their insistent portrayal of the scribes and Pharisees as hypocrites, and with the chilling cry in Matthew (27:25), "His blood be on us and on our children!" provided most of the scriptural fuel for the fires of Christian anti-Semitism. As we have seen, Marcion thought the letters of Paul as we have them were far too sympathetic to Judaism.

During the past century, partly as a result of the distinction drawn between the "original Christianity" of Palestine and the antithetical "Hellenistic Christianity" of Paul, a distinction widely assumed by nineteenth-century scholars and one with lingering influences even today, Paul has come to be treated as the great apostate from Judaism. It has been characteristic of Jewish scholars and spokespersons to say Jesus, Yes; Paul, Never. And even many whose response to Paul is less violent nonetheless see him as opposed in spirit to Jesus, and hence to the heart of Jewish piety.[8]

The leading characteristic of the investigation of Paul's Jewishness today is a move away from questions of particular terminology to more elusive, but more fundamental, matters of attitude and feeling. W. D. Davies, about a quarter of a century ago, wrote a book called *Paul and Rabbinic Judaism,* in which he set forth in great detail the parallels that can be drawn between rabbinic statements and things Paul says in his letters.[9] A number of Jewish scholars have pointed out, however, that such an approach may not characterize the evidence properly, since often the same terminology in a context of different attitudes and feelings can mean something very different indeed.

Hans Joachim Schoeps has argued that Paul's dependence on the Greek translation of the Hebrew Scriptures, which uses the Greek legal term *diathēkē* ("testament," "will") for the Hebrew *berith* ("covenant"), led him to miss the very framework in which the law is set: the covenant of mutual obligation.

When in 2 Corinthians 3:14 he speaks of the palaia [old] diatheke, which is superseded in Christ, diatheke becomes for him a sort of collection of ancient statutes identified with the nomos [law], while the kaine [new] diatheke is equated with justification which includes the forgiveness of sins. Palaia and kaine diatheke become for Paul the antithesis between Judaism and Christianity, and indicate the stark contrast between the religion of the law and the religion of grace. Because Paul had lost all understanding of the character of the Hebraic berith as a partnership involving mutual obligations, he failed to grasp the inner meaning of the Mosaic law, namely, that it is an instrument by which the covenant is realized. Hence the Pauline theology of law and justification begins with the fateful misunderstanding in consequence of which he tears asunder covenant and law, and then represents Christ as the end of the law.[10]

As he so often does, Samuel Sandmel comes forward with a sober judgment, chastened by patient attention to the evidence and a willingness (not a satisfaction, but a willingness) to remain in uncertainty where the evidence will not support anything else. He suggests that Paul is a genuinely remarkable phenomenon, whose individual genius cannot be accounted for by establishing all the influences on him and all the echoes in his writing. In any case, the influences are quite obscure. As Sandmel insists, we know nothing about Pharisaism in Dispersion Judaism of the early first century except what we can gather from Paul—that is, we cannot use Dispersion Pharisaism to account for Paul; on the contrary, the most we can do is to use Paul as evidence for that kind of Pharisaism.

Sandmel makes some careful distinctions between different ways in which early Christians conceived of the relation of Christianity to Judaism, and he finds that of the three main interpretations, Paul's is the most "conservative": Paul "affirmed a basic, general overarching continuity, and the discontinuity was limited to the laws"; Marcion and other Gnostics held that "the discontinuity was both general and specific, and, moreover, was total, to the end that it must be asserted that Christianity was never born out of Judaism, and owed no debt to it"; the letter to the Hebrews, and less explicitly Luke-Acts, present the view that "there is what one might call a higher continuity between the ancient Judaism and the new entity; . . . Hebrews is not concerned with Jews, but rather with the relation of the new 'Judaism' to the old."[11] When Paul is seen in this kind of comprehensive scheme, he appears to remain much truer to basic Jewish notions than Schoeps suggests.

B. The Greeks

When people think of Paul and the Greeks, they usually think first of the vivid scene in Acts 17: Paul standing among the scholars of the Areopagus at Athens, quoting Greek poetry to them and telling them that Christianity is really the answer to their intellectual quest. It is true that in his letter to the Romans (ch. 1), Paul presents an argument for "natural theology"—that is, human beings can figure out some true things about God by looking attentively at the universe around them—but the intention is very different from that of the apologetic speech on Mars Hill in Athens. In Romans, the whole point is to demonstrate that nobody has any convincing excuse for bad behavior.

Most scholars today agree that Acts 17 is a key to understanding Luke's conception of the spread of Christianity, but that Paul's attitude toward the Greeks—what he meant when he said he had become as one of them in order to win some of them—must be derived, if at all, from his letters. F. F. Bruce has argued that the speech in Acts 17 is just what we would expect Paul to say in that sort of situation, given what we know from his letters about his general ideas and methods of argument. There is much sound sense in Bruce's suggestion, and indeed in his entire effort to show the basic identity of the Paul of Acts and that of the letters. But even Bruce has to depend on the letters to confirm that the Areopagus speech is "just what we would have expected Paul to say in such a situation," so we are thrown back on the letters in any case.[12]

The question of Paul's approach to the Greeks is now complicated by the new awareness of the extensive Greek influence in Judaism. Once we recognize that Jewish Hellenism or Hellenistic Judaism provides a very wide spectrum of possibilities, we then have to ask whether Paul can plausibly be placed somewhere in that spectrum, or does he move clear beyond the bounds of permissible flexibility? Is there symbolic value in the fact that Paul's birthplace, Tarsus, lies between Athens and Jerusalem, but is closer to Jerusalem? Paul certainly thought of himself as a good Jew, although his

letters and Acts provide strikingly different warrants for his thinking so:

> [In Acts] Paul himself appears as a fully observant Pharisee through-
> out his life, while the Jews who refuse his message are categorically
> read out of the People of God. Thus in Paul's letters he rejects
> "Judaism," in the sense of the covenanted life structured by com-
> mandments, but not the Jews, while in Acts he remains true to "Juda-
> ism" but rejects the Jews.[13]

The question, then, is this: Was there a Diaspora Judaism sufficiently Hellenized so that when Paul looks most Greek to us, he
could imagine himself, *and be perceived by his contemporaries,* as being
a kind of Jew to that kind of Jew? When one thinks of the philosophical and theological speculations of Philo of Alexandria, Paul's
older contemporary and one who we know was an observant Jew,
the possibilities for Greek attitudes blended with Jewish piety become almost limitless. When one reads the allegories Paul draws
from the Hebrew Scriptures, one is tempted to think that Paul has
completely misunderstood the Jewish theological method of revelation through stories, a method that Jesus appears to have used and
developed. Surely in the allegorical reading of texts we have evidence of Paul the Greek. But Paul's allegorizing is almost amateur-
ish compared to Philo's. The judgment of subsequent generations
of Jews on both Philo and Paul has not been favorable, but during
most of the first century A.D. the lines were not drawn as hard and
fast as they were later.

The judgment of George Bernard Shaw, with which this chapter
began, reflects, at least indirectly, the view of "Paul and the
Greeks" that was widely held at the beginning of this century. Paul
was seen as having imported into the Christian community a form
of religion characteristic of the "mysteries," a catchall term used to
designate religious movements of initiation into secret rites and
esoteric knowledge.

There were dozens of "mystery" traditions in Paul's day; some
were already ancient among the Greeks, others were more or less
recent importations from Egypt or Syria or from points farther east.
With a good deal more imagination than they usually admitted,
scholars attributed this or that element of Paul's thought to the
influence of the mysteries: his notion of the Eucharist, baptism as

dying and rising with Christ, various levels of spiritual knowledge. What Shaw called "the limitations of Paul's soul," and what Harnack called the uniting of the gospel with the world's amassed "intellectual capital," was thought of as the influence of Greek philosophy and religion, both deeply colored by centuries of interchange with the cultures surrounding the Mediterranean.

Scholars of seventy-five years ago would be disoriented if they were to read studies of Paul that are being written today. There are still of course references to the mysteries, but they are definitely subordinate to discussions of Hellenistic Judaism. In a limited sense, this is simply the old discussion transposed into a new key, since some of the characteristic features of the "mysteries" are now found in Hellenistic Judaism. But Judaism, even Hellenized, remained Judaism, and as Sandmel reminds us, even Jews very far apart on the scale had, in their Jewish identity, more in common with one another than they had with those beyond the scale on either end. And as we shall see shortly, the recognition that the "Greek Paul" is to a remarkable extent also the "Jewish Paul" has both supported, and found support in, careful studies of the nature of Christian belief and practice prior to the writing of Paul's letters.

C. The Gnostics

The questions of "Paul and the Jews" and of "Paul and the Greeks" come to focus in the question of "Paul and the Gnostics." As we have seen, there are intricate (and frequently insoluble) problems of definition and delimitation in dealing with Gnosticism, and if the phenomenon is defined simply in terms of its clear second-century manifestations, then the subject of Paul and Gnosticism is the stuff of fantasy. If one is persuaded, however, that a gnosticizing tendency or spirit can be detected in the first century, then we have an important context in which to talk about Paul's Jewishness.

In the face of a genuinely radical development within Judaism (or within the Christian movement viewed as a form of sectarian Judaism)—a development which would invert everything, and make the creator god who chose the Jews a demonic being—Paul asserts categorically the identity of Creator and Redeemer. The distinction between law and grace is not, then, primarily an attack on Pharisaism; the real point of the distinction is the insistence that both law and grace come from the same God—and that amounts to an attack on Gnosticism. Despite his failure to appreciate the full and rich meaning of the covenant relation as the setting for the law, Paul is holding on to the conviction that the God who makes covenants is the God who made the world, and is the only God there is.

Until very recently, the only major evidence taken as pointing clearly to Paul's controversy with Gnostics was the letter to the Colossians, and that letter's apparent concern with Gnosticism was one of several reasons for doubting its authenticity (since scholars assumed that Gnosticism developed only later, Paul could not have been directly concerned to refute it). It is notoriously difficult to reconstruct the "Colossian heresy" from the letter's refutation of it; it appears to have been an amalgam of doctrines about spiritual beings and various rules about eating and sexual relations. It does not correspond to any of the later Gnostic systems known to us, but it has elements which would later be parts of various ones of those systems. The author of the letter appears to say that Christ is superior to all that heavenly host and that Christ therefore eliminates the need for all those regulations.

A significant new direction in Pauline study has resulted from the intense scholarly interest in Gnosticism and from a fresh assessment of the evidence of Paul's undoubted letters. This new development has highlighted the difficulty the historian faces in figuring out a complex situation, when all the evidence available is from one partisan in what was a fierce debate.

Nearly every reader of the New Testament has felt quite confident of knowing who the "Judaizers" were who hounded Paul around the Mediterranean and tried to undo the work he had just done. Because we read the law/gospel distinction as directed mainly against Judaism, we assume that the "Judaizers" would have been agents of the Jerusalem Christian community, who resented Paul's easy opening of this new Jewish movement to Gentiles. Paul's struggle with the "Judaizers" becomes, then, the crowning evidence for the nineteenth century's favorite thesis: that Palestinian Jewish Christianity was countered by Paul's Hellenistic Christianity, and that the battle was a head-on collision.

Recent studies of Paul's letters, especially the Corinthian correspondence, have done with the "Judaizers" what the blink of an eye will do to an optical illusion drawing: suddenly what were the black squares on a white background become white squares on a black background, or the boxes that appeared to be coming out of the page suddenly appear to be behind the page. The "evidence" is the same (no new manuscript of Paul's letters has turned up, nor do we have writings from the "Judaizers" themselves), but it looks very different.

The "Judaizers" have been turned upside down, or inside out. They no longer appear as emissaries of James and the Jerusalem church, as agents of reaction to Paul's more radical activities. It is now believed that they are Gnostics, not necessarily even Jews, but persons who have found in the basic Christian message themes and motifs that suit their purposes. For instance, avoidance of certain foods can be the result either of adherence to the law of Moses for the sake of righteousness, or of belief that the material world is unworthy of human beings. A gnostically inclined person might welcome Paul's distinction between law and gospel, and then turn around and want to reinstitute various abstentions, but for quite new reasons.

There is no doubt that Paul opposed any effort to retain the following of the law as a means of establishing one's own righteousness. Such an effort, however, appears not to have been the primary aim of the "Judaizers." Paul is chiefly concerned to indicate how limited is his own championing of an ascetic style of life: no one should conclude that when Paul says it is better not to be married, he thinks sex and the world of matter will "tarnish" the pure human spirit. The "Judaizers" are not those who think Paul has gone too far; they are those who think he has not gone far enough.[14]

For an understanding of Paul himself, a clear sense of who his opponents were is peculiarly important, since his thought or "doctrine" was hammered out in the heat of controversy. This new understanding of the direction from which his most persistent attackers came—from the "left" rather than from the "right"—will require a thorough reevaluation of Paul's role in the developing Christian community. There is probably an element of overstatement in the case that has been made for the "Judaizers" as Gnostics, or at least we must be careful not to lose sight of Paul's challenge to the Pharisaic evaluation of the Law.[15] But there can be no going back to the sharp Jerusalem/Paul antithesis of an earlier scholarly generation. And, indeed, the next "enigma variation" is directly related to this new understanding of Paul and his opponents.

III. Variation II: Already but Not Yet

Paul's thought is hard to grasp as a whole; indeed, the problem may lie in the systematic prejudice hidden in the very concept of "Paul's thought." But there is a consensus among scholars today that if the particular things Paul says are to make any sense to us, we have to understand something of the special twist he gave to eschatology. We must, in short, come to grips with one of the supreme ironies of history: that one of the world's most effective organizers believed that the world he was organizing was about to end. The key is in a paradox of adverbs: "already but not yet."

A. Paul and the Original Apostles

Nearly everybody agrees that Jesus' message had a large dose of eschatological concern in it—the kingdom of God is at hand; repent, the mighty will be put down and the lowly raised. Nearly everybody agrees that that emphasis would have characterized the beliefs and preaching of the early Jerusalem church. It is likely, too, that the Jerusalem church added to (or developed, as the case may be) whatever Jesus may have said about the relation of his own activity to the coming of the kingdom. It is clear that Paul had eschatological concerns near the center of his preaching too, and that the return of Christ to complete the work begun in his earthly career was an assumption of Paul's whole scheme of history and salvation. The pattern of "already but not yet," then, seems to be a plausible link between the teaching of Jesus and the teaching of Paul, with the Jerusalem church as the mediating factor.

Paul of course claims that he got his message direct from the risen Christ. This undoubtedly carried great weight with some of his hearers, but from the end of the second century comes a highly instructive document, almost certainly directed against the tradition springing from Paul, a document in which the relative values of companionship with Jesus and direct revelation are debated.

[The figure representing Paul says to Peter:] "You assert that you thoroughly understand your teacher's concerns because, in his physical presence, you saw and heard him directly, but no one else could gain such understanding by means of a dream or a vision. But I shall show that this is false. One who hears something directly cannot be quite certain about what was said, for the mind must consider whether, being merely human, it has been deceived by the sense impression. But the vision, by the very act of appearing, presents its own proof to the seer that it is divine. First give me an answer to this."

And Peter said, "The prophet, once he has proved that he is a prophet, is infallibly believed in the matters which are directly spoken by him. Also, when his truthfulness has been previously recognized, he can give answers to the disciple, however the latter may wish to examine and interrogate him. But one who puts his trust in a vision or an apparition or dream is in a precarious position, for he does not know what it is he is trusting. For it is possible that it is an evil demon or a deceitful spirit, pretending in the speeches to be what he is not. Then if anyone should wish to inquire who it was who spoke, he could say of himself whatever he chose. Thus, like an evil flash of lightning, he stays as long as he chooses and then vanishes, not remaining with the inquirer long enough to answer his questions."[16]

This second-century document, with its interesting parallels to modern discussions of the reliability of perception and eyewitness testimony dealt with in Chapter 6, shows us Peter making an accusation not far removed from Shaw's, that Paul stole Jesus as the figurehead for his salvationist vessel. But both Shaw and the document's "Peter" are far removed from current reconstructions of the relationship of Paul and the Jerusalem church.

The new understanding of Paul's chief opposition as coming from a gnosticizing left instead of from a legalist right has reinforced conclusions, based on earlier investigations of Paul's language, that the apostle to the Gentiles and the original apostles were not so far apart as used to be thought. Once proper attention is paid to the nature of the community which produced the New Testament as a worshiping community, and as a worshiping community *from the very beginning,* Paul's letters sound rather different from the way they do if the language of the letters is all attributed to Paul's own genius and inventiveness.

Many passages of his letters are almost certainly allusions to, or even direct quotations of, hymns and other liturgical formulas already in use in the churches before, or as soon as, Paul appeared on the scene. And some of these quotations are among the most theologically "advanced" passages in Paul's letters. The most conspicuous example is the meditation on the "self-emptying" of Christ

in Phil. 2:6–11; there is a consensus among scholars today that Paul
did not compose those lines, but is quoting a hymn that will be
familiar to his readers. Numerous other parts of his letters (e.g.,
Rom. 1:3–4; 1 Cor. 15:3–7; Col. 1:15–20), including his statements about the Eucharist (especially 1 Cor. 11:23–26), are now
thought to use language already stereotyped, and if these investigations have diminished slightly the range of Paul's originality, they
have expanded enormously the range of our understanding of the
Christianity that Paul found when he ceased persecuting it and
joined it.

The results of a great deal of patient research by several scholars
can be summarized briefly in the following words: What used to be
thought of as typically (and originally) Pauline Christianity, "with
sacraments, cultic worship of Jesus as Lord, Gentile members, and
the doctrines of pre-existence and atoning death of the Christ—had
already been 'founded' before Paul became its first persecutor and
then its missionary."[17]

This is still, to be sure, not quite the same as demonstrating the
similarity of Paul and the Jerusalem church, but it does amount to
saying that the very first missionary thrust of the Christian community was characterized by motifs and themes that used to be thought
of as Paul's "importation" into Christianity, the "imposition" of the
limitations of his soul on the soul of Jesus. It now appears that the
portrayal of the early Jerusalem community in Acts may be remarkably accurate. We see there, at the origins of the church on the Day
of Pentecost, the presence in the church of Jews from Palestine and
those from the Diaspora. The distinction we think of as that between James and Paul was already there in the distinction between
Peter and Stephen. If there was a fundamental distinction between
the religion of the Jerusalem church and the religion of the Pauline
churches, it was rooted in some of the differences between Palestinian and Diaspora Judaism—differences which, as we saw in
Chapter 4, have been in many respects modified and moderated by
recent study.

Scholars are beginning to suspect that the most important clue to
Paul's whole conception of the church is his dogged insistence on
seeing through to successful conclusion his project of a collection
for the church at Jerusalem (Rom. 15: 25–28; Gal. 2:10; 1 Cor.
16:1–4; 2 Cor. 8:9). It may be that Paul's opposing Peter to his face,

which he says (Gal. 2:11–12) he did in Antioch when Peter withdrew from table fellowship with Gentile Christians as soon as some emissaries from James arrived, was not the battle royal it is often pictured as being, but was rather a stern rebuke perceived very much to be a quarrel between brothers. Indeed, Paul's sternness makes sense only if Peter was in fundamental agreement with him on the basic issue, that of Gentiles' full access to the gospel. Paul accuses Peter not of having the wrong idea, but of failing to act according to his convictions.

It is not simply new appreciations of Paul's problems in the Gentile mission that complicate the question of his relations with the Jerusalem church. It is increasingly clear that "the Jerusalem church" is itself a general term covering a great variety. Very likely, Acts conveys only the faintest echo of what could easily have been sharp debates among the original followers of Jesus about the proper evaluation of Paul. It is further likely that the estimate of Paul's activities changed as time went on, or rather that it fluctuated, as reports either direct or indirect reached Jerusalem—some reports from Paul's champions, some from his detractors, none, probably, from "objective" observers, since the issues raised by Paul's teaching were the sort to evoke passionate argument.

B. Ethics

Everyone who has read Paul has been puzzled by the way his declarations that "law is no way to salvation" are followed by detailed regulations about the way Christians should act. Interest in Paul's ethics has increased in recent years. This has resulted, at least in part, from developments in the field of ethics itself. Various ethical theories (e.g., existentialist, contextual, situational) have taken "freedom from the law" as their starting point, and have then tried to see what happens if no further regulations (except, perhaps, a generalized admonition to "love" or to aim at "authentic existence") are imposed. Many such ethicists would argue that they are being true to Paul's insight, and that it is merely an unfortunate historical circumstance (or lack of clear vision on Paul's part) that he does not leave all matters of specific choice up to his readers. They are claiming to be, in effect, more Pauline than Paul himself.

In addition to this specifically ethical interest in Paul, there are also developments in politics and society that appear to call some of Paul's specific positions seriously into question. Among these are the questions of civil disobedience (in relation to Rom. 13:1—"Let every person be subject to the governing authorities"), women's liberation (in relation to Paul's attitude toward women and their place in the church), and gay liberation (in relation to Paul's statements on sexual deviance).

It is very easy to demonstrate how extensively Paul's prescriptions are influenced by the culture of his day. Women were locked into subordinate roles throughout society, and it can even be argued that in comparison to the norm of his day, Paul is quite liberal in granting institutional rights to women. Slavery was a basic fact of social and economic life, and while Paul says that Christian masters should treat their Christian slaves as fellow Christians, he does not say that Christian masters should, as part of their Christian duty, free their slaves. Genuinely democratic ideas had not appeared in political thought, even in the heyday of Greek philosophy, so we should hardly expect Paul to have differed significantly from the normal view, that the given political authority was part of one's world, and was to be accepted as such. Jews had a particularly harsh view of homosexuality as being the direct reflection of the polytheism of the Gentile world, and hence as directly opposed to the worship of the one true God. Finally, the most thoroughly developed ethical thinking available in Paul's day was that of the Stoics, and lists of duties in Paul's letters can be paralleled in Stoic writings of the same period. Much of what Paul tells his readers to do is simply the conventional ethical wisdom of his time.

The chief difficulty in interpreting Paul's ethics arises from the need to make distinctions between the general ethical principles Paul declares to be grounded in the nature of the gospel itself and the specific rules he derives from those principles. What goes in each category? And what, if any, of the specific rules would Paul himself be willing to say were applicable to his time and not to some other?

One's instinctive response to the latter question is: None. To make such a distinction between his time and another time would not come naturally or easily to Paul, and anyway, he was persuaded that there was very little time left. However, there was built into Paul's thinking a principle of revision. The law of Moses had been appropriate for its time, but it had been superseded. Of course Paul attributed a finality to the gospel that was not characteristic of the law, but even under the heading of that "finality" there was the need to "press on toward the goal" of the calling in Christ. That is, in the "already but not yet" paradox there is the basis for an *ongoing* dynamic development of ethical understanding, in the light of newly confronted situations.

The basis for ethical thinking in Paul then turns out not to be a safe and sure thing; the basis is a tension, the "but" which holds together "already" and "not yet." Paul provides a great deal of practical advice to his congregations, and he appeals to many different kinds of reasons—to nature, to freedom, to the example of Christ, to the building up of the congregation. But these reasons are themselves grounded in two fundamental principles: the transformation of the person by the grace of God, and the identity of the person as a member of the Christian community.

The first of these principles, transformation by the grace of God, is another way of putting the basic Pauline doctrine of "justification by faith." Paul believed that the surest evidence of remnants of the "old Adam" in Christians was the lingering suspicion that the full achievement of transformation was in their own hands. Paul sensed that to strive after perfection in behavior is to sow "the seeds of division—between group and group, man and man, and within the self."[18] This did not mean that any behavior was as good as any other, even though some who heard Paul thought it followed that they should sin all the more in order that grace might abound all the more. It meant only that virtue is a response to divine action, not a way of invoking or provoking such action. But it also means, at least by implication, that notions of virtue may alter as new responses to divine action come to seem appropriate.

The second principle serves as a provisional check on totally arbitrary developments coming out of the first. Christians do not belong to themselves as individuals, but to one another as members of the church, and Paul insists that one must never use freedom in such a way as to harm another. One must be free even from bondage to one's freedom. And one must be prepared to take very seriously the collective wisdom of the community. This is not by any means to say that the majority is always right, but it is to say something which is not particularly popular in our own day: the chance is better (only slightly better) that true wisdom is to be found in a community judgment than in the opinion of an individual. We tend to assume that the free individual, opposing institutions and systems, is the highest expression of human personhood. Paul sets up another model: someone who has no scruples about eating meat offered to idols abstaining in the company of one whose conscience is disturbed by such behavior (1 Cor. 8).

These two principles cannot by themselves provide the necessary guidance, and that is why Christian ethics must be something other than a branch of biblical interpretation. Transformation by grace and concern for another's scruples could become the basis for a passive form of behavior, devoid of prophetic bite. I might justify keeping silent about racial injustice on the grounds that while I am "free of prejudice," my neighbor has scruples about race, and I would not want to do anything upsetting to my neighbor. It can be argued that Paul sets a dynamic in motion when he declares that all the old distinctions are undone in Christ: circumcision/uncircumcision, Jew/Greek, slave/free, male/female, but it is clear that in terms of *practical* instruction to his churches this dynamic did not break fully through the conservative confines of the two basic principles.

Perhaps the proper function of the dynamic element in Paul's ethics is to provide energy for the "already" to encroach steadily on the "not yet." To put it that way raises immediately the danger of misunderstanding: it would appear to say that "every day in every way things are getting better and better." Such would of course be a travesty, for Paul believed that it was God's business, not ours, to complete the new age. But the Christian living now, in a time when it is clear to virtually all Christians that slavery is incompatible with the gospel, must be prepared to oppose those further arbitrary distinctions which are used by one group to hold another group down. Paul's continuing ethical importance for the church lies not in his list of duties (although these are worth meditating on—not everything he said is of use only to the first century), but rather in the dynamic of new creation operating through principles of transformation by grace and identification with the community.

To take Paul's specific behavioral instructions as being equally authoritative with his underlying principles is to run the risk of a kind of legalism he was determined to combat, and can serve to shut down the very process of responsible ethical reflection he appears to have wanted to stimulate in his converts. The attempt to sort out what is normative from what is conditional in Paul's ethical scheme is the business both of New Testament students and of students of ethics. Historians of early Christianity are paying more and more attention to the social organization and functioning of the Christian community, and Paul's success at translating theological ideas into social practice is a subject of great interest from the point of view of social theory. There is a ferment in the field of ethical philosophy, too, and Paul's blend of historical, philosophical, theological, and psychological theory and insight is bound to intrigue both Christian and non-Christian students of ethics.

The full impact of sociological investigation of the New Testament materials has yet to be felt, and it may be a long time before an even tentative assessment of Paul's ethics from the sociological viewpoint can be made. A suggestion might be put forward now, however, about one of the keys to understanding the puzzling relationship between Paul's theology of freedom and his specific ethical instructions.

It has often been said, either directly or indirectly, that Paul was a Pharisee who adopted an apocalyptic viewpoint (that of Christianity) and, as a result, rejected the Pharisaic tradition because the two were incompatible. As we saw in Chapter 4, however, Davies and others have demonstrated that ways of thinking which appear "incompatible" to us were held simultaneously by ancient persons, and specifically, there were Pharisees who did not find apocalyptic ideas out of character with their traditional regard for the written Law and the oral tradition.

In this context, Paul's whole stance takes on a new coloring. He could, *as a Pharisee,* believe both that God would have to bring in a whole new age *and* that the forms of this age, while passing away, were still of use. His catalogs of instructions might even begin to look like an extension of the Pharisaic tradition of "oral interpretation" of the law of Moses, designed to make it relevant to new situations. In any case, the possibility that Paul's blend of apocalyptic eschatology and sober admonitions to his churches represents, to a special degree, his Pharisaic identity may help explain his success as an organizer. As we shall see in the next chapter, there may be no better way to get a group going and growing than to predict an event which turns out not to happen (and this has been, to date at least, the experience of apocalyptists); and in terms of organizational staying power, there is nothing to match what the Pharisees accomplished following the destruction of Jerusalem by the Romans, for despite all the attempts to eliminate it from the face of the earth, Judaism survives. Perhaps "an apocalyptic Pharisee" would be the best answer to the question, "Whom would you nominate to organize the world?"

IV. Variation III: Psychology of the Religious Life

My own sense of "breakthrough" in the understanding of Paul came when I found myself reacting to him in his capacity as a psychologist of the religious life. The words are chosen carefully: I found myself reacting. It was not a conscious decision on my part. I am sure the way was prepared by reading various interpretations along those lines, but it was only when I had experienced for myself the alarming degree to which we are not the masters of our fates and captains of our souls that I came to have a sense of what Paul was talking about, indeed, to have a sense that he was making sense. A secular psychiatrist once told me that in his judgment the most helpful insights are those of Augustine and Luther, and of course each of them would point right back to Paul.

Those of us who find the psychological variation of the Pauline enigma particularly appealing have to be careful not to be oversold by it. Recent scholarship has fairly well demolished the romantically attractive hypothesis that when Paul talks about the inability to do the good that one wills (Rom. 7:19), he is talking primarily about his own experience, either before or after his conversion. There are simply too many places in his letters where he says directly that he did not have particular trouble living the life of an upright Jew under the law, to make it likely he is giving us autobiography in Romans 7. So, we must not draw a picture of Paul that makes him the model of our sense of frustration. If we are going to journey with Paul himself, we have to go up with him to "the third heaven" (2 Cor. 12:2–4), not down into the depths of despair.

A. Paul and Introspection

It is difficult, perhaps impossible, for us to read Paul as if Augustine, Luther, Kierkegaard, Barth had never read him and reported what they found there. Harnack, who knew the Christian tradition thoroughly, said that "one might write the history of dogma as a history of the Pauline reactions in the Church, and in so doing would touch on all the turning points of the history."[19] Paul liberated Augustine from philosophical dualism, Luther from gnawing despair, Kierkegaard from dizzying absurdity, Barth from liberal disillusionment. That the apostle to the Gentiles has been able to speak so directly to spiritual virtuosos in cultural and historical situations so strikingly different from his own and from those of one another is testimony to his capacity to make the abstract concrete —that is, if Romans 7 is Paul's description of the general condition of a human being prior to the reception of divine grace, and prior to the recognition that grace is the only alternative to self-devouring pride ("I have done what God requires, and look what a good person I am!") or self-destructive despair ("I cannot possibly do what God requires, so hope is groundless").

However Paul came to his understanding of the powerlessness of the will, whether from his own experience or through careful listening to other persons or through his reading of Scripture (or, more likely, "all of the above"), he did give expression to a frustration known by many persons in many times and places. But we must not assume that because Paul rescued Luther from the onslaught of devastating attacks of despair, Paul himself was subject to such attacks. Paul's speaking directly to all sorts and conditions of persons is a prime example of what Ricoeur calls the capacity of texts to create audiences of their own, audiences unintended and unanticipated by their authors. Once a process of communication has started, no one, least of all the one who started it, has the power to determine the direction it will take.

When Paul touches us deeply, it is easy to think that our problems were his problems. The danger that we may thus get a distorted view of Paul has been highlighted in an article published in 1963 by Krister Stendahl, Dean of the Harvard Divinity School. Called "The Apostle Paul and the Introspective Conscience of the

West," the article sets out to show that Paul was himself not a man of tormented conscience, and that for him the central problem was the meaning of history, not his own peace of mind.

Stendahl has shown that Paul's concern was, in the first instance at least, to resolve a problem in biblical theology (the mystery of the election of Israel on the one hand and the Jewish rejection of Jesus as the Messiah on the other hand, and how this paradox fits into an understanding of God's sovereignty) rather than to break a logjam in his own psyche. Stendahl puts the point succinctly:

[For the first 350 years Paul meant relatively little for the thinking of the church; it seems that his great insight into justification by faith was forgotten.] It is, however, with Augustine that we find an inter-pretation of Paul which makes use of what to us is the deeper layer in the thought of the great Apostle. A decisive reason for this state of affairs may well have been that up to the time of Augustine the Church was by and large under the impression that Paul dealt with those issues with which he actually deals: 1) What happens to the Law (the Torah, the actual Law of Moses, not the principle of legalism) when the Messiah has come?—2) What are the ramifications of the Messiah's arrival for the relation between Jews and Gentiles? For Paul had not arrived at his view of the Law by testing and pondering its effects upon his conscience; it was his grappling with the question about the place of the Gentiles in the Church and in the plan of God, with the problem Jews/Gentiles or Jewish Christians/Gentile Chris-tians, which had driven him to that interpretation of the Law which was to become his in a unique way.[20]

Stendahl goes on to point out that once the genesis of Paul's argument is forgotten, when the great historical question about the Gentile mission is no longer a pressing concern, and the criterion for meaning becomes not the direction of history but the personal anguish of an Augustine, the whole argument even of Romans 7 is distorted: for Paul never says that the will is depraved, as the Augustinian tradition (including, in this respect, much of Protes-tantism) would have it. The will to do the good is genuinely there, it is simply powerless. The move from powerlessness to depravity is perhaps a subtle one, but it is a decisive one, and makes Paul our contemporary in a way that would baffle him.

Paul will continue to work revolutions in the lives of individuals who have no inkling of the nature of the problems he was himself trying to sort out; he will always be a ferment in Christian life and thought. Nevertheless, careful study of Paul can help to guard against serious distortion of his words. We have just seen one such instance: a doctrine of the total depravity of the will cannot claim Paul as its patron. Another equally serious distortion that can arise from the "introspective conscience" interpretation of Paul is a "rugged individualism" which would be as strange to him as the notion of a depraved will.

We are easily blinded to Paul's sense of the importance of community, both the social community of the church and the historically continuous community of Israel. And even if Paul misinterpreted the ancient Israelite covenant in the way Schoeps has suggested, Paul nevertheless believed that persons continue to live in a community which has a covenant relationship with God. For Paul, life in the body of the church is at least as important as life in freedom from legalism, and if someone were troubled in conscience, Paul would probably say that the solution was in community at least as much as it was in the proper understanding of justification by faith.

B. Paul and Freud

A most stimulating recent study of Paul starts directly counter to Stendahl's argument. Richard Rubenstein begins his *My Brother Paul* with a declaration that in his opinion Romans 7 contains a retrospective account of Paul's life as a Jew under the law. "What Paul did in the light of Christ, I did in the light of my psychoanalytic experience."[21]

The book is rich in suggestive insight, and we shall be concerned with it in some detail in Chapter 9, in a discussion of the significance for New Testament interpretation of new ways of studying religion. For now, perhaps a brief indication of some of Rubenstein's conclusions will hint at the freshness (or, as one might want to say, brashness) of his understanding of Paul.

Rubenstein challenges the Judaism/Hellenism distinction not in the way a historian such as Hengel has challenged it (by demonstrating that Judaism had been thoroughly Hellenized), but by probing beneath such distinctions to the depth-psychological level. "The whole question of whether a particular mode of religious thought or action was originally Hellenistic rather than Jewish is subordinate to a far more important issue: what was psychologically at stake in the shift from one type of belief or practice to another?" Rubenstein rings a number of changes on the observation of Freud that "dark traces of the past lay in [Paul's] soul ready to break through to the regions of consciousness," and under the general heading of Paul's capacity to "make manifest the unmanifest" Rubenstein analyzes baptism as a return to the waters of the womb, the Last Adam as a symbolic way for human beings to return to their origins, and the Eucharist as a ritual eating of the elder brother. In all this, Paul becomes a supreme symbolist of humankind's unconscious drives and motivations.[22]

When described briefly in this way, the whole scheme sounds grotesque, and Rubenstein's book has been greeted by some reviewers with a good deal less than enthusiasm. But as Chapter 9 will attempt to show, Rubenstein is bringing to the reading of Paul a set of categories and a point of view that have been of enormous significance culturally in this century, and no matter how extensive the revisions that psychologists find they have to make in Freudian theory, there can be no going back from Freud's demonstration of the dynamic power of the unconscious.

Rubenstein's effort is bound to be clumsy in places, since he is something of a pioneer, but even in those places where his book requires not just a pinch of salt but a whole shakerful, his argument is invigorating and stimulating. And the argument is not simply about an understanding of Paul: it includes a sweeping generalization about the "preparation of the ground" for Freud:

> If any single idea dominates the way I have come to see Paul, it is this: Under the impact of the Christian religious revolution, which was at least initially an internal Jewish revolution, Paul came to understand, as did later Jewish mystics, that reality as apprehended by common sense offers only hints of the deeper and truer meaning of the human world. Paul thus prepares the way for and anticipates the work of the twentieth century's most important secularized Jewish mystic, Sigmund Freud.[23]

V. THE ENIGMA OF PAUL TODAY

That quotation from Rubenstein includes the first mention of the term "mystic" in this chapter. There is very little attention being given these days to the element of mysticism in Paul. Such lack of attention is, up to a point, healthy. Previous generations that saw Paul primarily as a mystic forgot his compulsion to understand history, and could overlook his constant concern to establish and nurture communities. Mystics are not necessarily individuals cut off from society; in our time Thomas Merton has illustrated in an unmistakable way the paradoxical truth that the pursuit of mystical vision can lead right into involvement with the world at its most sensitive points. But mysticism as popularly understood often implies a thoroughgoing individualism, and it is important that Paul not be seen in that light.

However, it may be significant for future study of Paul that mysticism talk reemerges *in a positive sense* in a Freudian psychological interpretation of Paul. Mysticism is perhaps to be sought in Paul not in the third heaven or, as Schweitzer thought, in the notion of incorporation "in Christ," but rather in Paul's instinctive use of symbols and images that have resonance with religious realities that are not limited to the biblical tradition.[24]

The enigma of Paul in the past has been a warrant for all sorts of competing views as to what he really was, what stood at the center of his theology, how he differed decisively from his opponents (who themselves were thought to have had clear and distinct ideas). The enigma of Paul today goes deeper than that. We know enough now to ask whether the search for "the center" of his theology, for clear lines between him and opponents, for what he "really" was, is not after all a misdirected search.

The distinction between Jesus and Paul was not anything like as sharp as Shaw thought, and the Jewishness of Paul went far deeper than Harnack recognized. To make into a systematic theologian a man who set out to demonstrate the danger in all systems is something of an indignity, and runs the risk of reducing Paul to the confines of what we can conceive of as a "system." If Paul could become all things to all persons, perhaps we can understand him only if we are willing, with some prodding from him, to become more things than we are.

CHAPTER EIGHT

THE SOCIAL REALITY
OF THE NEW JERUSALEM

The author of The Letter to the Hebrews (13:14) says, not with regret but in a tone of triumph, "Here we have no lasting city, but we seek the city which is to come." A recent development in the study of Christian origins asks of this passage, and others like it, not "What do they tell us about the content of the hopes that early Christians held for the future?" but "What does the holding of such hopes for the future tell us about the social existence of communities that make such statements?"

The New Testament itself, of course, provides many hints of the character of various Christian communities. Paul says to the Christians in Corinth that few of them are wise and powerful, and he exults in the marvel that God has chosen to shame the wise by the foolishness of the gospel (1 Cor. 1:18–29). In the Corinthian correspondence we can see already the emergence of economic class distinctions within the church, as well as sharp arguments between the spirit-filled and those more committed to order and decorum. The Gospels themselves suggest some of the ideals of early Christianity, particularly poverty. It does not take a psychologist or a sociologist to figure out that "the last will be first, and the first last" (Matt. 20:16) would have a special appeal to people whose social experience was that of being last.

The trouble with analysis of this sort—that is, the detection of social evidence "between the lines" of the texts—is that it is haphazard and depends mostly on the investigator's intuition. The study is not operating on the basis of any theory of social dynamics, and therefore it has no convincing way of interrelating the diverse and fragmentary pieces of evidence to one another.

In a book published in 1975, John Gager of Princeton University has written a charter for a new sociological investigation of early Christianity. The book, *Kingdom and Community: The Social World of Early Christianity*, draws on some earlier efforts along these lines, but Gager's book is a major stride ahead in this kind of approach to the subject, and *Kingdom and Community* will be the main object of attention in this chapter.[1]

I. THE SOCIOLOGICAL PERSPECTIVE

Kingdom and Community is a series of five studies of particular problems in the history of early Christianity that are tied together by a consistent concern about method. This concern—to apply to the evidence from the early Christian period schemes and models that have proved useful in the study of other religions—grew out of Gager's puzzlement as he taught his first courses:

> Why is it that the study of early Christianity, as normally practiced, seems so different from the study of more exotic religions in Africa, Australia, and Melanesia? . . . A combination of theological, cultural, and historical factors has conspired to create a protected enclave for this particular religion. As a consequence, methods and techniques that are taken for granted in the treatment of other religions have been ignored or discarded in dealing with this one (p. xi).

Gager is arguing for a new understanding of early Christian history by a systematic application of techniques of interpretation developed in the social sciences.

Gager is quite aware of the radical nature of his enterprise, and attempts to forestall criticism by those who will (inevitably, he admits) misconstrue his intentions: the critics will tend to lay "greater emphasis than the author himself on the incompatibility of his own work with that of his predecessors in the field (the author sees his relationship to previous work as a matter of both/and, whereas his critics perceive him as advancing a claim of either/or)" (p. xii). He states clearly that the answers you get depend on the questions you start with, and the questions you start with reflect the inclinations you bring to the problem.

Gager disclaims any desire to supplant more traditional forms of approach, and specifically includes "the theological" among valid ways of coming at the evidence. He does, however, believe that theological concerns have dominated the study of early Christianity for too long, and that such concerns have, in particular, got in the way of doing history. As we shall see toward the end of this chapter, Gager does make some claims on the basis of his analysis which have serious implications for theology, and yet it can be shown that some of Gager's findings, *within his own frame of reference,* point to conclusions different from those he reaches. But before we get there, we must consider how he arrives at his judgments.

Gager takes his fundamental model from the sociologist Peter Berger, who asserts that every human society is an enterprise of "world-building"—that is, every community constructs its scheme of order and value, in terms of which it perceives reality: "The social world in which we live determines our experience of what is real" (p. 9). It must be made clear at the outset that Gager, following Berger, is not saying that our thought is determined by our social surroundings (for example, that middle-class people have middle-class prejudices); to the extent such determination of our thinking may happen, it is only part of the much larger scheme with which Gager is working. Construction of a "social world," and subsequently the maintenance of that world, involves language, rituals, institutions, doctrines, indeed everything we recognize as elements of human society. The use of "social world" in this sense is roughly equivalent to what is meant by saying that novelists "create whole worlds" in their books.

Gager distinguishes between a concern with the details of early Christian society, which is not his concern, and a concern, which is his, with the social world created by the early Christian community, in terms of which its rites and beliefs made sense: "This is not a book about developed theologies of God or salvation in early Christianity but about the ways in which it, like other new religions, created a world so that certain ideas of God and salvation, and not others, seem peculiarly appropriate" (p. 10). As a corollary to this, Gager goes on to state his "basic conviction that the process of generating a sacred cosmos or a symbolic universe is always rooted in concrete communities of believers" (p. 10). This conviction directs attention away from single individuals (whether they be Paul or Jesus) to the Christian communities themselves—and in so doing brings the sociological study of the New Testament into parallel with developments in more traditional lines of New Testament research. As we have seen in previous chapters, the understanding even of Jesus and Paul is increasingly set in a communal framework.

If the Christian social world is so directly the product of the community, then it is important to know as much as we can about that community. Gager acknowledges his debt to the development of redaction criticism in the study of the Gospels (pp. 8–9), for when the focus is shifted from the isolated units of tradition (with the goal of "getting back to Jesus") to the overall "world" of the individual Gospel texts, we suddenly find ourselves with a great deal of evidence for "social worlds in the making" in various parts of the Christian movement. While there is, through redaction criticism, a direct link between Gager's work and more traditional New Testament study, his main intellectual affinities are with sociologists who have studied religion and society in a variety of "laboratory" situations. Gager is, for the first time, from the perspective and training of a historian of early Christianity, seeking to apply systematically to the historical evidence the methods and theories of such social scientists as Max Weber, Anthony Wallace, and Victor Turner.

Many early Christian writers, and some of their scholarly descendants, have argued that the growth and triumph of Christianity are a testimony to its divine origin—indeed, in Acts (5:34–39) the Pharisee Gamaliel is presented as the original formulator of this view, when he says there is no point in trying to stamp the church out, since if it is of God, nothing can eliminate it, and if it is not, it cannot survive. Such arguments are even theologically vulnerable; in terms of both the rapidity and extent of its spread, the growth of Marxism in the past century has far exceeded that of Christianity in the first three centuries. But Gager argues the specifically historical point. According to his analysis, the emergence and rise of Christianity are dynamically no different from the emergence and rise of many other religious movements. There are some unique features of Christianity, just as there are to any group creating a social world, but these unique features can themselves be worked into a sociological analysis.

II. Christianity as a Millenarian Cult

There can be few things so obvious as the crisis presented to the early Christian church by the nonreturn of Christ. Historians have almost without exception looked for ways in which the Christians adjusted their thinking and behavior to take account of the dashing of their hopes. The historical problem becomes: how to explain the Christian survival of a crisis that should have done the movement in. When viewed sociologically, however, what has been thought of as a threat to the church turns out to have been an immense blessing. There can be circumstances in which the best way to assure a religious community's growth is to commit the community to a prediction that does not come true.

Gager's treatment of Christianity as a millenarian movement is the longest chapter of his book; the argument has many facets, and is rich in detail. We can here consider no more than a few of its leading features.[2]

A. The Disprivileged

When sociologists tell us that "have-nots" want to be "haves," they do not go beyond what we could figure out for ourselves. But when they go on to describe the ways in which have-nots come to terms with their difference in status from the haves, they frequently alert us to psychological and social mechanisms we might have missed. In addition to detecting some of those mechanisms, modern studies have also developed a way of breaking the notion of "deprivation" loose from some clear (though arbitrary) "poverty line"; in social dynamics "relative deprivation" is an important force. When people sense a significant discrepancy between what they have (in terms of wealth, power, status, etc.) and what they can reasonably aspire to, the stage is set for something to happen. A poor person whose expectations do not go much beyond the current poverty may experience less deprivation in this sense than one relatively well off who aspires to go much higher. In terms of social dynamics, deprivation is a function of one's sense of being deprived.

Millenarian movements are, in sociological terms, drastic responses to a sense of deprivation. At the most obvious symbolic level, the movement projects the replacement of this world order with a totally different one, in which those who are have-nots here become the haves there, and vice versa. At a deeper level, the evaluation of this world is simplified by resolving "the complexities of moral judgments that typify a complex society . . . into a series of binary oppositions: poor-rich, good-evil, pious-hypocrite, elect-damned" (p. 25). And one can go beyond the straightforward interpretation of New Testament statements on poverty as evidence for the generally low economic level of Christian converts. "The ideology of poverty does more than simply mirror social reality. It exaggerates and idealizes this reality" (p. 28).

Gager draws on various sources, including the New Testament, to present a picture of Palestinian life, particularly in the region of Galilee, in the first century, and he finds that "a premillenarian mood of political alienation and active resistance was abroad in Palestine during and beyond the time of Jesus' activity there" (p. 23). When reading Gager's description, one begins to hear Sandmel's voice in the background, warning against the assumption that we know more than we can know—Gager leans particularly heavily on the hypothesis that the original Christians were drawn from the 'am ha'aretz (the "people of the land"), and while that may well be so, Sandmel has questioned whether we really know very much about such people at all.

Gager is of course aware of the difficulties and dangers in doing sociological analysis on historical data. We have severely limited numbers of sources, and no way of controlling them by questionnaires or by reliable statistical information. He is right that we may even learn something from necessarily circular arguments: the theory of the relation of deprivation to millenarian movements may itself help substantiate connections (for example, Christianity was a millenarian movement, it appealed to the 'am ha'aretz, therefore the 'am ha'aretz were a deprived group). But Gager goes farther than the evidence warrants, and he goes farther than his own introductory remarks suggest he intends to go.

After giving a catalog of sayings and activities of Jesus that illustrate sharp conflict between him and the Pharisees, Gager asks: "What is this catalogue of charge and countercharge but an expression of the resentment, with its peculiar mixture of religious and social factors, between Pharisees and *'am ha'aretz,* a resentment that is amply attested in rabbinic sources themselves?" (p. 26). The implied answer is, "Nothing else."

Gager is here overstepping the "both/and" limits he set for his own program, for he is, at least by implication, ruling out other explanations for the charges and countercharges. Mention is made of "religious factors," but they are simply part of the more general category of "resentment." Jesus' keeping company with tax collectors and sinners may be of interest to theologians or ethicists, but their explanations of what such behavior might mean do not get to the heart of the matter, which is an expression of resentment on the part of people excluded by the religious establishment. It is very tempting for anyone offering an explanation of something to assume that while other ways of approach may cast some light on the subject, *this* explanation tells us what is *really* going on.

B. Charisma

Every millenarian movement has a founder, or at least looks to someone as its originator. The term "charisma," given wide currency by the writings of Max Weber, has often been taken to mean a personality type—indeed, we often say that someone has a "charismatic personality." Recent study has modified the notion of charisma in a very significant way.

> To the sociologist, charisma . . . can only be that which is recognized, by believers and followers, as "charismatic" in the behaviour of those they treat as charismatic. Charisma is thus a function of recognition: the prophet without honour cannot be a charismatic prophet. Charisma, therefore, sociologically viewed, is a social relationship, not an attribute of individual personality or a mystical quality.[3]

It follows from this definition that even in the absence of sure historical knowledge about Jesus, we can speak of him as a charismatic figure, since we have a great deal of evidence of the responses to him, and it is in the interaction of response that charisma is realized.

The role of the millenarian prophet is to articulate "within a common religious tradition . . . new definitions of power, value, and truth as well as new paths of access ('redemptive media') to them. . . . In this respect, Jesus' activities in the Gospels reflect a perfect image of the millenarian prophet, for he combines criticism of the old with a vision of the new" (p. 29). Time and again Jesus appears as the one who teaches with authority, and he does so by specifically contrasting the old way of access to God with the new way he is proclaiming. From this perspective, then, Jesus' role as prophet can be seen in a context more general than that of a revival of ancient Israelite practices and expectations. He is a charismatic figure who emerges in a premillenarian situation to articulate the hopes of disprivileged members of the religious community, and in that articulation *and in the followers' response to it,* a new social world is born as a new community comes into being.

C. When Prophecy Fails

Whatever predictions Jesus may have made about the end of the world and about his part in the hastening of that end, it is clear that the earliest Christians believed the end was coming soon and that the events of Holy Week had been decisive in starting the process. The early Christians may never have been so specific as to name the hour at which Christ would return, but the experiences of groups in our own day who have confidently set the timetable for the end of the world suggest how the early Christians may have come to terms with the fact that history went on happening.

Recent studies have suggested strongly that the disconfirmation of a millenarian prediction—that is, you wake up the morning after the day on which the world was scheduled to end and find you are in the same old world—does not necessarily damage the group that makes the prediction, but may serve to spur the members on to greater feats of doctrinal definition and missionary zeal. The explanatory concept in these studies is "cognitive dissonance"—when your belief structure and the reality you experience are sharply out of phase with one another, you will make various moves to reduce the "dissonance" this creates in your thinking. And the move we would logically expect—the rejection of the belief that had been contradicted by experience—is not always the move that is made.

Of course some groups whose predictions prove wrong fall apart. There are prior conditions which must be met, and sociologists who have studied contemporary millenarian cults, most notably Lionel

Festinger and others who collaborated with him on the book *When Prophecy Fails: A Social and Psychological Study of a Modern Group That Predicted the Destruction of the World,* have quite carefully spelled these conditions out. They include the relevance of belief to action, the followers' having done something, such as breaking family ties, that is difficult to undo, the specificity of the belief (that is, events may really refute it) and the actual occurrence of the disconfirming evidence, and social support for the believer.[4] For our purposes the main interest is not so much in the conditions, although Gager points out that early Christianity can be shown to meet the conditions, but in the discovery of Festinger and his colleagues that when the conditions are met, not only does some revision of the belief take place (at least the date has to be recalculated) but an impulse toward "proselytism almost always occurs. The assumption, often unconscious, is that 'if more and more people can be persuaded that the system of belief is correct, then clearly it must, after all, be correct' " (p. 39).

One has to be careful in this kind of analysis not to attribute too much to the theory. If the missionary expansion of the church is what is up for explanation, it is worthwhile remembering that there were probably many motivations. Instructions of Jesus to his followers to go out and proselytize may not all be later rationalizations of the church; it is possible, even likely, that someone who believed the hopes of Israel had been fulfilled would set about to spread the word, since the Hebrew Scriptures contain many references to the coming universalizing of the worship of the Lord God of Israel.

There is no reason whatever to dispute the application of the findings of *When Prophecy Fails* to the early Christian evidence; it does help us to understand how the nonreturn of Christ actually aided and abetted missionary zeal. But the theory overextends itself when it reads all of the evidence in such a way as to support itself. That early Christianity had many of the features of a millenarian movement is clear; that the evidence is properly organized according to the framework of the millenarian theory is not quite so clear.

III. SOCIAL DYNAMICS

There is a widespread romantic view of the early Christian church as an urban proletariat furtively worshiping in the catacombs to escape the ever-watchful eye of the Roman police. But the evidence of second-century Christian writers, who claim that one of Christianity's distinctive features is its appeal to a wide range of social classes, is supported by a remark in a letter of Pliny the Younger, governor of a province in Asia Minor, to the Emperor Trajan about A.D. 112, in which he asks for instructions on the way to deal with Christians. Pliny says that the church has attracted persons "of every social rank."[5] Gager points out that the notion of "relative deprivation" makes it possible to speak of Christianity as a community of disprivileged persons and at the same time to accept the evidence of Pliny's letter: "The category of disprivileged persons may well include individuals who are neither poor nor ignorant, e.g., intellectuals" (p. 95). But Gager's main concern is not with what Christians or governors say about the social origins of the Christians, but with an adequate understanding of the society from which the Christians came.

A. Rigidity and Fluidity

Gager gives a clear account of the nature of society in the Roman Empire. The various social classes depended on birth and legal status, not on wealth or education or even on ethnic origin. The class lines were sharp in the first century; toward the end of the second century and during the third they blurred, and thus the way was prepared for a convergence. Christianity, through the writings of its intellectuals and through the moderating of its ideal of poverty, accommodated itself more and more to social classes in which there was little sense of deprivation, while at the same time all sorts of "new persons" made their way into the upper social classes as the structure of the Empire began to fall apart at the end of the second century. As the Roman historian A. H. M. Jones puts it, "the emergence of Christianity as a major force in the fourth century 'coincided with a social change which brought to the front men from the middle and lower classes.' "[6] Knowing what happened in the fourth century is, of course, not directly of concern to anyone wanting to understand the New Testament, but it is nevertheless of indirect importance. When reading the New Testament, we may instinctively think of a social context something like our own, in which there can be serious disputes among analysts about where the class lines are. The same was true to a considerable extent in the third- and fourth-century Roman Empire, but it was not true in the first century. The social structure then was quite rigid, with legally defined classes.

The evidence we have for the social class of Christians within that structured framework points almost exclusively to the lower classes: slaves, freedmen, perhaps some municipal bureaucrats. Within each class there was a wide variety of conditions, and it was possible to hold that it was a happier fate to be a rich person's slave than to be a poor, freeborn citizen (p. 102). But the overwhelming impression conveyed by the evidence for Christianity is not so much that of classes as that of setting: the cities. It is true that Pliny talks about the spread of Christianity in the countryside as well as in urban areas, but it is clear that the tone of the Christian movement was set by urban groups: the familiar names are Thessalonica, Corinth, Philippi, Rome, Antioch, Ephesus, Smyrna, Jerusalem.

Jones has argued that even in the fourth century, when Christianity had triumphed, its strength was still "predominantly in Greek-speaking urban areas among the lower classes and . . . aristocratic aversion to the movement was still widespread." After citing this, Gager calls to mind the observation of Max Weber:

> The religion of nonprivileged classes bears three distinctive marks: a strong tendency toward congregational units; future-oriented systems of compensation (salvation); and a rational system of ethics. He further proposed that these are not accidental features, but that they derive directly from the particular position of disprivileged classes in an urban setting.

And it follows from this that "earliest Christianity was just such a religious movement." The universalizing tendency in Christianity, wherever it came from, was at best a theoretical possibility until two changes—the accommodation of Christianity to classical culture and the democratization of the aristocracy—had made the spread of Christianity beyond the disprivileged residents of the cities practical. A rigid class structure and a rigid millenarian message both had to become more fluid before they could intermingle.[7]

B. Tolerance and Persecution

In his letter to Trajan, Pliny says that a systematic exercise of imperial force could eradicate Christianity. Gager takes this as a sober observation, and perhaps it should be—although governmental promises that conflicts will soon be over, that the enemy is about to capitulate, and that there is "light at the end of the tunnel" may have been as hollow in imperial Rome as we have come to realize they are in our own day. In any case, however, Gager does make a strong case that when the Roman government started seriously persecuting the Christians, in the middle of the third century, the moment had arrived when it was no longer possible to stamp the movement out. By the time the Romans decided on an all-out policy of persecution, the Christian church was so well established that persecution only strengthened its cohesion and will to resist.

As for the earlier period (first and second century), Gager makes the important point that in recent discussion

> the significance of Roman toleration in religious matters may have been overemphasized. . . . At the start, Christianity was not really tolerated; it was simply unknown or thought to be a Jewish sect. Later on, it enjoyed a degree of toleration, but only so long as the internal stability of the empire was assured. In other words, toleration was a political luxury (p. 126).

However, one must not overlook the frequent statements in Christian writings of the second and third centuries (not to mention Paul's letter to the Romans and 1 Peter, both of which prescribe obedience to earthly authority) that Christians are under religious obligation to be good citizens and to pray for the emperor even though they refuse to worship him.

It may be that the revolutionary implications of Christian belief, and indeed of Christian notions of community, were not perceived by the authorities because Christian behavior gave them no reason to be apprehensive. I would agree with Gager that an unstable Empire had to have scapegoats, and that Christians' refusal to participate in the civic cultic ritual made them prime targets for official suppression. But the toleration prior to that time may have been something more positive than simple inadvertence on the part of the government.

It is necessary, too, in order to complete the story, to note that following the persecutions of the 250's came a half century of almost uninterrupted peace for the church. Indeed, the great persecution of the early fourth century stunned as much by its novelty as by its ferocity. Most of the Christians alive when that persecution broke out had not even been born when the previous persecution had come to an end. The toleration of the latter half of the third century does not easily fit Gager's pattern.

C. Conflict

Only the most narrow-minded dogmatist can read the early Christian evidence, including the New Testament, without noticing that there was conflict and disharmony within the Christian community from the very beginning. Indeed, even in the Gospels there is no attempt to hide the rivalries among the apostles, their misunderstandings of Jesus, and their different interpretations of what he said and did. Many Christians wish it were not so, and have tried to construct for themselves a picture of the apostolic community according to the statement in Acts 4:32, that they had all things in common and were *of one heart and soul.* Modern social theory casts a highly skeptical eye on any declaration that a group of persons is without conflict, and insists, on the contrary, that conflict is natural to groups, and even more, is essential to them.

This sociological viewpoint has far-reaching implications for the analysis of orthodoxy and heresy. In a clear and unequivocal statement of these implications, Gager says:

> In dealing with a religious movement like early Christianity, where we confront diversity and disharmony from the very first, any effort to single out one point of view as more authentic than others will necessarily compromise a thoroughly historical orientation. Such an approach may be justified in an ecclesiastical or theological setting, but it will not find, nor should it seek, any historical justification (p. 79).

In short, the search for a *historical* answer to the question, "What is normative or essential Christianity?" is declared invalid. The

THE SOCIAL REALITY OF THE NEW JERUSALEM   193

most we can do is characterize the initial diversity, trace the development of other forms of belief and practice as well as the survival (perhaps in altered terms) of some of the original forms, and eventually describe as "orthodoxy" what triumphed, with an attempt to account for that triumph.

The issue raised here is a serious and complex one, but before we deal directly with the issue as Gager poses it we need to consider further what he says about the role of conflict in groups. He cites in support of his view the work of Lewis Coser, who has argued that conflict actually serves to bind groups together.[8] Coser's scheme provides for Gager a general theory for interpreting the church's opposition to heresy within and to Jews and pagans without.

Within the early Christian community itself we can seen the emergence of tension between what Gager calls "a 'populist' majority and an intellectual minority." Specifying further the function of conflict, Gager notes that conflict becomes particularly intense when ideologies are in competition, especially "competing views of the same ideology": for example, Christians and Jews each claimed the proper understanding of the religion of Abraham and Moses, Irenaeus and Valentinus each claimed the proper understanding of the religion of Jesus (pp. 81–82). To use some of Gager's own terms, we might say that in both these cases of conflict each of two groups was claiming dominion over a social world, one constructed through many centuries by the Jewish community, the other constructed during a century and a half by the Christian community. It was a kind of territorial struggle; given the terms in which it was fought, there could be no truce, no compromise. And if the conflict drove the competing groups apart, it served to define each of the groups more distinctly, and to strengthen group structures.

Many searching questions grow out of a recognition of the positive function of conflict. The most searching of all is the question of whether groups have to invent enemies.

As has already been noted in the discussion of Gnosticism in Chapter 5, there are many interpreters of the New Testament today who regard the New Testament not as the charter for Christianity, but as the trophy of the politically victorious party in the battle among the many original Christianities. Such interpreters point to areas of overlap between some New Testament documents and the writings of some of the Gnostics, and suggest that the orthodox leaders of the end of the second century, notably Irenaeus and Tertullian, have greatly exaggerated the difference between themselves and the Gnostics, and between "the apostolic tradition" and the Gnostics, in the interests of holding their own party together. The whole notion of an authentic tradition going back to a restricted group of apostles is considered to be an invention of second-century partisans; some scholars have suggested that it was Gnostics who first proposed a principle of "apostolic succession," and that the orthodox then responded with their own version, which has been accepted as historical fact ever since.

That the whole story is more complex than the church fathers would lead us to believe cannot be doubted for a minute. That orthodoxy and heresy were categories in flux until the end of the second and the beginning of the third century cannot be doubted. That the New Testament is a selection from a huge array of documents that had been produced in various parts of the Christian community cannot be doubted. But there is a question about Gager's unqualified denial that there can be a *historical* answer to the question of normative Christianity. Was everything up for grabs, and do we simply have the story the winners wanted us to hear?

First, it can be noted how extraordinarily complex the New Testament is. The fact that it has been subject to such different interpretations, the fact that it embodies differing and occasionally contradictory pictures of Jesus, the fact that Paul's justification by faith is set alongside the justification by works of The Letter of James—all these facts and many others raise questions about the thoroughness of the ideological screening process through which books had to go to become part of the church's Scripture. As Gager notes, the early fathers of the church, particularly Tertullian, did not believe that Scripture could be interpreted properly apart from the guidance provided by the church's "rule of faith," a kind of creedal summary which is viewed by some modern scholars as simply the expression of the group's ideology. But a case can at least be argued that the "rule of faith" is itself a fairly accurate reflection of original Christian views, particularly in its insistence on the close relation of creation and redemption.

Second, the theory that "apostolic tradition" is a fabrication is not dictated by the evidence. Paul of course breaks free of what may

have been an original special regard given to Jesus' earliest followers: Paul insists that he is an apostle just as they are. But he goes
out of his way to be in touch with Peter, James, and John, and there
does not seem to be any particular reason for doubting the tradition
that both Peter and Paul ended their careers in Rome, and thus
would at least have had the chance to transmit their preaching
directly to that congregation. Furthermore, the recent scholarly
conclusion that Paul and the Jerusalem church were not nearly as
far apart theologically and practically as was once thought gives
further weight to the notion that the New Testament may reflect
the form of Christianity with the soundest *historical* claim to connection with the original followers of Jesus.

Third, as we noted in the discussion of Gnosticism, it does not
seem necessary to say that the Gnostics had as good a claim as their
enemies to be Christian, and that they just happened to lose. Gager
poses a "what if" question that implies his own firm commitment
to the unavailability of any historical answer to the search for normative Christianity, a search which he declares is thoroughly theological. "It might also be interesting to ask whether the reaction to
Marcion and Valentinus would have been appreciably different had
they advanced their views in more settled times" (p. 88). Questions
of that sort can be multiplied: one might ask whether Marcion and
Valentinus would have advanced their views had the times been
more settled—and I should think such a further question would
seem entirely appropriate to Gager, since he appears to consider
that all the group actions in a given period are to be understood in
terms of the social dynamics of the time. One should not say simply
that Irenaeus had to "make" Marcion into a heretic; one would
have to say also that Marcion had to "make" those in Irenaeus'
camp into heretics.

In much writing about Gnosticism these days there is a sympathy,
often overt, for the Gnostics as those who fought the good fight and
lost. But from a purely historical perspective, it has to be remembered that in the second century nobody had yet won. The historical goose and the historical gander should both be served with the
same sauce.

I maintain, as I have already argued in Chapter 5, that the reaction against Marcion and Valentinus was a Christian reaction. The
case is easier to make, in my terms at least, for Marcion, but I would

argue it for Valentinus too, and by means of a device which Gager himself employs for other purposes.

The sociologist Max Weber designed a methodological tool called "the ideal type."[9] A complex and ambiguous social phenomenon can be "boiled down" to its fundamental components and structure, and this "ideal type" of the phenomenon can then be used for comparison and contrast with other "ideal types" extracted from similar phenomena. Weber never claimed that the types corresponded to actual living situations, though some of his critics treated his argument as if that were what he was saying. Gager himself recognizes the value of the "ideal type" method of analysis, and uses it in several different contexts.

I believe that the church fathers, in their heightening of the differences between their views and those of the Gnostics, including Valentinus, were engaging in a kind of rule of thumb "ideal type" analysis. They saw that for all the similarities of language, of spirituality, of theology between the various Gnostic groups and themselves, there were fundamental disagreements, disagreements which could be clarified and highlighted by boiling the two systems down to their essentials. This is not to deny that there is polemical distortion in what the fathers wrote, and it is not to imply that they were "anticipating" Weber as amateur sociologists. It is to say, however, that in the light of what we now understand about the Jewish nexus of earliest Christianity, it can be argued *on historical grounds* that the New Testament, with the "rule of faith" as a norm for interpretation, has greater claim to being Christian than do the writings that were rejected as "heretical" by those whom we have come to know as the church fathers. I believe, in short, *on historical grounds,* that the reaction to Marcion and Valentinus would not have been appreciably different had they come along at some other time.

IV. WHY CHRISTIANITY?

Virtually everything Gager says is suggestive, and as should be clear by now, much of it is provocative. The most interesting of all his chapters, and the one with potentially the most impact on the direction of the study of early Christianity, is the final chapter, "The Success of Christianity." Gager asks whether a *historical* explanation can be given for the growth of Christianity to the status of the Empire's official religion.

A. Traditional Views

Gager first sets forth types of views that have governed the telling of the Christian story. There are the apologists for Christianity, who assume that there really is no question to be asked, since the divine nature of the faith assured its appeal and hence its victory. There are those opposers of Christianity, Edward Gibbon and his successors, who blame Christianity for "the decline and fall of the Roman Empire," and then declare that the church inherited a corpse. Arnold Toynbee has cast the whole problem into a new light with his theory of a universal church following on a universal empire; in terms of this theory, the flight of persons to monasteries in the fourth century is not an avoidance of political responsibility, but is rather the farseeing establishment of the vanguard of a new civilization. Gager questions all of these on the grounds that they impose one sort or another of clear bias on the evidence. Gager sets out to see whether the question of why Christianity succeeded when its competitors (and they were many) did not can be approached without a pronounced theological—either pro or con—bias.

B. The Heir of Hellenistic Judaism

Earlier in his book, Gager has argued that it is inevitable for an originally millenarian movement to pass out of its unstructured, freely changing form into a structured organization concerned to maintain and perpetuate itself. He notes that it is absurd for people today to "regret" that Christianity became "routinized." Millenarian movements cannot, by definition, survive as millenarian movements; they have to change their character, they have to come to terms with the world. For a Christian today to lament the transition from the free-floating charismatic gifts of Paul's letters to the hierarchical organization of the pastoral letters is to lament the condition that made possible the survival of Christianity beyond its first few generations.

In his final chapter Gager develops more fully an explanation for the nature of early church organization. He indicates what the church found once it moved "beyond the confines of its Palestinian cradle."

> Diaspora Judaism provided a blueprint, precise to the finest detail, for the adaptation of Christianity to the Greco-Roman world. It is definitely not the case, as is sometimes imagined, that this outward expansion marked a departure from Judaism and Jewish influence. In leaving Palestine and embarking on the uncertain course of cultural accommodation, Christianity simply took as its model a different sort of Judaism. The literature, thought, and institutions of Hellenistic Judaism in the diaspora not only influenced their Christian counterparts; in a real sense, Hellenistic Christianity alone preserved the legacy of Hellenistic Judaism (p. 126).

Gager's substantiation of this is detailed and convincing. From the church's use of the Greek translation of the Old Testament, through methods of biblical interpretation and the adoption of many Jewish writings (the Apocrypha) in addition to those we know as canonical, to the influence of Philo on Christian writers and the correspondence between the Christian church service and the pattern of synagogue worship, the case not simply for inheritance but also for continuity is built up.

Of the greatest importance is the adaptation of synagogue organization, which included not only a structure but also a spirit, a sense of community solidarity that was reinforced by regular weekly meeting.

> One might argue that the availability of the synagogue as a model for the religious community helped to preserve primitive Christianity from extinction. As the initial impetus for the formation of community, namely, the expectation of the End, began to fade, it is quite conceivable that the energies of the movement could have dissipated from want of communal structure. This surely would have happened if the churches had adopted the institutional pattern of the so-called mystery cults. By following instead the pattern of the synagogue, the early enthusiasm was redirected toward the community itself and historical continuity was ensured (p. 129).

As we saw in Chapter 4, there are reasons for believing that the move from the Palestinian "cradle" into the adventure of "cultural accommodation" did not in itself necessitate quite so large a shift as Gager suggests; or rather, the "different sort of Judaism" found in the Diaspora was not so different from the Palestinian variety as we used to think. On this basis one might add, very tentatively, a fourth to the list of arguments for a historical answer to the question of normative Christianity: the maintenance by "orthodoxy" of the main elements of Hellenistic Jewish practice, especially organization, is one of the *historically traceable* links to the earliest Christians.

C. The Unique Factor

The full significance of the synagogue pattern becomes apparent when, in his analysis of the factors which Christianity did and did not have in common with its competitors, Gager concludes that

> for all of its success as a missionary cult, . . . the winning of converts cannot be regarded as the key to the continued growth of the Christian movement. In a world that offered an unlimited variety of religious options, there needed to be something further to retain the loyalty of converts through time. This something was the sense of community. With one major exception (Judaism), no other cult engaged its adherents at so many levels or covered so wide a range of human activities (p. 130).

According to this analysis, the key to Christian success is the lively sense of really being members one of another. While the city here might not be lasting, the experience of group solidarity in the Christian community provided for the members stability and a sense of identity. The Christians met often; they frequently had the common bond of having been rejected by their friends and family because of their new allegiance; they cared for the needs of their sick and indigent with a systematic thoroughness otherwise unknown in the ancient world. By creating a social world over against the world of Roman society, the Christians were able to perceive reality in a way that made current deprivation bearable, and indeed desirable. There is plenty of evidence from pagan sources of a longing for a sense of place, a scheme of meaning that would alleviate a widespread uneasiness and loneliness as Rome the Eternal became increasingly Rome the besieged.

V. HISTORY, COMMUNITY, AND EXPLANATION

There are always surprises in New Testament study, and one that will have to be added to the list is the correlation between the major conclusion of Gager's radical study and the starting point of the moderately conservative textbook by Kee, Young, and Froehlich, *Understanding the New Testament.* In Chapter 6, I contrasted the approach of Kee, Young, and Froehlich, who begin with quests for community in the ancient world and then proceed through Jesus to Paul and the early church, with the approach of Norman Perrin, a recent convert to the Bultmann position, who puts Jesus in the last chapter and then puts the Jewish and Hellenistic worlds into an appendix. I indicated then that I found the Kee, Young, and Froehlich approach more nearly adequate to the subject matter, and there is more than a little fascination in finding that Gager suggests it was the community sense of Christianity which was its unique feature. It appears, in fact, that Gager's radically historical and sociological approach to the New Testament material is more nearly compatible with Kee, Young, and Froehlich's moderate theological interpretation than with Perrin's radical theological interpretation.[10]

Gager's point can be pressed further. In his terms it is simply a historical fact that the Christian sense of community was suited to the needs of the time. In strictly historical terms (at least in the perspective of strict history as Gager wishes to apply it), the sense of community is no more the essence of Christianity than any other aspect of it. It just happens to have been the right thing for the time. But, if that which makes the Christian movement in its astonishing variety a coherent body is the sense of community, then there would appear to be justification for moving from the historical observation—that is, Christianity's unique factor was its effective sense of community—to a declaration that such a sense is *essential to* Christianity. In any case, one would want to ask how it came about that Christianity had this particular characteristic.

One has to carry forward from Gager's crucial point about the Christian inheritance from Judaism. The Christian self-identification as the New Israel then becomes normative, and while Israel, whether old or new, is subject to an enormous range of interpretation and explication, the fact remains that some things are inadmissible. You cannot be the New Israel if you believe that the God of creation who chose Israel is an inferior deity; the New Jerusalem, the "city to come" which the Christians are seeking, makes sense only if it is the dwelling of the God who chose old Jerusalem as the place where his name would be honored. While the notion of a crucified Messiah is a stumbling block to Jews, the notion of a disembodied phantom as the Lord's Anointed would be a road-block, so a form of belief and/or practice which considers the incarnation illusory on the grounds that only in such a way is God preserved, undefiled, from contact with the world, cannot claim to be Christian.

It is true that the Jewish community in Jesus' day was concerned with distinctions: each sect was accusing the others of unfaithful-ness. But part of the historical genius of Israel has been its inclusive-ness, and Jesus was being "essentially" Jewish in his insistence that the outcasts were full members of the religious community. The Christian church is being true to its "essential" nature when it is emphasizing inclusiveness. This is not to say that anything goes; there are some interpretations of the tradition that amount to deni-als of it. But the boundaries are very wide. The ecumenical move-ment of the twentieth century can be interpreted in many ways. One way would see it as an attempt on the part of splintered Christendom to recover, from its original Jewish heritage, an un-derstanding of how sisters and brothers can dwell together in peace, or at least in an acknowledgment that they are all part of the same family.

Once we have isolated the Christian sense of community as its unique characteristic and the one that had the most sustained appeal in the ancient world, we have to switch from low-powered magnifi-cation to high-powered and ask—perhaps it is also a basically histor-ical question—how (and why) this *particular* sense of community came to be. There are all kinds of communities: clubs, churches, lodges, unions, sports teams, political parties, colleges. The early Christian church was not just "community" in the abstract. It was a particular kind of community, although with enormous variation.

The best clue to the kind of community the church was is the early Christians' assumption that the Hebrew Scriptures were the place to read their own history. Gager says that the church "was neither totally religious, as were many pagan cults that met only for ritual activities, nor totally social, as were numerous voluntary associations. The key to its success lay precisely in the combination of the two" (p. 131). This is an indirect way of saying that the success of the Christian religion depends on its having adopted and adapted a leading characteristic of the Jewish religion, which was "neither totally religious . . . nor totally social."

Indeed, Gager suggests that had it not been for the Roman defeat of the Jewish revolts, with a consequent pressure to exclusivism and isolationism among Jewish leaders, Judaism might well have become a strong competitor with Christianity for eventual social superiority. Be that as it may, there is an interesting correlation to be made not only between the conclusions of Gager and the moderate position of Kee, Young, and Froehlich, but also between Gager's conclusions and the approach to the history of Christian doctrine in the work of Jaroslav Pelikan, who suggests that the main tendency of dogmatic development is not what Harnack and his successors thought, the "Hellenization" of Christianity, but rather its "de-Hellenization"[11]—which we might put positively as its "re-Judaization." Out on the frontiers of study there are some close encounters of unexpected kinds.

CHAPTER NINE

WATER, BREAD, WINE:
PATTERNS IN RELIGION

The world—as far as it has not completely turned its back on tradition —has long ago stopped wanting to hear a "message"; it would rather be told what the message means. The words that resound from the pulpit are incomprehensible and cry for an explanation. How has the death of Christ brought us redemption when no one feels redeemed? In what way is Jesus a God-man and what is such a being? What is the Trinity about, and the parthenogenesis [virgin birth], the eating of the body and the drinking of the blood, and all the rest of it? What connection can there be between the world of such concepts and the everyday world, whose material reality is the concern of natural science on the widest possible scale? At least sixteen hours out of every twenty-four we live exclusively in this everyday world, and the remaining eight we spend preferably in an unconscious condition. Where and when does anything take place to remind us even remotely of phenomena like angels, miraculous feedings, beatitudes, the resurrection of the dead, etc.? It was therefore something of a discovery to find that during the unconscious state of sleep intervals occur, called "dreams," which occasionally contain scenes having a not inconsiderable resemblance to the motifs of mythology. For myths are miracle tales and treat of all those things which, very often, are also objects of belief.[1]

In this rather intimidating series of questions, Carl G. Jung poses the problem of the interpretation of the New Testament from the psychological perspective. If, as Gager says, New Testament study has remained until now a special "enclave" in its resistance to sociological analysis, it has been even more resistant to the viewpoint of psychology. This chapter, more than the previous one, is at least as much a prediction about the future course of New Testament study as a description of what is going on currently.

I. Christianity and Religion

Jung's answer to the question of New Testament interpretation meshes at a number of critical points with the findings of scholars who have searched for common themes and motifs in the religions of the world, and in addition to considering the potential impact of psychology on New Testament study, this chapter will also deal with the significance of "history of religions" (or "comparative religions") for New Testament interpretation.

At one level, resistance to the psychological and comparative religion approaches to the New Testament is easily understandable. Traditional Christian claims to uniqueness and finality appear threatened by a manner of thinking that will place Christianity, and even more important, Christian origins, in a wider context.

There is another level of resistance, however; if the one we have just characterized is "conservative," this other one might be called "radical." Rudolf Bultmann in effect asks Jung's questions, but then proceeds to give a very different answer. Initially, the answer does not look so very different. "Demythologizing" is an effort to find terms meaningful to persons today in which to present or convey the message contained under outdated forms in the New Testament. However, while Jung moves away from the particular to the general, from the conscious to the unconscious, Bultmann heightens consciousness to its most intense expression in the existentialist focus on crisis, decision, authenticity. Jung finds the deepest meaning of the gospel message when historicity has faded virtually into oblivion, while Bultmann finds it when historicity is, so to speak, at a fever pitch.

It is interesting to speculate what direction New Testament studies might have taken if a scriptural scholar of the immense learning of Bultmann had had his basic outlook influenced by Jung instead of by the existentialist philosopher Heidegger. As it is, the existentialist remedy for the plight of "the modern person," rather than the psychoanalytic remedy, has shaped the main tradition of New Testament interpretation in this century, and because they are not easily compatible—indeed, they may be fundamentally incompatible—New Testament study has seen very little of the latter.

What I have called the "radical" resistance to this approach to the

New Testament does not say simply that this approach fails to appreciate the special character of the Christian religion. It says that the approach is at fault in the first place for putting Christianity in the category "religion."

Throughout the nineteenth century there were efforts to describe Christianity as being other than a religion; this was a way of finessing the problem created by the rapidly increasing awareness of the variety of religions in the world. The effort to extract Christianity from the "religion" category has reached a kind of climax in our own time, with the advocacy of "religionless Christianity" by Dietrich Bonhoeffer and those influenced by him, and with Bultmann's insistence that the Christian gospel is the interpretation of human existence as such.[2] In one way or another modern interpreters of the New Testament have looked for ways to skirt the "scandal of particularity"—the inconvenient assertion of the Bible that God makes arbitrary choices, that revelation comes through particulars (the Jews, Jesus, the Hebrew and Greek languages, and so on), not through universal and abstract ideas.

There may indeed be a legitimate way of talking about a principle of transcendence in the gospel that calls even the Christian religion under judgment, but such a principle does not sever the connection between Christianity and religion. To draw a very rough analogy: Bultmann's rejection of concern with *any* of the details of the career of Jesus has given way among his own pupils to an interest in determining whether Jesus can actually support the message which presupposes him; so we might expect those who advocate prying Christianity loose from the Christian religion will become more concerned to understand the lines of connection that are very hard to snap. In any case, one's commitment to a gospel principle of judgment on all religion should not be allowed to get in the way of an appreciation of the meaning of aspects of Christianity that are, by any definition, religion.

The conservative resistance (Christianity will be dissolved into a sea of myths and religions) and the radical resistance (why step backward into myths when we can step forward out of them?) are reinforced by a specifically academic resistance: with the field of psychology in such ferment as it is now in, is there not great risk in attaching the New Testament wagon to any one particular star which may prove to be no more than a passing meteor? Formally, of course, that is an argument for never saying anything, and there is always the chance that the theory you call to your aid will be scuttled by the experts in the field from which you have called it. Psychology is developing and changing so rapidly, there are so many sharp divisions of opinion within it that the outsider is wary of entering the fray at all.

To look to Jung for insight into the New Testament cannot fall under the accusation of "jumping on a bandwagon." Jung receives little attention among psychologists today. He has a small and deeply devoted following, but the vast majority of psychologists consider him quite beside the point. That of course may change; fashions in every field are notoriously unpredictable.

But even if Jungian theory remains on the professional periphery, it repays investigation by New Testament interpreters. Jung's break with Freud came about partly because of Freud's insistence that the sexual libido theory be treated as dogma, and a dogma in terms of which everything, including religion, was to be explained. Jung would have none of that kind of rigidity; for him, openness to new insights, formulations, theories was a presupposition of investigation, so his scheme, at least theoretically, is one in which exploration is not only unhindered but is also positively encouraged.

In addition, there is a remarkable convergence of Jung's theories about the psyche and the findings of historians of religion about the patterns of belief and practice in diverse times and places and traditions. Indeed, Jung himself drew on many of these findings, and offers suggestions from his clinical experience for ways in which to account for initially inexplicable similarities. Jungian psychology and history of religions have been mutually reinforcing, and they provide a powerful analytical procedure for interpreting a wide range of data.

The discussion in this chapter will draw primarily on Jung himself (mainly on the book *Aion: Researches Into the Phenomenology of the Self*) and on the leading historian of religions, Mircea Eliade. Each of them is a complex figure with an enormous list of publications, and what is offered in this chapter can be only a tentative evaluation of their significance for New Testament study. One other scholar will appear with some frequency: Richard Rubenstein, whose *My Brother Paul* has already occupied our attention briefly in Chapter

7. What is of special interest about the book for our purposes is its total dependence on Freudian psychological theory and terminology. There is a suggestive irony in the discovery that when analyzing New Testament data, both Freudian and Jungian approaches lead to strikingly similar results.

There are three subjects at which we will look: baptism, the Eucharist, and Christ himself. These are not small subjects, and the psychologist and historian of religions are usually interested in the development of these well beyond their origins in the apostolic age, and hence beyond their significance in the New Testament. But just as John Gager was able to argue plausibly that Christianity caught on because it offered a sense of community to people isolated and fearful, so the Jungian and the Freudian and the Eliadean can argue plausibly that Christianity caught on because at its origin it gave expression to basic needs and longings of the psyche. The adherents of those three approaches are arguing that the early Christians were wiser than they knew.

II. BAPTISM

The question of baptism to which New Testament scholars have characteristically addressed themselves is the historical question of the relationship of early Christian baptism to the practice of John the Baptist. That leads to the question of the relation of John's baptism to Jewish proselyte baptism more generally and, since the discovery of the Dead Sea Scrolls, to the ritual washings of the Qumran community. Of course such questions themselves imply some attention to the meaning assigned to these various rites by their practitioners, and the relation of baptism to the eschatological hopes and expectations of the Christians has been investigated from many angles. But New Testament scholars have not, on the whole, set their discussions of the meaning of baptism in contexts as wide as those of initiation rites and water symbolism. Historical concerns have tended to overshadow symbolic concerns.

A. Initiation

Eliade has argued that "it is not even necessary to suppose that an initiatory theme was 'borrowed' by Christianity from some other religion. As we have said, initiation is coexistent with any new revelation of spiritual life."[3] From Eliade's perspective, the theological framework in which baptism is usually discussed by New Testament scholars—its intimate connection with the preaching of the imminence of the kingdom of God—is too restricted a framework. For Eliade, the interpretation put on baptism by Paul—the experience of dying and rising with Christ—is not the importation of some alien religious influence, but rather an expression of the fundamental meaning of a rite of initiation.

Eliade traces virtually all initiatory rituals back to puberty rites, which signify the transition from one level of existence to another, always within a communal setting, and in such terms the Christian rite of baptism is properly tied to a theory of passing from an old life to a new life. The meaning of the rite is too restricted if it is simply the washing away of sins, or even an anticipation of a new life in the future. Eliade speaks of a "psychodrama," the acting out of a genuine psychological transformation. "It is impossible to attain to a higher mode of being, it is impossible to participate in a new irruption of sanctity into the world or into history, except by dying to profane, unenlightened existence and being reborn to a new, regenerated life."[4]

B. Water Symbolism

In a curious sixth-century Byzantine treatise there is an account of an emergency baptism in the desert. A Jew who has joined some Christian refugees from war falls desperately ill, and asks to be baptized. No water is available, so one member of the group pours sand over the man's head and pronounces the trinitarian formula ("I baptize you in the name of the Father, Son, and Holy Spirit"). The illness abates, the man recovers, and when the refugees get back home they ask the bishop whether the baptism was valid. There is no problem with the lay status of the one who did the baptizing; from very early times the church recognized the right of lay persons to perform the sacraments in emergencies. But the use of sand is another matter. The bishop gathers his clergy, and after a long discussion they agree that the baptism was not valid. The man, still a Jew, is taken to the nearby Jordan River, where he is properly baptized and becomes a Christian.[5]

At one level this story is quaint, but at another level it suggests a religious instinct on the part of the bishop and his clergy that finds resonance across barriers of time and place and culture. Water symbolism is one of the most basic of all religious forms of expression. In a chapter of nearly thirty pages on "The Waters and Water Symbolism" in his book *Patterns in Comparative Religion,* Eliade gathers a wide range of evidence to support his sweeping contention that "in cosmogony, in myth, ritual and iconography, water fills the same function in whatever type of cultural pattern we find it; it *precedes* all forms and *upholds* all creation."[6]

According to Eliade's analysis, the "dying and rising with Christ" in the Pauline characterization of baptism implies more than even the cessation of life and the renewal of it. Baptism involves a return to the beginning of things, to the chaos over which the Spirit of God brooded (Gen. 1:2), and from which order was created. Speaking of water symbolism generally (that is, not with specific reference to Christian baptism), Eliade says:

> Immersion in water symbolizes a return to the pre-formal, a total regeneration, a new birth, for immersion means a dissolution of forms, a reintegration into the formlessness of pre-existence; and emerging from the water is a repetition of the act of creation in which form was first expressed. Every contact with water implies regeneration: first, because dissolution is succeeded by a "new birth," and then because immersion fertilizes, increases the potential of life and of creation.[7]

There is of course much water imagery in the New Testament. In addition to various baptisms there is also the living water referred to in the Gospel of John (4:7–15), and "the river of the water of life, bright as crystal, flowing from the throne of God and of the Lamb" in the book of Revelation (22:1). From Eliade's point of view, the best place to look for the nature of early Christian experience would be not the primitive kerygma (preaching), but rather the symbols, such as water, which relate Christian experience to a wide range of religious data.

Attention would focus not so much on Paul's doctrine of justification by faith as on the imagery of 1 Peter, which is considered by a growing number of scholars to be an early Christian baptismal sermon altered slightly into the form of a letter. The text addresses its hearers: "Like newborn babes, long for the pure spiritual milk, that by it you may grow up to salvation" (2:2); here is what Eliade would call the true note of initiation—a return to the beginning, a starting from scratch, a genuine *starting,* for salvation is presented as a process of growth. Later in 1 Peter we have the earliest expression of what would become in later centuries a much-used image for baptism: in Noah's ark, eight persons "were saved through water. Baptism, which corresponds to this, now saves you" (3: 20–21). With Noah, God started the world of living things all over again, so the imagery here also points to Eliade's understanding of water symbolism.

None of this analysis denies that the immediate occasion for the early Christian use of water imagery was the preaching of the coming of the kingdom of God and the sense of renewal in preparation for its arrival. The analysis does, however, suggest an important modification of the particular understanding of the kingdom-preaching that has been dominant in this century. The individual was, to be sure, confronted with a radical demand—"Repent, and believe in the gospel"—but the individual was *also* initiated into a community, and the initiation itself was understood as a once-and-for-all act of re-creation, the beginning of a process. One did not have to go back to "Start" in every new situation.

Rubenstein, in his analysis of Paul's interpretation of baptism, draws a somewhat smaller circle than Eliade does. The Freudian has a more restricted theory of the origins of religious images than does the historian of religions.

Perhaps the central insight of psychoanalysis is that all the "higher" productions of the human psyche—such as art, myth, and religion— are ultimately objectified expressions of the organism's developmental vicissitudes and its strivings for bodily gratifications within the emotional matrix of the nuclear social unit, the human family. Psychoanalysis has sought to uncover the organic, developmental, and familial realities underlying the symbolism of religion. Paul's bodily "materialism" and his persistent tendency to utilize the metaphors of paternity, fraternity, and filiation in his religious thought expressed a similar insight intuitively. The very crudeness of Paul's images testifies to their emotional honesty and their overwhelming power. The crudeness also makes it possible for depth psychology to comprehend Paul's theology in terms of its own symbolism.[8]

This is only a fragment of the impressive pattern of Freudian meaning that Rubenstein finds in Paul, but it relates particularly closely to Eliade's findings. If for Eliade the meaning of baptism is the return to creation in a cosmic sense, for Rubenstein its meaning is a return to creation in a very personal sense.

> Paul was able to associate the death and Resurrection of Christ with the experience of the newly baptized Christian because he understood intuitively and gave theological expression to the identity of womb and tomb in the subliminal consciousness of mankind. By his association of baptism with Jesus' death and Resurrection, he was able to bring to consciousness some of mankind's oldest and most profound responses to water.[9]

Rubenstein cites Eliade as support for his view, and there is of course a fair degree of correspondence between them. But the close ties of the Freudian interpretation to the central myths of familial relationship make Rubenstein's enterprise quite different from Eliade's. Rubenstein, before he is through discussing baptism, will have gone on to say that "Baptism promises escape from the hostility of the Divine Infanticide; baptismal rebirth thus involves the hope for a noninfanticidal Parent" (that is, a parent who will not seek, either actually or symbolically, to kill the child); and, beyond that:

> In the course of psychoanalysis, fear of the father is usually uncovered first. Fear of the mother is older and less subject to therapeutic amelioration. If baptism involves the hope for the noninfanticidal Parent, the rite carries with it the assurance that the believer, after his return to the watery womb, has been rescued and need no longer fear his original mother.[10]

Rubenstein certainly does not argue that Paul had figured all of this out. Psychoanalytical interpretations of texts seldom if ever claim to be reporting what was going on in the author's conscious thought. The terminology Rubenstein applies to his understanding of Paul is thoroughly uncommon in the field of New Testament study; literary criticism more generally has become accustomed to such ways of speaking, and in that field, techniques for judging the particular applications of the Freudian approach have been developed. It will be a while before New Testament scholars figure out just what to make of Rubenstein's book, and even more, of his whole manner of approach. But the strangeness of the effort should not in itself get in the way of appreciating Rubenstein's central argument. He attributes Paul's genius to his intuitive capacity to "make manifest the unmanifest," that is, to bring to the surface of powerful symbolic expression the hidden dynamics of the human unconscious. "Paul was able to express some of the deepest and most archaic emotional strivings of mankind because he was able to give objectified expression to his own unconscious mental processes."[11]

III. EUCHARIST

Few formulas can have occasioned so much controversy as "This is my body" and "This is my blood." The dispute over leavened or unleavened bread played a part in the schism between Greek and Latin Christianity, and of course the doctrines of transubstantiation, consubstantiation, real presence, and, as Jaroslav Pelikan has remarked, "real absence," have been shoals on which the unity of Western Christendom has shattered into hundreds of fragments. The fact that the Eucharist has been such a bone of contention is enough to make clear how central it has been in the practical definition of Christianity.

As in the case of baptism, so with that of the Eucharist: New Testament scholarship has emphasized the close relation of the rite to early Christian eschatological expectations. It is a foretaste of the messianic banquet, a proclaiming of "the Lord's death until he comes" (1 Cor. 11:26). Students of religion more generally see in the Christian ritual of the sacred meal an example of a widespread practice, one that can be found frequently in the Old Testament as well as in religions having no organic connection to Christianity. Old Testament scholars have made good use of comparative materials in clarifying the meaning of ritual eating in ancient Israel, but so far New Testament scholars have been more concerned to figure out exactly what Jesus said in that upper room than to probe the Christian meal in terms of more general evidence for the importance of eating together in the creation and maintenance of religious communities.

Rubenstein suggests that there is meaning in the Lord's Supper that goes deeper than doctrine usually supposes, and that Paul intuited this deeper meaning. Indeed, Rubenstein implies, though he does not make the point directly, that the later Catholic tradition, with its insistence that the Mass is a sacrifice, is a further specification of this deeper and psychologically rich meaning.

To summarize Rubenstein's complex argument: Christ is presented as the elder brother with whom we wish to identify, particularly when we realize that he has achieved immortality and omnipotence. Those are states approximated in the womb, states for which we have all been striving, which is to say, to which we have all been longing to return. Beyond that, with the substitution of the elder brother for God the Father, persons are enabled to reenact what Freud called the "primal crime," that of parricide (killing of the father), without incurring the destruction threatened by the divine parent. "Because of his resurrection, Christ cannot be destroyed in the act of being consumed. He is therefore the perfect sacrificial offering."[12]

Paul's understanding of the Eucharist in "crudely physical" terms is thus, in Rubenstein's view, an answer at the deepest levels of the psyche to what Freud perceived to be the main barrier to psychological health, the repression of the memory of the primal crime (whether Freud considered the primal crime to have been a specific historical event, or rather, an event repeated many times at the origins of the human race, is not entirely clear). Through the Lord's Supper, Christ becomes effectively elder brother, father-substitute, and mother-substitute: "Unlike our natural mother, our earliest source of nurture, the Risen Christ can neither perish nor run out of milk."[13]

The significance of the Eucharistic sacrifice passes beyond the individual psyche to its relation with human community, which is, however, seen in Freudian sexual terms.

Sacrificial worship is the most perfect form of human worship. It effects a convergence of the destructive and the loving, the sinful and the hopeful, the latent and the manifest in human consciousness and experience. Furthermore, in true sacrificial worship the believer achieves at least momentarily the goal that men will only achieve decisively if and when they return to the Garden, an end of repression. In sacrificial worship little, if anything, is repressed: the life-giving originator is consumed, the yearning for omnipotence expressed, and the ultimate goal of true sexual union is achieved in that men cease to be their separate selves and become, if only momentarily, "one body."

For Rubenstein, the essence of Paul's intuitive genius is in his insistence that "Christians are one body in Christ because they partake of a single loaf," whereby the "latent expressions of archaic sacrificial ritual in Judaism," which had been relegated to the rituals of the home table, "became explicit in Christianity."[14]

The "crudely physical" character of the Eucharistic bread is what gives it contact with Freudian theory. The Eucharistic wine serves to confirm for Rubenstein the thoroughness of the Christian religious revolution. The radical nature of the return to the womb in baptism is matched by the shock delivered to the Jewish religious system by the command to drink blood as a religious duty.

Rubenstein suggests that the strong taboo against drinking blood, which persists to this day among those who keep the kosher regulations, betokens a strong temptation to do what is forbidden, and that in "the awesome rite of the Lord's Supper" this repressed temptation in Judaism surfaces to symbolic expression. The lusting for blood can easily be related to ancient and deeply rooted beliefs about blood's life-giving and power-bestowing qualities, and when the blood is that of the one who has achieved immortality and omnipotence, the desire to drink it is enhanced that much more. The intoxicating power of both blood (as in the rites of worship of the god Dionysus in Greece) and wine was a link between the two substances, so the drinking of wine as blood was a very direct challenge to the Mosaic taboo.[15]

It is quite safe to say that most people, when they participate in a Eucharist, whether it be a Roman Mass or an Orthodox liturgy or one form or another of Protestant service, are not conscious of doing what Rubenstein says is happening in that activity. His analysis presupposes that the ritual is a symbolic expression of something which the consciousness resists admitting.

In his discussion of the Eucharist, even more than in his analysis of baptism, Rubenstein uses terms and concepts that jar on an ear accustomed to the tamer language used by most New Testament interpreters. There is much in his theory that is questionable, but what he says is provocative, and should by no means be dismissed as outrageous. If the twentieth century has learned anything, it has learned that much of our life takes place outside the bounds of consciousness, in places, to use the title of a popular children's book by Maurice Sendak, "where the wild things are." Maybe the New Testament's "understanding of human existence" corresponds more closely to modern depth psychology than it does to modern existentialist philosophy.

IV. CHRIST

New Testament study is concerned to account for and interpret the names and titles attributed to Jesus. We have already dealt briefly with the problems surrounding the title Messiah (= Christ in Greek); there are equally murky problems connected with the titles Son of Man, Son of God, Lord, Servant, and the like. What the historian of religions and the psychologist suggest, however, is that there is a typological significance to Christ that transcends the historical questions about the origin and development of various divine titles.

A. Incarnation

Despite his encyclopedic knowledge of world religions, and his convictions about the need for humility in religious dialogue, Eliade is an advocate of Christianity, very much in the tradition of Justin Martyr, who in the second century declared that whatever had been well said by anyone was the property of Christians.[16] Just as the early Christian fathers argued that there was a Greek "preparation for the gospel" through philosophy to parallel the Hebrew preparation through prophecy, so Eliade argues that there is a kind of preparation for the gospel of the incarnation in all religious experience and traditions, since every manifestation of "the sacred" is a partial incarnation.

Eliade's analysis of religion is grounded in his conception of two realms, "the sacred" and "the profane," and religious experience occurs when the sacred manifests itself in the profane, thereby creating holy places (Jerusalem is not just "any place") and sacred time (the experience of "new birth" interrupts secular or profane chronology). Eliade says we are justified in studying primitive and other, more advanced hierophanies (a technical term meaning "appearances of the sacred" or "manifestations of the sacred") in the light of Christian theology, since the structure of religious experience is the same everywhere, and the Christian expression of the basic religious message of incarnation is the fullest possible expression of it, since for God to become fully a human being is as far as God can go. He quotes a text from the Vaisnavite school of Indian mysticism that shows a striking similarity to the Christian view of the *kenōsis,* or "self-emptying," of Christ, as that is particularly expressed in the hymn quoted by Paul in the second chapter of Philippians. The Vaisnavite text is as follows:

> Though he is omniscient Visnu shows himself in the *arkas* (material objects in which he is venerated) as if he were without knowledge; though a spirit, he appears material; though truly God he appears to be at the disposal of man; though all-powerful he appears weak; though free of all care he appears to need looking after; though inaccessible (to sense), he appears as tangible.[17]

There are some real problems with Eliade's view. There is quite a long jump from manifestations of "the sacred" to the incarnation of the God of the Bible, and Eliade's arguments arouse the suspicion to which any vast, general scheme that has in it a place for everything must be subject. Apparent parallels have to be examined with a skeptical eye; the Vaisnavite text speaks only of Visnu's "appearances." For Eliade, that observation would amount to no more than saying the Vaisnavite text is still only hinting at the full meaning of the sacred's manifestation in the profane; but one must be cautious when saying that a text is "really" pointing to something other than what it says.

While we must not be carried away by the exhilaration of Eliade's immense sweep through evidence from sources and areas of the world we have never heard of, we need to consider seriously his central point: the New Testament declaration that the Word became flesh is not a unique paradox, but is rather the full expression of the pattern of paradox that is characteristic of every religious event. And Eliade sees religion everywhere. Indeed, he says that there is scarcely any human activity, any human gesture, that has not at some time or some place been for someone a conveyor of the sacred, of that combination of awesomeness and fearfulness and power that constitutes the experience to which the characteristic human response is worship, often coupled with repentance.[18]

Eliade's importance for New Testament study is in the way he approaches the material. He comes at the evidence with a particular attitude, a frame of reference in terms of which some of the traditional New Testament scholar's overriding concern with detail appears not trivial, but shortsighted. The incarnation is paradoxical, yes; but "this paradox of incarnation which makes hierophanies possible at all—whether the most elementary or the supreme Incarnation of the Word in Christ—is to be found everywhere in religious history."[19] The incarnation may have been, as Paul said it was, a stumbling block to Jews and foolishness to Greeks, but according to Eliade it was what most religiously sensitive people have experienced and expected in most times and places.

B. Perfection and Completion

Carl G. Jung came under frequent fire from the Christian faithful for what they took to be his "explaining religion away" in terms of psychic phenomena. He was at pains to point out that since he firmly believed the psyche was real, he was not explaining something away when he explained it psychologically. He even went so far as to answer the question, "Do you believe in God?" with a declaration that he did not have to "believe" because he *knew* God through his own psychological experience and that of his patients.[20]

Jung found in years of clinical experience that psychic processes simply do not operate according to the principles of logic and order that we expect in our conscious experience. Dramatic, mythological language is required for talking about such processes. We cannot translate the myth into the language familiar to us in our conscious thinking without losing something essential to the meaning of the myth.

We should not assume, however, that just because the processes of the unconscious are not logical, they are therefore arbitrary. Jung insists that the basic patterns of myth and symbol he discovered in analyzing literature and his own dreams and the dreams of his patients, patterns that he calls "archetypes," are not here today and gone tomorrow, but are constant factors in the life of the human race, functioning at a level deeper than that of cultural and racial divisions. And Jung believed that to neglect those factors, to pretend they are not there, is to risk grave danger:

> Anyone who identifies with the daylight half of his life will therefore declare the dreams of the night to be null and void, notwithstanding that the night is as long as the day and that all consciousness is manifestly founded on unconsciousness, is rooted in it and every night is extinguished in it. What is more, psychopathology knows with tolerable certainty what the unconscious can do to the conscious, and for this reason devotes to the unconscious an attention that often seems incomprehensible to the layman. We know, for instance, that what is small by day is big at night, and the other way round; thus we also know that besides the small by day there always looms the big by night, even when it is invisible.[21]

From this groundwork, Jung builds up the structure that is his most characteristic contribution to psychological theory, the process of "individuation." The term refers to the uniquely personal assimilation by the individual of those impersonal components of the unconscious which are expressed in the archetypes. For Jung, the term "self" serves to locate the point where unconscious forces converge, and in these terms Jung can speak of Christ as exemplifying

> the archetype of the self. He represents a totality of a divine or heavenly kind, a glorified man, a son of God sine macula peccati, unspotted by sin. As Adam secundus [the "Second Adam"] he corresponds to the first Adam before the Fall, when the latter was still a pure image of God.[22]

All this sounds rather abstract; that is partly because a complex argument is here necessarily condensed, partly because Jungian terminology is even less widely familiar than that of the Freudian tradition. But despite its sounding abstract, Jung's way of thinking is meant to be thoroughly concrete. "It is precisely our experiences in psychology which demonstrate as plainly as could be wished that the intellectual 'grasp' of a psychological fact produces no more than a concept of it, and that a concept is no more than a name." "In psychology one possesses nothing unless one has experienced it in reality. Hence a purely intellectual insight is not enough, because one knows only the words and not the substance of the thing from the inside."[23]

If abstractions are ineffective, it follows that the Christ-symbol will *do* something only insofar as human beings have experience of its reality—that is, only insofar as they respond to it as a force for wholeness and integration in their lives. And it is with the insertion of the notion of wholeness into the discussion that Jung raises a most remarkable issue.

In his clinical experience Jung became aware that the archetypes of wholeness, which appear spontaneously in the unconscious, are characterized by "fourness"; such motifs are found historically in a number of Asian traditions, in the designs known as mandalas which serve to focus the attention during meditation, but the motifs often appear in the dreams of Westerners who know nothing of those Asiatic traditions. Jung reports many variations on the basic pattern, the four points or four arms of a cross arrangement.

The meaning he attaches to the motifs is what he calls the "coincidence of opposites," with the self being located at the center of the cross. The practical implication of this is the following: a truly integrated self will not deny either part of the pairs of opposites (e.g., good/evil, feminine/masculine) which converge at the point where the self is located. Jung believes that when a pair of opposites is not held together by the self, the part of the pair that is denied will seek its revenge through the mechanisms of the unconscious —the person will literally be unconsciously haunted by that which has been consciously thrown out.

What follows from this is Jung's belief that Christ has come to be only half an archetype. Jung theorizes that the earliest Christians experienced Christ as the symbol of wholeness; as evidence he offers the crucifixion itself (the cross corresponding exactly to the unconscious patterns), the cry of dereliction ("My God, my God, why have you forsaken me?" Mark 15:34; Matt. 27:46), indicating that Christ was not denying his own sense of abandonment by God, and the positioning of Christ's cross between two thieves. Jung goes on to say that this original Christian experience soon was corrupted by the adjustment of Christian thought and symbolism to the Greek philosophical understanding of God, according to which God could be only good and the source only of good. As a result, the symbol of Christ gave up completeness to gain perfection. And at this point Jung sees the emergence of the figure of Antichrist as the inevitable darker side of the divine nature when Christ himself is purified beyond the shadow of a doubt.

Jung would argue that the figure of Antichrist is not to be accounted for simply in terms of developments within Jewish apocalyptic; rather, the Antichrist is an inevitable corollary to the figure of Christ. And then comes the radical suggestion: Antichrist is the completion of Christ as the archetype of the self. What would this mean for New Testament interpretation?—that the full meaning of Christ is not to be found in the historical Jesus or in the kerygmatic Christ, but rather in the paradoxical combination of Christ and Antichrist, in the setting beside one another of the Gospels *and* the book of Revelation, instead of treating them in separate categories.[24]

The fact that both Jung and Gager, from very different starting points and with different explanatory schemes, devote a good deal of attention to the book of Revelation, is an important clue to new directions in New Testament study. That book, which is seldom read today in establishment churches and was for a long time in many areas of the early church treated with suspicion, is coming into its own in scholarly discussion as a way of getting at the social and psychological reality of early Christianity. Some modern interpreters, who want to characterize Christian origins, shy away from the book of Acts—which purports to tell the story—and instead puzzle over intricate visions full of numerology and strange beasts.

John Gager, in *Kingdom and Community,* devotes several pages to a careful structural analysis of the last book of the New Testament. He finds that it fits well into a pattern of opposites, and while he does not use Jung's term "coincidence of opposites," the table of correspondences he draws up illustrates just such a theory. And Gager, in discussing the *social* function of the book, draws on psychotherapy for his terminology: "The writing is a form of therapy, much like the technique of psychoanalysis, whose ultimate goal is to transcend the time between a real present and a mythical future." One result of Gager's analysis of Revelation is a modification of the "truism" that millennial movements, by definition, always fail (since if they survive, they become something else). The images of the book of Revelation may have been powerful enough to create the millennium for the community: "For hearers of this book, even a fleeting experience of the millennium may have provided the energy needed to withstand the wrath of the beast."[25]

Jung's interest in the book of Revelation is shaped by his own convictions concerning what is required in an archetype of whole-ness. His analysis extends to the question of the authorship of the book, and his suggestion is intriguing, to say the least.

Many scholars have been willing to posit common authorship for the Gospel of John and the Letters of John (or at least one or two of them), but most have stopped short of admitting that their author could also have produced Revelation; the differences in style, lan-guage, outlook are so extreme that it appears impossible for one person to be responsible for the entire collection.

Jung describes the position of the author of the Johannine letters, who says that complete love must characterize the Christian and excludes all consideration of evil in the Christian life. Then Jung makes his characteristic move: nothing would be more likely in such an author, whose conscious life was devoted to denying the "shadow" part of the self, than the appearance of dreams just like those of Revelation. Jung, in other words, treats Revelation as being exactly what it says it is: a report of visions. Jung is suggesting that we look behind and beneath the stylistic differences between the letters and Revelation to the psychological reality of the coinci-dence of opposites. In terms of that reality, the two apparently irreconcilable styles and points of view in the Johannine literature may actually be the definitive statement of the psychic price Christi-anity paid in trading the experience of wholeness for the virtue of perfection.[26]

V. Myth and Modernity

The lines of approach to the New Testament discussed in this chapter are probably unfamiliar to most readers; they are equally unfamiliar to most New Testament scholars. It is easy to imagine a thousand (or at least half a dozen) ways in which an interpreter following one of these lines could end up talking preposterous nonsense, and some readers may have concluded we need not wait —that Jung or Eliade or Rubenstein has already achieved that dis-tinction. However, these "new" approaches are not entirely un-precedented, and they may help us recover some neglected parts of the Christian heritage.

Clement of Alexandria, the teacher of Origen, says explicitly that all Scripture speaks in a mysterious language of symbols, and Pope

Gregory the Great, who called the Bible a river for wading lambs and swimming elephants, wrote that "Holy Scripture by the manner of its speech transcends every science, because in one and the same sentence, while it describes a fact, it reveals a mystery."[27] The church fathers' allegorizing is looked upon with some embarrassment by most Christians today, and there is, to be sure, in much early Christian biblical speculation an arbitrary, uncontrolled quality.

What such investigators as Eliade and Jung and Rubenstein have shown is that there are in worldwide religious patterns and in fundamental human psychological experience controls by which we can distinguish between an intelligible mysterious language of symbols and sheer arbitrary inventiveness. Adolf Harnack "scornfully dismissed Origen's work with the epithet 'biblical alchemy.'"[28] There is a delicious irony in that term, since one of Jung's significant contributions to culture is his recovery of the tradition of alchemy, and his demonstration that what is usually dismissed as "trying to turn lead into gold" was in fact a rich and complex understanding of human nature, an understanding which incorporated some of the deepest psychological insights of the ancient world. In Jungian terms, an interpreter of Scripture could be awarded no higher praise than the title of "biblical alchemist."

Christian thinkers have of course for a long time been considering the implications of the psychoanalytic revolution for Christian theology generally. A recent article by Patrick Vandermeersch has posed the question of the relative compatibility of Freud and Jung to a Christian view of the world. Vandermeersch admits that at first glance Jung seems more "comfortable," and at no point does Vandermeersch deny Jung's capacity to enlighten and stimulate new insight.

Vandermeersch does, however, contrast Jung's notion of the ego (or, roughly speaking, the self) as a *product* of unconscious processes with Freud's notion of the ego as an *agent;* and, even more significant, he notes that Jung's theories are, in social terms, thoroughly individualistic (the self develops through the interaction of elements in its own psychic experience), while Freud's theories at every point presuppose a model of interaction between persons.

What is important in Freud's so-called "pansexualism" is that everything in it contains some interpersonal value. To reduce everything
to sexuality in the brute biological sense is precisely what Freudian
analysis does not do. Though it links with the body and sex the
representations with which it deals, it always shows that they bear an
interpersonal meaning. . . . For the Freudian, the power of the image
is an interpersonal power.

   This interpersonal aspect has no place in Jung's conception, or at
least, in his system. Jung seems to take it for granted that the power
of the image is bound up with what one can only feel in one's own
depths.[29]

Vandermeersch notes that there is no necessary opposition here;
we may say that Jung simply chooses not to deal with interpersonal
relations. But the fact remains that the Jungian system as such may
not be, in the long run, as germane to Christianity as is the Freudian
with its emphasis on the person as creative agent and on the fundamental importance of human community in the development of the
self. The development of personal *identity*, which has been so brilliantly illuminated by the neo-Freudian Erik Erikson, may prove
more fruitful as a way into the New Testament than Jungian *individuation*.

   This may all seem very remote from New Testament interpretation—but so would discussions of existentialist philosophy have
seemed remote in the 1920's. There is perhaps more than simple
whim in the suggestion that New Testament scholarship will see an
increase of attention to such figures as Freud, Jung, Eliade, Erikson.
In one respect, such a suggestion is entailed by another development discussed in this book. A very substantial part of Paul Ricoeur's thought has been his interpretation of Freud, and if Ricoeur
does in fact work his way into the fabric of New Testament study,
some Freudian threads will get worked in too. And certainly whatever use is made of psychological concepts in New Testament study
will reflect more general developments in the appropriation of such
concepts by Christian theology.

   So it very much remains to be seen what will come of all this. On
the basis of the work done thus far, it is possible to say that the
implications of the kind of study dealt with in this chapter are
surprising.

   Most people instinctively think of psychological and comparative approaches to religion as radical, reductionist, destructive. But the Freudian Rubenstein goes so far as to recommend a thoroughly physical conception of the Eucharist to all religions as a model for effective integration of persons into a larger communal whole; for Rubenstein, any attempt to "spiritualize" the Eucharist, to make it palatable not to the senses but to the intellect, is to rob it of its power. Jung, persuaded that the Trinity is a truncated symbol of wholeness, does not recommend that the Christian church jettison the whole notion of the Trinity; rather, he hails the Roman Catholic recognition of a "quaternity," a fourfold symbol and hence a symbol of wholeness, by the dogma of the Assumption of the Blessed Virgin Mary into heaven, proclaimed by Pope Pius XII in 1950.[30]

The psychologists are saying, in short, that what religion has to offer the world is not less mystery, but more mystery; not the resolution of all paradoxes, but the multiplication of paradoxes in order that they may be truly confronted and transcended. While New Testament scholars shy away from transcendence talk, Jung works it into the very marrow of his thinking. The results of historical study and existentialist analysis of the New Testament are considerable, and their value is undeniable, but it may be that in future the perspectives of comparative religionists and of psychologists will have more direct influence on New Testament scholarship than they have had so far.

If that happens, a whole new understanding of and appreciation for myth could alter the tone of New Testament interpretation. Gager writes, concerning the book of Revelation, "Just as the therapeutic situation is the machine through which the patient comes to experience the *past* as present, so the myth is the machine through which the believing community comes to experience the *future* as present."[31] In other words, the *myth* is precisely that which makes effective what the existentialist considers to be the whole point of the kerygma. And against what has been the reigning orthodoxy in New Testament interpretation, the "modern person" who cannot accept the mythological mode of thought, it is worth pondering an insight of the novelist Thomas Mann, that "while in the life of the human race the mythical is an early and primitive stage, in the life of the individual it is a late and mature one."[32]

CHAPTER TEN

THE APOSTOLIC BOOK
AND THE APOSTOLIC SEE

In Chapter 1 we noted Reginald Fuller's catalog of bombshells that had unexpectedly struck New Testament studies in the twentieth century: Barth's commentary on Romans (1919), Bultmann's essay on demythologizing (1941), and Käsemann's call for a revival of the quest of the historical Jesus (1956). When the whole development of New Testament study in our time is taken into account, those explosions appear minor compared to one that is not mentioned anywhere in Fuller's book. The date was 1943, and the bomb burst in Latin, not in German: the encyclical *Divino afflante Spiritu* of Pope Pius XII.[1]

It might appear strange that in a book that has dealt broadly with New Testament themes there should be a separate chapter devoted to scholarship within one particular ecclesiastical tradition. However, there is no more dramatic evidence of the new context of New Testament study than the sudden emergence of Roman Catholics into the front rank of biblical scholars. And this emergence was made possible by a document which genuinely deserves to be called revolutionary. A proper understanding of new directions in New Testament study requires knowledge of that revolution and what it means, both in terms of results already visible and in terms of future prospects.

I. "No Wrong Without a Remedy"

George Bernard Shaw has appeared earlier in this book, as a caustic critic of the apostle Paul. He appears again, in the same combative guise, but with a different aim. In the preface to his play *Saint Joan* (about Joan of Arc), Shaw defends the Catholic Church at a time when, in his own intellectual society, it was not fashionable to do so.

> In the Catholic Church, far more than in law, there is no wrong without a remedy. . . . Many innovating saints, notably Francis and Clare, have been in conflict with the Church during their lives, and have thus raised the question whether they were heretics or saints. Francis might have gone to the stake had he lived longer. It is therefore by no means impossible for a person to be excommunicated as a heretic, and on further consideration canonized as a saint. Excommunication by a provincial ecclesiastical court is not one of the acts for which the Church claims infallibility. Perhaps I had better inform my Protestant readers that the famous Dogma of Papal Infallibility is by far the most modest pretension of the kind in existence. Compared with our infallible democracies, our infallible medical councils, our infallible astronomers, our infallible judges, and our infallible parliaments, the Pope is on his knees in the dust confessing his ignorance before the throne of God, asking only that as to certain historical matters on which he has clearly more sources of information open to him than anyone else his position shall be taken as final. The Church may, and perhaps some day will, canonize Galileo without compromising such infallibility as it claims for the Pope.[2]

Catholic biblical scholarship during the past hundred years has produced heretics, and there is no particular reason to think they may one day become saints. But the history of biblical studies in the Catholic Church during the century from Vatican Council I (1870) to the present day is one of the most persuasive possible illustrations of Shaw's claim that in the Catholic Church there is "no wrong without a remedy."

For the first four decades of the twentieth century the serious Catholic biblical scholar was often confronted with the kind of choice classically formulated in the *Spiritual Exercises* of Ignatius Loyola, founder of the Jesuit Order: If the Church tells me that white is black, I will believe it is black.[3] The Pontifical Biblical Commission issued a number of directives on specific matters that made it impossible for a Catholic scholar to be faithful both to the findings of biblical criticism and to the teaching authority of the Church. For example, when the overwhelming majority of scholars were persuaded that Mark was the first of the Gospels to be written, the Catholic scholar was required to maintain that Matthew was written first (the *obligation* put the Catholic scholar in a totally different situation from scholars who are today reviving specifically historical and critical arguments in favor of the view that Matthew is the earliest of the Gospels).

Decisions on disputed points in biblical study were made test cases of ecclesiastical authority, and rules by which controversies in other fields would be settled were pushed aside by the exercise of disciplinary penalties. The task of the Catholic scholar was not to find answers to the questions, but to try to justify the answers arrived at already on grounds other than those of the scholarly discipline.[4]

There are many non-Catholics, and perhaps many Catholics too, who today still think that Catholic biblical scholars are simply apologists for dogma, that they look to Rome for the answers, and then construct the question to lead to the prearranged result. It is certainly true that many academics think a Catholic cannot in good conscience be a free scholar; indeed, the suspicion that a Catholic scholar is not free from authoritarian restraints seems to have outlived the now outworn suspicion that a Catholic politician cannot be truly independent.

The working conditions of the Catholic biblical scholar were so radically changed by *Divino afflante Spiritu* that the year 1943 deserves a place in a select list of momentous dates in the history of Christianity. The year 1943 presented the opportunity of a "semicentennial"—fifty years earlier, in 1893, Pope Leo XIII had promulgated the encyclical *Providentissimus Deus,* which made some small steps in the direction of freedom of movement for biblical scholars. But Pope Pius XII's *Divino afflante Spiritu* went far beyond anything that had been said earlier. Before considering the details of that encyclical, however, we should look briefly at the developments in the period preceding it to get a vivid sense of its revolutionary quality and to see why Pius XII is genuinely the patron of modern Catholic biblical studies.

II. FROM VATICAN I TO VATICAN II

The First Vatican Council (1870) was not in a liberalizing mood. It declared the dogma of Papal Infallibility, which, as Shaw points out, is a strictly limited claim; but in the political and intellectual atmosphere of the time, the dogma was seen as a victory for reactionary forces. Under military pressure the Council had to disband prematurely, and there was not sufficient time to work out a clear and comprehensive statement on Scripture. Vatican I did, however, reaffirm the position of the Council of Trent, held in the middle of the sixteenth century, which had set itself against the Protestant claim that the Bible was the supreme authority, outside and over ecclesiastical authority.

In 1870 and for several decades afterward the Church thought of itself as still in much the same conflict situation as three hundred years before. This is borne out not only by the actions of Vatican I but also by one of the emphases of Leo XIII's encyclical *Providentissimus Deus.* He states: "The sense of Holy Scripture can nowhere be found incorrupt outside the Church and cannot be expected to be found in writers who, being without the true faith, only gnaw the bark of Sacred Scripture and never attain its pith."[5] The chief effect of this statement was to discourage cooperative efforts between Catholic and Protestant biblical scholars. If the criterion for excellence was not scholarly competence, but rather adherence to the dogmatic tradition of the Church, then there could be nothing to gain and potentially much to lose by consorting with those who were merely gnawing the bark.

As popes necessarily do, Leo XIII had in mind not simply the welfare of the scholars but also the welfare of the multitude of the faithful, and he knew well how unsettling to faith the positions being advanced by some Protestant biblical scholars were. It would be reassuring to the Catholic laity to tell them that Protestant scholars, no matter how many academic degrees they had and no matter how many languages they could read, could not *by definition* properly understand the Bible. There is no use being unsettled by something that cannot be true.

Leo did look cautiously forward when he suggested that biblical writers were not invested with infallibility when they spoke on matters in the realm of natural science, but that was hardly revolutionary in comparison with the radical suggestions about the nature of biblical literature being made by the leading Protestant scholars. Still, the way was opening up, and Catholic biblical study might have accelerated steadily had the Modernist crisis not intervened.

The Modernist controversy is a complex subject in itself, and in its details is not germane to our discussion. But the general suspicion into which it cast any application of new ways of thinking to the materials of Catholic faith does bear directly on the gloomy history of Catholic biblical studies in the first forty years of this century.

Modernism was a *tendency* that got characterized as a *program* in the encyclical *Pascendi Dominici gregis* of Pope Pius X in 1907. The pope claimed to detect a concerted effort to reduce all matters of religious faith to the expression of certain human inner needs, and to exalt the individual conscience above every expression of ecclesiastical authority. The implications of this "Modernist program" for the understanding of dogma, of Scripture, of the Sacraments, of the Church, were, in the pope's judgment, deadly blows to the whole system of Catholic truth. He denounced the tendencies as the importation into the bosom of the Church of the most serious attacks being made on the Church from outside. In the name of reform the Modernists were, he believed, threatening to destroy the Church.

One of the leading Modernists was Alfred Loisy, a New Testament scholar, who, following the completion of his doctoral dissertation in 1890, became more and more radical in his application of critical method to the Scriptures, until he finally denied both the intention of Jesus to found a church and Jesus' consciousness of his own divinity. Loisy was excommunicated in 1908, the year after Pius X's encyclical, and he died in 1940, just three years before the publication of Pius XII's *Divino afflante Spiritu.*

The condemnation of Modernism was, above all, a denunciation of an attitude: the critical methods were seen as a pretext for overweening arrogance on the part of individuals about their ability to solve problems conclusively, and even more important, their ability to dispel mystery. To a certain extent, Pius X was right, for nineteenth-century scholarship did on occasion express a sense of its own infallibility (indeed, one wonders how scholars escaped inclusion in Shaw's catalog of infallible thises and thats). There is irony in the fact that, just two years before the issuance of *Pascendi Dominici gregis,* a scientific paper had been published that would later prompt James Bryant Conant to say that after it he could never consider any theory about the physical world to be the last word. The paper was by Albert Einstein, on relativity; it signaled the dismantling of the whole scheme of physical reality on which nineteenth-century science had been based.[6] Indeed, it was not to be long before the natural sciences themselves provided examples of a tentativeness, an exploratory quality very different from the confident skepticism of such a historical critic as Loisy.

Loisy had the very unfortunate effect of providing, for all the gathering forces of reaction in the Catholic Church, a scary illustration of what could come of unrestricted appropriation of modern tools of criticism. The condemnation of Modernism in general had the specific impact on biblical studies of a series of conservative decisions by the Pontifical Biblical Commission, which had been established by Leo XIII in 1902. The regulations were not quite so restrictive as they might have appeared on first reading, but their effect was virtually to silence some of the leading Catholic biblical scholars.

An espionage network grew up for reporting to Rome any tendencies toward Modernism in the writings of biblical scholars, and the activities of this network became so despicable that they had to be censured formally by Pope Benedict XV. This pope's pronouncement on biblical studies, the encyclical *Spiritus Paraclitus* of 1920, was more defensive than Leo XIII's pronouncement nearly thirty years before, and by its unequivocal insistence on the historicity of the biblical narratives it indicated just how threatened the Church felt itself to be by the theological conclusions that had been drawn from critical study of the Bible.

When Pius XII became pope in 1939, then, the plight of Catholic biblical scholars was a grave and depressing one. There was really very little they could do without running a serious risk of getting into deep trouble.

The change instituted by Pius XII came swiftly, and it was astonishing.

His pontificate marked a complete about-face and inaugurated the greatest renewal of interest in the Bible that the Roman Catholic Church has ever seen. The signs of this change were visible in the new attitude of the Pontifical Biblical Commission, which in 1941 condemned an overly *conservative* distrust of modern biblical research. The encyclical *Divino afflante Spiritu* of 1943 was a Magna Charta for biblical progress. Although the Pope saluted the encyclicals of his predecessors, he announced that the time for fear was over and that Catholic scholars should use modern tools in their exegesis. . . . In

1955 the secretary of the Pontifical Biblical Commission took a very brave but most necessary step in stating that now Catholic scholars had complete freedom (plena libertate) with regard to the earlier Pontifical Biblical Commission decrees of 1905–15. . . . This meant that Catholics were now free to adopt modern positions on the authorship of the Pentateuch, Psalms, Isaiah, the Gospels, etc.[7]

There were two aspects of the encyclical that were particularly momentous. First, the pope said that Catholic scholars should no longer do their critical work on the basis of the Latin Vulgate (a translation made by Jerome early in the fifth century), but should work from the original languages (Hebrew and Greek) of the biblical texts. Second, and even more important, the pope emphasized the necessity of studying the various kinds of literature that go to make up the Bible. Truth was no longer limited to historical truth, and a Catholic scholar could, for instance, undertake to show the central religious message of Jonah without having to defend the view that a popular folktale about a man being swallowed by a fish and regurgitated alive three days later was a straightforward narrative account of something that actually happened. The truly startling feature of this encyclical is that it does not give grudging approval to modern biblical criticism, but positively enjoins it on Catholic scholars. The Church states officially that the Church's purposes are not well served by reactionary, rearguard actions.

This is not to say there was no reactionary, rearguard action, however. In the last year of the pontificate of Pius XII, when he was very ill, and in the first years of the reign of John XXIII, there were moves to condemn some recently published studies of the New Testament, and two professors were removed from their posts at the Pontifical Biblical Institute. The draft resolution on divine revelation prepared for presentation at Vatican Council II was strongly critical of recent progressive developments in Catholic biblical scholarship, and there was good reason to believe that much of the advance of the previous two decades (since Pius XII's encyclical) would be undone.

In 1964, however, two years after the Council had begun, the Pontifical Biblical Commission issued an Instruction which permitted a thoroughly historical treatment of the problem of the Gospels, and the decree on Divine Revelation passed the following year by the Ecumenical Council reflected the tone of that Instruction. The earlier draft of the decree had in fact generated such strong opposition from the Council fathers that it had been sent back to a committee, which now included more biblical scholars than previously, for thorough revision. To give visible expression to his own commitment to modern biblical research, Pope Paul VI restored the two dismissed professors to their chairs.

It begins to look as if the wrong of the early part of this century has found its remedy, and a remedy that it would be very hard to undo. For now the practitioners of modern biblical study in the Roman Catholic Church have behind them the combined force of papal encyclical and conciliar decree. Perhaps even more important in establishing the place of such study in the Church are the solid accomplishments of Catholic scholars, and it is to a consideration of some of these that we now turn.

III. ACHIEVEMENTS

The contrast between the warning of Leo XIII, against the collaboration of Catholic and non-Catholic biblical scholars, and the admonition of Vatican Council II, that Catholics should work together with Protestants in the fundamental task of biblical translation, should thoroughly discredit the suspicion that the Catholic Church is a rigid, unchanging monolith. And when one notices that a recent editor of the *Journal of Biblical Literature,* the publication of the Society of Biblical Literature which has been appearing for nearly a hundred years, has "S.J." (Society of Jesus = Jesuits) after his name, it is clear that potentially anything can happen.

The biblical movement has brought Catholics and Protestants into close contact. It has also had a special effect within the Catholic Church in the United States. One of the leading characteristics of American Catholicism has been, traditionally, its preoccupation with other than intellectual tasks. There have been exceptions, of course, but very few Americans have stood in the front rank of Catholic thinkers. In the Catholic biblical movement, however, America has made some leading contributions, and such scholars as Joseph Fitzmyer (the recent editor of the *Journal of Biblical Literature*), Roland Murphy, and Raymond Brown have produced works whose authority has been universally recognized.

The most convincing testimony to the vitality of American Catholic biblical scholarship is *The Jerome Biblical Commentary,* a two-volume treatment of the entire Bible published in 1968 and edited by the three scholars just named. In their preface they write:

> This work is a compact commentary on the whole Bible written by Roman Catholic scholars according to the principles of modern biblical criticism. . . . The principles of literary and historical criticism, so long regarded with suspicion, are now, at last, accepted and applied by Catholic exegetes. The results have been many: a new and vital interest in the Bible throughout the Church; a greater contribution of biblical studies to modern theology; a community of effort and understanding among Catholic and non-Catholic scholars.[8]

They go on to say that the commentary is designed for those who *want to study* the Scriptures, and they hope this will include large numbers of the laity as well as seminarians and professors.

In considering what would be of use ecumenically, the editors decided against asking non-Catholics to contribute to the volume.

> Everyone now knows that generally Catholic and non-Catholic biblical scholars work very well together and have the same approach to and interpretation of most biblical passages. But there remains a feeling or suspicion both within and without the Roman Catholic Church that such cooperation represents a private endeavor of only a few and that it is without any official backing in the Church. The question of *the* Catholic interpretation of the Bible constantly reappears. It seemed to the editors that the best way to expose the misunderstanding implicit in this question was to produce a commentary written entirely by Catholics. . . . Naturally some are more critical than others in their approach to the Bible and thus exemplify the variation to be found in any community of scholars. But this variation itself should destroy once and for all the myth of *the* Catholic position, as if there were a series of biblical interpretations or positions that all must profess.[9]

Running through the *Jerome Commentary* is a kind of excitement often lacking in Protestant commentaries; this probably has something to do with the exhilaration of finally being able to say publicly what you really want to say about subjects that interest you deeply both intellectually and spiritually. The reader has a sense of being present at a real beginning.

It is a beginning that does not need to start from scratch. As the editors point out, every page of the commentary demonstrates the dependence of Catholic scholarship on the groundwork laid by Protestant scholars. Thus *The Jerome Biblical Commentary* serves to reassure Catholics not only that they have scholars who are up-to-date and can make a contribution but also that the resources of Protestant scholarship are not to be distrusted or neglected. In a practical sense, *The Jerome Biblical Commentary* relegates to the status of historical artifact the warning of *Providentissimus Deus* against associating with those "who only gnaw the bark."

By its very name the commentary signals a new age in the Church: it is the *Jerome Commentary,* not a "Commentary on Jerome's Bible." To insist, as the Church used to do, that all work be done on the basis of the Latin Vulgate, was to do homage to Jerome's *translation.* The work of Catholic scholars today is homage to Jerome himself and to his activity of *translating,* of using the tools of his day to understand the Bible. It is as if the Church has finally heard Jerome saying "Do as I do," not "Now, I have done it."

IV. The Special Contribution

Despite the acknowledged use made by Catholic and Protestant biblical scholars of one another's work, there remains the potential for a particular Catholic contribution to the understanding of the Bible. Important elements of this potential can be set out under three headings.

A. Institution

One of the central claims of all modern study of the Bible is that the church produced the New Testament, not the other way round. Rather ironically, it has been the Catholic Church that has most stoutly resisted this conclusion, claiming for the New Testament an immunity from the shaping tendencies of historical development in the earliest Christian generation. However, it is now officially mandated by the Church that scholars take seriously the processes by which the teaching of Jesus was remembered and shaped by the apostolic generation. This means that the church which most strongly asserts its right to the inheritance of the apostolic community (the bishopric of Rome is called "the Apostolic See") is now beginning to understand that the *interpreting* of the faith, which it claims to have the right to do, is in fact an activity which was going on from the very beginning—that the New Testament is itself part of the church's development of doctrine.

Many people deplore what they call the "institutionalization of Christianity"; for them, the Roman Catholic Church (or probably any church, for that matter) is a shackling of the free spirit which Jesus came to let loose in the world. But scholars today of all sorts of religious and academic persuasions are challenging the simplistic notion, popular until recently among New Testament interpreters, that a clear distinction can be drawn between "original Christianity" and what has been called "early Catholicism." Jesus is reported to have said (Matt. 18:20) that wherever two or three were gathered in his name, he was there among them. Modern scholars, informed by social theory and data, are saying, in effect, that wherever two or three are gathered for any purpose, the beginnings of "institutionalization" are present.

Catholic scholars, with their deep, almost instinctive sense of the church as an institution (even as an institution with which they are sometimes in serious tension), should be peculiarly well situated to appreciate the way in which institutionalization was built in to the very process of spreading the gospel. The activity of the apostles necessarily implied some measure of organization, and Catholic scholars, as a result of the interweaving of their own sense of identity with the structures of an institution, might well have a "sixth sense" for the nature of the apostolic church as communal institution and institutional community. They know in their bones that institutions are not only organizations and structures but also tradition and momentum.

Catholic New Testament scholarship can help call Protestant scholarship back from its overemphasis on individualism, and it can also help Catholics see that the validity of the church does not depend finally on the church's having been projected in detail by Jesus. The key here is not simply a recognition of the institutionalization inherent in any apostolic activity, but beyond that, a recognition of what is implied in the fundamental Christian claim to continuity with Israel. As John Gager has pointed out, the early Christian church takes over much of the organization of the Jewish community, and what modern "free spirits" see as the unfortunate increasing institutionalization of the church within the New Testament period may be simply the gradual emergence into the light of the New Testament documents of references to organizational structures that had been in use all along. Because of the importance of the Old Testament in the shaping of original Christian ideas of the church, it is especially fortunate for Catholic study of the New Testament that the biblical movement in the Catholic Church is focused as much on the Old Testament as on the New.

B. Pastoral Concerns

As was mentioned early in this book, one of the striking differences between the age of the church fathers and the past hundred years of Protestant scholarship is that most of the biblical commentary in the first five centuries was done by bishops, while recently it has been done by university or seminary professors. Bishops in the early centuries were pastors at least as much as they were administrators, and they knew that their interpretation of the Bible had to speak to all sorts and conditions of persons. Many Protestant scholars have of course also been pastors, but they have not characteristically had the day-to-day contact with the laity that was a large part of the life of patristic bishops.

In this respect, modern Catholic study of the Bible is more like that of the ancient church. It is certainly true that the institutional affiliation of nearly all the contributors to *The Jerome Biblical Commentary* is academic, but most of the contributors are priests, and will in the normal course of their duty have contact with some of the laity. This may make them at least relatively more sensitive to the need to relate the results of scholarship to concerns that people actually have. Even more basically, Catholic scholars tend to have a well-developed sense of the total responsibility of the church, a responsibility that is only partly academic and intellectual.

Another way of putting this is to say that Catholic scholars may have a more compelling sense of their obligation to serve the church than Protestant scholars tend to have. There is of course always the danger in this that scholars will sacrifice their sense of "where the argument leads" to the interests of "protecting the sensibilities of the faithful." But that is in most cases a remote danger, and it is not a foregone conclusion that relating scholarship to human concerns risks a greater distortion of the truth than doing scholarship in an academic isolation which gets lost in a welter of technicalities and is dogmatically devoted to what is at the moment perceived as fact. One must certainly master the literature and its intricacies, but to stop there is the abiding temptation of the ivory tower. Perhaps Catholic biblical scholars can help all of us learn better than we have so far the skills of genuinely humane scholarship.

C. Sense of Tradition

This third heading is the least specific of the three, but it is the most important. In *The Jerome Biblical Commentary* there is a lengthy and learned appreciation of the achievement of Rudolf Bultmann, whose name prior to 1943 would have been anathema in the Catholic Church. Along with the acknowledgment of Bultmann's genius, however, the commentary's critique gets at the essential flaw: Bultmann's radical individualism and his ahistorical sense of the religious life, his conviction that one can start from scratch, that Christianity begins afresh with everyone who finds God at the end of the road of despair or meaninglessness.[10] Against all Protestant notions of "starting from the beginning," Catholic scholars have an instinctive sense of being surrounded by a great cloud of witnesses, witnesses whose sense of what the Bible means has a claim on our attention today which is not obliterated by their lack of acquaintance with modern methods of historical and literary criticism.

Catholic scholars, by virtue of their sense of tradition and of their place in it, might have a readier sense than their Protestant counterparts of the provisional quality of any conclusion reached about the particular meaning of a passage—if we cannot go along with Augustine in this or that case, then it is likely our successors will not be able to go along with us in that or this case. But every interpretation seriously made with a concern for the upbuilding of the church becomes a contribution to the whole tradition of the faith, and the value of that interpretation will survive whatever changes in scholarly fashion may occur.

V. OPEN WINDOWS

It will of course be a long time before anything like a balanced verdict can be rendered on the achievements of the Second Vatican Council (1962–1965). We are now nearly a decade and a half past its conclusion, and while much has happened in that period to carry forward the Council's impetus of *aggiornamento,* "updating," "throwing open the Church's windows to let in air from the outside world," there has also been a great deal that looks like recoiling from that impetus. That this is a time of acute crisis for the Church is evident.

The pronouncement of recent times with the deepest long-term implications for the Church is not the opposition to artificial birth control or to the ordination of women or to the marriage of priests. It is the "Dogmatic Constitution on Divine Revelation" of Vatican II. It is characteristic of our time that people tend to overlook matters of "mere dogma." The very title *"Dogmatic* Constitution on Divine *Revelation"* would be taken by many as a signal that this document could safely be skipped over if one's main intention is to find out what is *really* going on inside the Catholic Church.

Neither "dogma" nor "revelation" is a fossil by nature, however. They are both dynamic terms, and if they are properly understood, a title that includes both "dogmatic" and "revelation" will suggest that the document may have extraordinary potential for doing something.

The "Constitution" concerns itself with both Scripture and tradition, but in a way far more pronounced than ever before in Catholicism, it gives pride of place to Scripture, at least in terms of the attention paid to it. There are two chapters (out of a total of twenty-six) that are directed primarily at biblical scholars, and they deserve quotation as indicating both the general freedom of the scholar and the authority of the Church.

12. Seeing that, in sacred Scripture, God speaks through men in human fashion, it follows that the interpreter of the sacred Scriptures, if he is to ascertain what God has wished to communicate to us, should carefully search out the meaning which the sacred writers really had in mind, that meaning which God had thought well to manifest

through the medium of their words.

In determining the intention of the sacred writers, attention must be paid to, among other things, literary forms, for the fact is that truth is differently presented and expressed in the various types of historical writing, in prophetic and poetical texts, and in other forms of literary expression. Hence the exegete must look for that meaning which the sacred writer, in a determined situation and given the circumstances of his time and culture, intended to express and did in fact express, through the medium of a contemporary literary form. Rightly to understand what the sacred author wanted to affirm in his work, due attention must be paid both to the customary and characteristic patterns of perception, speech, and narrative which prevailed in the age of the sacred writer, and to the conventions which the people of his time followed in their dealings with one another.

But since sacred Scripture must be read and interpreted with its divine authorship in mind, no less attention must be devoted to the content and unity of the whole of Scripture, taking into account the Tradition of the entire Church and the analogy of faith, if we are to derive their true meaning from the sacred texts. It is the task of exegetes to work, according to these rules, towards a better understanding and explanation of the meaning of the sacred Scripture in order that their research may help the Church to form a firmer judgment. For, of course, all that has been said about the manner of interpreting Scripture is ultimately subject to the judgment of the Church which exercises the divinely conferred commission and ministry of watching over and interpreting the Word of God.

13. Hence, in sacred Scripture, without prejudice to God's truth and holiness, the marvelous condescension of eternal wisdom is plain to be seen that we may come to know the ineffable loving-kindness of God and see for ourselves how far he has gone in adapting his language with thoughtful concern for our nature. Indeed the words of God, expressed in the words of men, are in every way like human language, just as the Word of the eternal Father, when he took on himself the flesh of human weakness, became like men.[11]

An entire book could be written on the interpretation of these two chapters of the Constitution—and this section of this chapter of this book is not the place for even a partial analysis. However, it should be noted that the insistence on Church authority is not the starting point, but is sandwiched between a recognition that a text's meaning is intimately bound up with the circumstances of its writing and a declaration that the language of the Bible is human language, not in itself different from any other human language. Scholarly research is enjoined to help the Church (of which the scholars to whom the words are directed are of course a part) "form a firmer judgment"—that is, the scholars are to help form the judgment, their work is not prejudged.

The final two chapters (Chapters 25 and 26) of the Constitution urge on all the Catholic faithful—clergy, members of religious orders, laity—the reading and study of the Bible. In a long historical perspective this is revolutionary. The Church in late medieval times excommunicated, and occasionally burned, persons who undertook to provide the Bible in a language the laity could read for themselves. The Bible is a book that has demonstrated through the centuries a remarkable capacity to get things started, to make a difference in the way people think and act. When an authoritative Council of the Church directs the faithful—all seven hundred million of them—to get about the business of reading and studying the Bible, who knows what might happen?

CHAPTER
ELEVEN

OPENING UP
AND BROADENING OUT

Several lines of scholarly development have converged to create a new climate for New Testament interpretation, and the field of New Testament study is moving in significant new directions. It is the purpose of this concluding chapter to sum up what has been said, and to suggest what the new directions in New Testament study mean in relation to the age in which we live.

First, however, we must look at other ways of relating New Testament study and current concerns—ways that are fundamentally different from what I have proposed, and that have a very wide appeal and influence today.

I. The Nuclear Age and the Age of Aquarius

Ernest Digweed is not a name familiar in the field of New Testament study. Nevertheless, Mr. Digweed has posed a problem in which New Testament scholars might be supposed to have a professional interest. A recent news report reads as follows:

Jesus Christ stands to collect some $44,000 on the occasion of his second coming.

A British man who died last year has bequeathed this handsome sum to Christ if he returns within the next 80 years, specifically to "reign on earth," and if he proves his identity to the British government.

The terms of this unusual will were disclosed last week in probate proceedings on the estate of Ernest Digweed, a retired teacher who stipulated that if anyone falsely claimed to be Christ, or if Christ failed to show up to claim the sum, then the money would go to the British crown.[1]

The procedural questions raised by this will are formidable. Is it a matter for the Foreign Office or for the Home Office?—that is, do you deal with Christ diplomatically or domestically? If Christ must "reign on earth" as part of his proof to the British government that he is genuine, then he would hardly need to "prove his identity" to them, since he would already have effective control over everything, including Great Britain. Perhaps the whole responsibility should be shifted to the archbishop of Canterbury—but the queen is the Supreme Head of the Church of England, and it is her government that stands to gain should no claimant, or only false ones, show up. Will Christ decide to return earlier than originally planned, to avoid erosion of his inheritance by further decline in the value of the pound sterling? It is, in any case, likely that in the best British tradition Mr. Digweed's eccentricity will be treated with proper respect, and a way found with full legislative and legal decorum to determine the final disposition of the funds.

A. Biblical Prophecy

Most New Testament scholars would plead "pressure of other business" if they were asked to serve as expert witnesses in court when someone claims the $44,000. There is enough of a problem figuring out who Jesus Christ was at the First Coming without getting involved in legal battles over his identity at the Second Coming. There are, however, some interpreters of the New Testament today who claim to be eminently qualified to answer any questions the British government might have—indeed, to draw for them a "portrait" of Christ as he will appear at the Second Coming so that should there be a lineup of claimants, the judge can say with confidence, "Behold, the man!"

Hal Lindsey's books, presenting an interpretation of the Bible, are among the true "best sellers" of our time. His best-known book, *The Late Great Planet Earth,* originally published in 1970, had sold eight and a half million copies by mid-1977.[2] The sort of New Testament study we have been talking about has had slight impact on our culture compared to the extraordinarily widespread interest in Lindsey's treatment of what he and many others call "biblical prophecy."

Hal Lindsey specializes in campus appearances, and he writes with a college-educated audience particularly in mind. His collaborator on *The Late Great Planet Earth* is a journalist, and the style has the pungency—as well as, at times, the superficiality—of a newspaper column. Lindsey treats academic biblical scholarship with scorn, and professors have responded in kind. It is worth looking at *The Late Great Planet Earth,* however, if only to try to understand its truly awesome appeal. Books that sell in the millions are major cultural forces.

There are three main themes in *The Late Great Planet Earth,* all of them interrelated: the Second Coming, the State of Israel, and God acting in history. We need to look briefly at each of them.

Lindsey's book is a helpful guide to those who have wondered what is meant by bumper stickers that read "In Case of Rapture This Car Will Be Unmanned." Lindsey states his own firm belief in the literal fulfillment of the statement in 1 Thess. 4:17 that we shall be caught up "in the clouds to meet the Lord in the air." This will happen in a moment, in the twinkling of an eye, so that you will not see people being carried away—it will simply be "now you see them, now you don't." Christ will of course take to himself in this way only those who genuinely believe in him—that is, according to Lindsey, those who believe without question in the virgin birth, the miracles, the physical resurrection, and so on. Those who experience the Rapture will return with Christ after the final battle of Armageddon to share his reign of a thousand years before he makes the new heaven and new earth.

Bultmann has said explicitly: "We can no longer look for the return of the Son of Man on the clouds of heaven or hope that the faithful will meet him in the air."[3] The popularity of Lindsey's book suggests otherwise—that there are many people who can believe it and who are prepared to announce it to everyone through bumper stickers. Paul said that the notion of a crucified Messiah was a stumbling block to Jews and foolishness to the Greeks. Is what Lindsey is presenting any more of an absurdity to us than the concept of incarnation was to Origen's pagan opponent Celsus or Justin's Jewish opponent Trypho? The question is posed simply for reflection. Ancient debates have a kind of remoteness that makes us insensitive to the heat the issues generated. If I try to think how hard it would be for me to accept Lindsey's teaching about the

Rapture, I begin to understand how hard it was for Greeks and Jews to accept the gospel.

The Second Coming itself appears only at the end of Lindsey's book. It comes as the culmination of gathering intensity on the world scene. Lindsey deftly interweaves current events and projections from them with what he presents as clear and precise biblical prophecies of past and current events. From this basis he concludes that prophecies of future events are also accurate. Lindsey is well aware that history is littered with reports of groups who have said that their own time is clearly the time predicted as the End by Daniel and/or Revelation, and he faces this one head on. Why, he asks, should anyone think it will be different this time? And his answer points to the decisive factor in the rapid growth of interest in what is called biblical prophecy.

Lindsey points out that the establishment of the State of Israel in 1948 has altered the pattern of world affairs in relation to biblical prophecy in a way that no political or cultural development for nearly two thousand years has done. With this new fact as the clue that solves the mystery, Lindsey compiles a carefully articulated set of predictions collected from many different parts of the Bible (particularly Isaiah, Ezekiel, Daniel, the apocalyptic material in the Synoptic Gospels, some parts of Paul's letters, and Revelation) to substantiate his claim that current events are fulfilling in detail what was predicted. Russia as the "foe from the north," the alliance of Arab states as the "foe from the south," China as the "hordes from the east," and the alliance of ten nations in the Common Market as the revival of the Roman Empire, in fulfillment of the predictions of Daniel about the "beast with ten horns"—all these fit the pattern he discerns, and Lindsey does not balk at predicting exactly what is going to happen as the nations of the world propel themselves headlong into World War III.

There is, undeniably, a kind of logically compelling quality to his prophecy—or, as he would say, his inspired interpretation of biblical prophecy. Everybody knows the Middle East is a powder keg, and not a few people would say, if asked where they think the superpowers will have their great showdown, that the Middle East is the most likely place. Lindsey would certainly take the repeated breakdowns in peace efforts in that area as further evidence that there is no real compromise between Israel and the Arabs. The appearance of this apparently irresolvable conflict in that part of the world at a time when nuclear weapons have proliferated is for Lindsey a "sign of the times" such as Jesus said his own generation was not able to read aright (Matt. 16:3). Lindsey would say that we are right to think the Middle East is where attention should be focused, but that we are blind when we do not realize it has all, *in detail,* down to strategic plans and tactical maneuvers, been set forth in the Bible.

The section of *The Late Great Planet Earth* in which Lindsey talks about the Second Coming is representative of his mode of argument.

According to Zechariah, "all nations will be gathered against Jerusalem to battle." The Jews who live in the area will be on the verge of annihilation when God gives them supernatural strength to fight. Then the Lord will go forth to fight for them and save them.

Jesus' feet will first touch the earth where they left the earth, on the Mount of Olives. The mountain will split in two with a great earthquake the instant that Jesus' foot touches it. The giant crevice which results will run east and west through the center of the mountain. It will go east to the north tip of the Dead Sea and west to the Mediterranean Sea (Zechariah 14).

It was reported to me that an oil company doing seismic studies of this area in quest of oil discovered a gigantic fault running east and west precisely through the center of the Mount of Olives. The fault is so severe that it could split at any time. It is awaiting "the foot."

Zechariah predicts a strange thing with regard to the ensuing split in the earth. The believing Jewish remnant in Jerusalem will rush into the crack instead of doing the natural thing of running from it. They will know this prophecy and realize that this great cavern has opened up for the Lord to protect them from the terrible devastation that He is about to pour out upon the godless armies all around. It will be used as a type of bomb shelter.

The nature of the forces which the Lord will unleash on that day against the armies gathered in the Middle East is described in Zechariah 14:12: "And this shall be the plague wherewith the LORD will smite all the people that have fought against Jerusalem; Their flesh shall consume away while they stand upon their feet, and their eyes shall consume away in their holes, and their tongue shall consume away in their mouth" (King James Version).

A frightening picture, isn't it? Has it occurred to you that this is exactly what happens to those who are in a thermonuclear blast? It appears that this will be the case at the return of Christ.[4]

The mixture of ancient imagery with modern (mountains split-
ting in two, geological faults, bomb shelters, thermonuclear war)
is compelling to many people, and serves as a kind of alternative
"demythologizing" to the sort Bultmann undertakes. Indeed, Lindsey in effect inverts Bultmann's argument. Bultmann has said that
what ancient persons could take as literal we no longer can, because
science and technology have altered our view of the world. What
was "reality" for persons of biblical times is "myth" for us. Lindsey
would say that what could have been for ancient persons no more
than vivid pictorial language (for example, the descriptions of the
Final Battle in the Bible) can become literal for us precisely *because
of* developments in science and technology. What was "myth" for
persons in biblical times is cold, hard "reality" for us.

Underlying Lindsey's presentation of both the Second Coming
and the role of the establishment of the State of Israel is his conviction that God acts in history in ways that are crystal clear, ways that
can be specified in detail. The judges and prophets and kings and
Jesus and the apostles saw God at work directly in the happenings
of their day; God acting in history was not a philosophical question
for debate (Can the divine get mixed up in the world of change and
matter?), it was simply the way they thought about what was happening. Lindsey and those who share his views would say it is
irrelevant to the Bible to agree that it says God acts in history, and
accept this as a premise, if you do not go ahead and get down to
cases.

The great appeal of Lindsey's book is that it makes available a
sense of purpose, meaning, direction in the apparently chaotic developments on the world scene. Discerning God's purpose in the
events of our own time becomes not a tentative, intricate weighing
of probabilities, but rather a confident perception of a pattern that
is linked to the entire pattern of history presented in the Bible.

B. The Occult

If the "biblical prophecy" approach to the Bible has a serious
rival for popular attention in our time, it is the approach that sees
the Bible as the storehouse of occult wisdom. A writer of the first
part of this century, Rudolf Steiner (1861–1925), is becoming
increasingly prominent as interest in the occult grows, and we shall

look at him briefly as representative of the approach. Steiner wrote 170 books, and gave over 6,000 lectures on subjects as diverse as most university curricula. He lived most of his life in Switzerland, where he began his career as a precocious editor of the scientific works of Goethe. By the time he was about thirty he had undergone some profound experiences in terms of which he came to view the world as primarily spiritual. He found support for his view in a study of what he characterized as the "tradition of Mysteries in antiquity."

In Steiner's opinion, the most interesting facts about antiquity are by definition not accessible to us directly. All the people who counted (the philosophers, the playwrights, the poets) were, according to Steiner, initiates into one or another secret mystery fraternity. The cardinal rule of the mysteries was that the initiates could not tell the uninitiated what they learned through initiation. There could be a kind of watered-down teaching for those outside, but that is all it was.

As a result of his own experience, Steiner came to believe that the leading characteristic of the mysteries was an *experiential* knowledge of the reality of the spiritual world. Steiner, brought up on natural science, believed that the greatest natural scientists made their discoveries because of their intuitive grasp of spiritual realities —in other words, he held that materialistic natural science was unable to account for the natural scientist. But Steiner was at great pains to insist that what he was talking about was mystical *fact,* not mystical fancy.

In *Christianity as Mystical Fact,* Steiner draws numerous lines from his theory of the mysteries in antiquity to the New Testament. For example, he solves the problem of the discrepancies among the Gospels by saying that each is the application of one particular mystery group's traditional portrayal of a divine man to the career and teaching of Jesus. But beyond the doctrinal differences, Steiner considers the problem of historical discrepancies entirely beside the point, since for him history is simply the shell in which mystical meaning resides.

Steiner's central point, however, is one that at first sight seems paradoxical. He claims that his deepest spiritual experience occurred when he perceived for the first time the "Mystery of Golgotha." In Steiner's own terms, the historical event of Christ serves to link the world of the senses with the spiritual world.

> In the Christ-experience a quite definite stage of initiation is to be seen. When the mystic of pre-Christian times went through this Christ-experience, then, through his initiation, he was in a condition enabling him to perceive something spiritual—in higher worlds—for which the material world had no corresponding fact. He experienced what comprises the Mystery of Golgotha in the higher world. Now when the Christian mystic goes through this experience, through initiation, at the same time he beholds the historical event on Golgotha and knows that in this event, which took place in the world of the senses, is the same content as formerly existed only in the supersensible facts of the Mysteries. What had descended upon the mystics within the Mystery temples in earlier times thus descended upon the community of Christ through the "Mystery of Golgotha." And initiation gives the Christian mystic the possibility of becoming conscious of this content of the "Mystery of Golgotha," while faith causes mankind to participate unconsciously in the mystical current which flowed from the events depicted in the New Testament and has been permeating the spiritual life of humanity ever since.[5]

The historical particularity of the Christian message is of use only as a way of getting to the universal, "the whole of humanity." The

> soul of the world is the Logos. If the Logos is to become flesh He must repeat the cosmic process in physical existence. He must be nailed to the Cross and rise again. This most significant thought of Christianity had long before been outlined as a spiritual representation in the old world conceptions. This became a personal experience of the mystic during "initiation." The Logos become man had to experience this deed as a fact, valid for the whole of humanity. Something which was a Mystery process in the development of the old wisdom becomes historical fact through Christianity. Thus Christianity became the fulfilment not only of what the Jewish prophets had predicted, but also of what had been pre-formed in the Mysteries. . . . Christianity as mystical fact is a stage of development in the process of human evolution; and the events in the Mysteries and their effects are the preparations for this mystical fact.[6]

Steiner's basic premise—that all significant figures in intellectual, cultural, and religious life in the ancient world were initiates into secret mystery fraternities—is a highly dubious historical claim, although there is of course no way finally to refute it, since the very lack of evidence becomes evidence (the fact that they did not write about it simply demonstrates the force of the basic rule of secrecy in the mysteries). Nevertheless, Steiner's way of approach to the New Testament is one with an appeal that does not depend on its connection to such a historical theory. If Lindsey says the Bible reveals a clear sense of purpose and direction in the apparent chaos of our world, Steiner says that the understanding of the world as spiritual provides a clear sense of the purpose and direction in the apparent chaos of Scripture. For Lindsey, a proper understanding of the Bible leads to a proper understanding of the world. For Steiner, a proper understanding of the world leads to a proper understanding of the Bible. In both cases, the meaning of that which is confusing is revealed by that which is crystal clear.

II. The Time of Pilgrimage

Lindsey presents New Testament interpretation keyed to the Nuclear Age, when the threat of a ghastly Armageddon seems all too immediate. Steiner presents New Testament interpretation keyed to the Age of Aquarius, when a new "wind of the spirit" (rather vaguely defined) appears to be blowing across the world. From the perspective of the Nuclear Age, the academic study of the New Testament is not historical enough, it does not take God's action in history at face value. From the perspective of the Age of Aquarius, the academic study of the New Testament is too historical, it gets bogged down in the details of history at the expense of the lofty spiritual meaning of the texts.

The age for which current academic study of the New Testament is suited is not one which can be easily characterized in a single phrase; it has many features, not all of which fit neatly into a general pattern. If we want a shorthand expression, we might call it the "time of pilgrimage."

"Pilgrimage" is certainly no new idea. It is one of the oldest of cultural and religious motifs.[7] It has fallen out of use because we have come to expect instant gratifications in our experience. We consider that the only alternative to a static life is a staccato one. Pilgrimage requires a spirituality of the long haul, prepared both to weather those times in our life when everything is chaotic, and not to get too complacent when everything "falls into place." Pilgrims are not always sure what they are seeking, and sometimes when they think they do know, they are surprised by what they find.

Pilgrimage is not a mere episode in our life, one of the "experiences" we chalk up in our pursuit of happiness. It is our life itself. And just as our life fluctuates between order and confusion, so does the Bible: sometimes it appears to make coherent sense, and other times it seems an impossibly diverse collection of partial insights which cannot be brought into any sharp focus. In short, we find ourselves persons in history dealing with a book produced in history: neither the world nor the Bible provides a straightforward standard in terms of which to interpret and order the confusion of the other.

It might now be asked: Why resist the biblical prophecy solution or the occult solution? Is an insistence on "pilgrimage" simply an academic prejudice, a rearguard action to rally a somewhat bedraggled group of professors who are facing steadily increasing assaults from a Nuclear "right," which cites geologists, and an Aquarian "left," which claims to know what scientists are *really* up to?

There are good reasons not to opt for the biblical prophecy solution or the occult solution, reasons which have nothing to do with justifying one's job or remaining respectable among one's academic colleagues. Unfortunately (at least in the short term), these reasons do not generate the sort of exhilaration people feel when they see for the first time the light of Lindsey's laser beam or the more suffused, aurora borealis kind of light that shines in Steiner's pages. The moderate illumination of the scholar's desk lamp may seem a paltry substitute, but it may last longer. Three of the reasons can be broadly classified: one as theological, one as specifically biblical, and one as personal. These three can themselves be summed up under one general term, that of "revelation."

The *theological* reason for sticking with pilgrimage as the designation for our life is the doctrine of the incarnation. To take that doctrine with full seriousness is to go all the way, as Vatican Council II did, and say that just as God became a human being, so God uses human language in the Bible.

The way Lindsey reads the Bible presupposes that biblical language is unlike any other language we know of, for he sees it all as having been dictated by God, and as presenting a complete picture of what is to come. That there is a future thrust to a great deal of biblical language is undeniable; but future hope and expectation are part of much human language, and we claim for little or none of it the kind of precise accuracy Lindsey claims to find in the Bible. Of course, Lindsey is able to find many striking "confirmations," but one could pick and choose other passages to create quite different patterns. And Lindsey's reading of New Testament apocalyptic language disregards the *caution* that is generally characteristic of biblical predictions; as Dunn has said,

> The first-century Christian apocalyptic writings never allowed enthusiasm to get out of hand; they deliberately set their face against speculating about dates and times; always the note of the not yet was present to prevent hope becoming too detailed, too certain about the details of God's future.[8]

The main point is this: Christian doctrine asserts that God became a human being, and dwelt among us—and in so doing, God subjected revelation itself to the limitations and rich possibilities of human language and to the ambiguities of history. There is a hidden inconsistency in asserting both that God acts in history and that the record of those acts is itself not subject to history. You must both *have and eat* your incarnational cake, even if it does not exactly suit your taste.

The occult interpretation of the New Testament shares with the "biblical prophetic" an unwillingness to take the incarnation with full seriousness. Steiner insists that the point of Christianity is that the mystical becomes historical fact, but it remains true that for him the historical fact is primarily an educational device. What *really* happens is a spiritual event: Christ undergoes in the flesh what is in reality a great cosmic happening. Historical life is simply the outer shell for vast, deep spiritual movements. And this makes it possible to overlook, or dismiss, the ambiguities of history, since by definition everything really means the same thing—the possibility that there could be genuinely irreconcilable understandings of Jesus is simply eliminated. Human experience is not bounded by language, but is always breaking through it; and since historical life is not our real life, there is no need for God to get intimately involved in history, except by way of teaching a lesson.

The second reason for keeping to the middle path of pilgrimage is *biblical.* The Bible itself contains several accounts of persons who were uncertain what the future would bring, and occasionally an event of the past is understood in two quite different ways. Jeremiah, as we noted earlier, had grave doubts about the accuracy of his message, to the extent of suspecting that God was playing tricks on him. Most instructive of all, the Book of Jonah caricatures the prophet who is annoyed when his confident prediction, made in God's name and at God's specific request, does not come true. The First Book of Chronicles (21:1) says that Satan incited David to take a census of Israel and Judah, though Second Samuel (24:1) says it was the Lord who "incited David." All these examples (and more could be given) are from the Old Testament, but there are New Testament ones too. Paul in his letters can be shown to have modified his eschatological ideas as he grew older, the "Synoptic Apocalypse" has different characteristics in each of the three Gospels, and John's Gospel has thoroughly reworked eschatology.

The Bible has passages that do not cohere, but that is not the heart of the argument against Lindsey's and Steiner's positions. Both men have ways of accounting for contradictions and absorbing them into their schemes of thought. Much more important is the Bible's own portrayal of the "piety of doubt," the "faithfulness of uncertainty." Even Paul said that "now we see in a mirror, dimly" (1 Cor. 13:12)—and that *now* is the time of pilgrimage. Paul reports a heavenly vision, and he believed Christ was coming back soon—that is, he is grist for the mills of both Steiner and Lindsey. But Paul also insists that we do not have certain knowledge of things to come, and he counts his vision as among his lesser spiritual benefits, in a considerably lower rank than abilities and skills which lead to the upbuilding of the community. The occultist could say that Paul is here simply veiling the truth, as any mystery initiate was supposed to do. At some point, however, one may want to call a halt to the special pleading, and rest content with a suspicion that Paul is saying exactly what he means.

The third reason for staying on pilgrimage is a *personal* one. Our life is an experience of growth, of development, with certain deep continuities running through it, and there is no clear reason why that growth should stop at a particular stage. Both biblical prophecy and the occult treat the Bible in a way that hinders the potential for human growth. The answers are all presented, the schemes are all worked out. One goes to the Bible to solve puzzles or delve into mysteries, but a valuable potential is eliminated: the sort of growth that can occur when a person has to work through—*and keep working through*—experience and Scripture, *both of which* are themselves moving back and forth on a line between certainty and uncertainty. This is the situation of the person who is prepared to risk growth, who is not content to stop short either at the assertion that the Bible is all literally true so all we have to do is read and believe, or at the assertion that all the variety of the Bible points to one eternal and timeless truth so all we have to do is get in touch with our true and timeless self.

To take the doctrine of the incarnation seriously; to take the complexity of the Bible not as a hurdle to be jumped but as the course to be run; to opt for the uncertainty of growth instead of the confidence of certainty—all these have direct bearing on the understanding of revelation. Interpretations of the New Testament which make of revelation either the direct voice of God or the mystery veiled by the language are simply not serviceable for persons on pilgrimage.

A view of revelation such as that put forward nearly forty years ago by H. Richard Niebuhr comes close to serving the purpose. Niebuhr talks about the way certain historical events illuminate others, though he insists that such illumination is dependent upon a community's interpretation of the illuminating event. For instance, outside the Christian community's interpretation, the crucifixion of a Jew nineteen and a half centuries ago on a charge of sedition does not serve to make sense of anything else, much less all of history. "God's action in history" is thus seen, in Niebuhr's terms, not simply as the life of Jesus Christ but also as the formation of the community which interpreted that life and transmits that interpretation to subsequent generations. And revelation is closely tied to *confession* of faith, for "we can proceed only by stating in simple, confessional form what has happened to us in our community, how we came to believe, how we reason about things and what we see from our point of view."9

This implies further that one stands *with* those who wrote the Bible, one does not stand looking *at* them (rather like doing a commentary in the spirit of Jerome instead of commenting on his translation of the Bible): "One must look with Isaiah and Paul, and not at them—participate in their history rather than regard it." The challenge is to get "from observation to participation and from observed to lived history."[10]

Revelation is for Niebuhr a *process* of interaction between ourselves as members of a community and the Bible. We may discover patterns of meaning in the Bible that make sense of the rest of our life, but the conclusion reached is subject to revision. One of the dynamic elements of revelation is its encouragement of remembering: "By reasoning on the basis of revelation the heart not only understands what it remembers but is enabled to remember what it had forgotten." And growth is, for Niebuhr, the *necessary* consequence of a proper appropriation of revelation: "Revelation is not only progressive but it requires of those to whom it has come that they begin the never-ending pilgrim's progress of the reasoning Christian heart."[11] What is revealed, then, at the most basic level, is this: that our lifetime is a time of pilgrimage. God does not set us forth on a pilgrimage and then suddenly propel us to the end of the journey by providing a book that has all the answers. Revelation begins a quest, it does not end an argument.

I am not writing a treatise on the doctrine of revelation, and what is said here makes no claim to being a thorough analysis of Richard Niebuhr's views, let alone an adequate treatment of the whole issue. However, perhaps enough has been said to indicate that a coherent understanding of revelation, compatible with current academic study of the Bible, is conceivable. The term "compatible" is carefully chosen. One of the merits of Niebuhr's understanding of revelation is his insistence that events are revelatory only for a community which interprets them in a particular way. One can certainly study the Bible academically without discovering revelation in it; but one can also find revelation in the Bible without having to abandon academic study of it. One who understands revelation in this way is denied whatever pleasure is provided by sharp and precise answers such as Lindsey offers, or by vast and general answers such as Steiner offers. But there is a special kind of pleasure that comes with understanding revelation as the impetus to pilgrimage: in words from W. H. Auden's Christmas poem, *For the Time Being,* "You will see rare beasts, and have unique adventures."[12]

III. Features of Current New Testament Study

Now it is time to begin a review of the territory covered in the previous ten chapters of this book. To suggest that this summary will put everything neatly into place, that it will provide a complete and balanced view of the current state of New Testament study, would be highly presumptuous; even more, it would contradict one of the premises of the argument—that history, even the history of New Testament study, is incomplete, has loose ends, is subject to varying judgments.

A. The Waning of Existentialism

The waning of the influence of existentialism is both the result of and prerequisite for the other developments. During the years of the predominance of Bultmann's authority there have of course been advocates of other ways of approach to the New Testament, but it has been hard for them to receive general attention while the whole question of demythologizing has so preoccupied New Testament scholars.

1. History and Historicity

The existentialists claim to be taking with full seriousness the reality of human existence as historical. We are all bounded and limited by our circumstances. Any assertions about "human nature" as such are unwarranted, since for everyone the full range of possibility from devil to angel is open, and we make the "essence" of our own individual "human nature" only through the collection of concrete decisions we make as life confronts us with the necessity to choose. We cannot take experience at secondhand.

The lasting value of this approach is its warning against letting literature substitute for life or letting somebody else's religion do service for your own. The danger against which the existentialist theologians set themselves in an ever-present danger. It is dramatized unforgettably by Søren Kierkegaard, the Danish originator of existentialism, when he describes the plight of a man who cannot even convince his wife that he has doubts about his own Christianity.

> Dear husband of mine, how can you get such notions into your head?
> How can you doubt that you are a Christian? Are you not a Dane,
> and does not the geography say that the Lutheran form of the Chris-
> tian religion is the ruling religion in Denmark? For you are certainly
> not a Jew, nor are you a Mohammedan; what then can you be if not
> a Christian? It is a thousand years since paganism was driven out of
> Denmark, so I know you are not a pagan. Do you not perform your
> duties at the office like a conscientious civil servant; are you not a
> good citizen of a Christian nation, a Lutheran Christian state? So then
> of course you must be a Christian.[13]

Kierkegaard is saying that the Danes have sacrificed the historical
nature of their immediate existence to the history of the relations
between state and church in Denmark. The challenge of the gospel
has been so blunted that you cannot even get a rise out of someone
by saying you take the whole thing seriously enough to doubt
whether it is true.

Nevertheless, history provides a context as well as a condition,
and the existentialist overlooks the way in which we *can* extend
ourselves by appropriating the experience of others. We must certainly not let literature substitute for life, but literature can extend
the range of life for us, and it might be the very strangeness of the
early Christians that makes them effective teachers for us. The
important fact about them and us is not that they are *ancient* persons
and we are *modern* persons, but that both they and we are *partial*
persons.

2. Centrality of Community

The existentialist approach isolates persons from their past. It also
isolates them from one another. The line from Luther through
Kierkegaard to Bultmann is one of ever-narrowing focus, until
finally all attention is riveted on the momentary response of the
individual to God's challenge in a particular situation in a particular
setting. Luther said it did no good to say that Christ died for our
sins; salvation was effective only when you could say that Christ
died for *my* sins. Luther himself, partly from conviction, partly from
habit, maintained confidence in the value of the Christian community with its sacramental activities that give vivid expression to
existence as members of the body of Christ, responsible to and for
one another. But with the further erosion of the medieval social and

religious synthesis, the potential for radical individualism embedded in Luther's "salvation by faith alone" came to full development, and one might say it has reached its logical conclusion in our time.

The emergence to prominence of the field of sociology has affected our view of reality, and not only of the present but also of the past. The "great man" theory and practice in history writing is itself out of date, and while the reading of a particularly jargonistic sociological analysis of a historical period may make us long for the good old days of heroes and villains, we know it would be difficult and basically unsatisfying to return to a more anecdotal history-writing.

"Consciousness and Society," to borrow the title of a book by H. Stuart Hughes, are for us inextricably bound together. This is the crucial aspect of "the modern person" that recent New Testament interpreters have overlooked. We simply do not conceive of ourselves in radical existentialist terms, and for many people today there is more need to demythologize Bultmann's individualism than there is to demythologize the New Testament's sense of the importance of community. The New Testament "myth" of existence in the body of Christ is more nearly intelligible than is Bultmann's "scientific" distinction between authentic and inauthentic existence.

When individualism is the ideal, the conclusion that Christianity gave anxious people a sense of belonging and provided for them a supportive community in a world from which (for a whole variety of reasons) they felt alienated, appears to convict Christianity of being opium for the people, a cop-out for those too weak to make it in the rough-and-tumble of life. At the very least, the "institutionalization" of the church appears as a betrayal.

When the ideal is different, when we see ourselves as *by our nature* (not simply by our choice) responsible to and for one another, Christianity's providing community does not look like an evasion of true humanity at all, but is seen rather as a condition for the realization of true humanity. The Christian community can no longer be viewed as the unfortunate and expendable shell for the timeless kerygma. One cannot be a Christian by oneself, and to try to distill from the New Testament a fundamental message which makes it both possible and necessary to be a Christian in isolation

NEW DIRECTIONS IN NEW TESTAMENT STUDY

is an attempt at alchemy by those who lack the genuine alchemist's sense of mystery.

3. Kerygmatic Variety

It is clear that many different kinds of people were deeply affected by contact with Jesus or with his immediate followers, and the New Testament is, among other things, a record of what the effects were. There seems to be no clear reason, however, why we should assume that all the effects can be boiled down to a single, central experience. For some, undoubtedly, the experience did correspond closely to what the existentialist theologians describe as the encounter with God's demand in the immediate, concrete situation for a decision: for or against faith. But others, surely, experienced the encounter with Jesus as in much greater continuity with their life and expectations as citizens of the religious community of Israel. Still others experienced the encounter with Jesus in terms of more or less developed philosophical and religious schemes, some of which we call Gnostic, some of which we call apocalyptic, some of which we call Platonic, and for some of which we are still searching for names.

At several places in this book I have suggested that there are legitimate, historical ways of judging some of these responses to be fundamentally at odds with crucial elements of Jesus' teaching and activity; that is, I believe "orthodoxy" and "heresy," while certainly not as precise for the first and second centuries as for the period subsequent to the fourth century, are nevertheless not totally loaded terms. Still, within the very broad limits covered by the term "orthodoxy" there were many different understandings and presentations of the kerygma—or rather, there were many kerygmata, for to say there were many presentations of the kerygma perpetuates the illusion that the different "presentations" are all shells containing the same kernel.

The existentialist approach begins with a portrait of the modern person drawn in bold strokes and in a single color, postulates a similarly monochromatic New Testament "world view," and through demythologization extracts from the New Testament a monochromatic kerygma which then confronts the monochromatic "modern person." Even if you cannot believe much, you can believe the little you do believe with full conviction, because it is *the* core of the New Testament—all else is beside the point, or is simply an elaboration of the point. There is some reassurance in having a proclamation, and it is even better when you know exactly what the proclamation was and therefore is. In this respect Bultmann, otherwise so unlike both the biblical prophecy advocates such as Lindsey and the occultists such as Steiner, shares a characteristic with them: Bultmann is sure he knows what the basic meaning of the New Testament is.

The situation gets murkier when you have to say that there is this point of view in the New Testament, but there is also that point of view, and indeed another one as well. The great appeal of the existentialist approach, as well as those of Lindsey and Steiner, is the availability of a short answer to the question, What is the Christian gospel? That which makes a genuinely historical approach harder to grasp, and indeed harder to get excited about, is the impossibility of giving a short answer to that question, and the necessity of saying that the question itself may be improperly put.

4. The Enigma of Jesus

The waning of the existentialist approach can be seen finally in the modifications that have been occurring within the Bultmann tradition itself. As long as the message of Jesus was thought to be a presupposition for the theology of the New Testament rather than a part of that theology itself, the quest of the historical Jesus could safely be left where Schweitzer left it—on the heap of outmoded nineteenth-century obsessions. But it eventually became clear to some of Bultmann's students that if there was to be a Jesus of history at all, he had to be a Jesus upon whom the kerygma could plausibly be based, not some other Jesus who would support some other kerygma.

The scholars were coming to understand what Origen knew seventeen centuries ago: that the particularity of Jesus is the guarantee against uncontrolled arbitrariness in the gospel—and particularity implies that we can make some statements about the activities and teaching of Jesus that are descriptions of things that actually happened and accounts of what he actually said. The new quest for the historical Jesus presupposes that what actually happened in the past is of concern to us now, indeed helps to constitute what we are now. This is a highly significant modification of the existentialist approach, an approach which holds that we are really free (and that means free from all past norms) in every moment.

The new quest for the historical Jesus is beginning to establish a relationship of dialogue between the *then* of Jesus and the *now* of our time, and it may be that Paul Ricoeur's account of what we do when we interpret texts will help to keep the dialogue alive and creative. As Henry Chadwick says, in such matters of interpretation we have to be very cautious and we must not let our hearts run away with our heads. There is another danger, however, to which New Testament scholarship has been subject: the head has been cut off from the heart. Ricoeur's potential value as a guide for New Testament study lies primarily in his understanding of interpretation as an activity of the whole person, and it is only on the basis of such an understanding that a real conversation between the human reality of a distant *then* and the human reality of a near *now* can take place.

As we saw in Chapter 6, even a latter-day convinced Bultmannian such as Norman Perrin concludes that there are a few things we can say with reasonable confidence about the historical Jesus. Two of the half dozen or so assertions he is willing to make are particularly significant for New Testament study generally.

First, the fact that Jesus was baptized by John suggests strongly that Jesus identified himself with the tradition of prophetic spiritual renewal deeply embedded in Israelite history. Despite the ambiguities surrounding Jesus' reported statements on the Law, and despite the obviously Christian bias in the New Testament reports of John the Baptist and his followers, we can say that in a highly charged symbolic action Jesus identified himself with the people of Israel, his people, and that his choice of a particular group of followers testifies both to his sense of continuity with the Israelite tradition and to his fundamentally Jewish conviction that religion is a matter of community, that the kingdom of God is *among* you.

Second, the fact that Jesus consorted with religious outcasts suggests that for him the proper response to God's challenge is not simply to move from inauthentic to authentic existence for oneself, but to find the Messiah where there is human need, and to disregard those artificial divisions by which we declare ourselves better than others. (My own advice to the British government in the matter of Ernest Digweed's will would be to assign responsibility for identifying Christ to the Salvation Army, that branch of the Christian community which has specialized in looking for Christ where he said he would be found—see Matt. 25:34–40.) There is a deep affinity between Jesus' behavior in his associations with others and the conclusion Paul draws from the doctrine of the new creation: that distinctions of slave and free, Jew and Gentile, male and female, are no longer of any effect. In both cases—the identification with a community, and the blurring of artificial distinctions—the *historical* Jesus can become normative for Christians.

B. The Jewishness of Christianity

The recognition that Jesus is inextricably woven into the fabric of Jewish tradition and life is part of a much larger development in New Testament study. The Jewishness of Christianity at its origins is being appreciated in a new way at the focal point of several converging lines of research, and particularly as a result of increasing awareness of the great variety within Judaism itself at the time when the Christian community began. Our previous failure to recognize these connections was a result of depending too much both on the Christian sense of sharp difference from Judaism, born out of conflict in the first several generations, and on the picture of first-century Judaism filtered through the biases of the Pharisaic party whose practice and belief became normative for Judaism following the Roman destruction of the Temple.

1. Qumran and John
The analysis of the Qumran documents has had at least one salutary effect on New Testament scholars in general: everyone now recognizes how risky it is to say about some motif or other in the New Testament that it "could not be characteristic" of Jewish thinking. So much in John's Gospel—the dualism, the apparent philosophical preoccupations, the symbolism—that was thought to reflect a Hellenistic milieu, is now seen to have direct analogues in the writings of a rigorously ascetic Jewish group who, in Palestine, meditated upon the Scriptures and waited expectantly for the end of the world. The discovery of what was contained in those caves by the Dead Sea has stretched permanently our capacity for conceiving variety within Judaism.

Given the Judaism within which Christianity emerged, there is potential for broadening our conception of Christianity if we take its Jewishness seriously. One could argue that Christianity was simply one sect among many others, just as exclusivist as the Sadducees or the Pharisees or the Essenes. But the book of Acts hints, at least, that the earliest Christian community found room within itself for both Palestinian Jews and Dispersion Jews (who as Christians did not get along in perfect harmony, to be sure), and perhaps the conviction of being the New Israel meant for the early Christians that they were to be inclusive of all of Israel, with its extraordinary variety.

2. Jerusalem and Paul

The new understanding of the relation between Paul and the Jerusalem church is even more indicative of a trend in New Testament study than is the influence of the Qumran documents, for this new understanding does not depend on the appearance of unanticipated source material, but on a reassessment of texts that have been available since the first century. Until quite recently the lingering influence of the Hegelian analysis of early Christianity has colored the portrayal of Jerusalem and Paul: the Palestinian gospel of Jerusalem is the thesis, the Hellenistic mystery religion of Paul arises as the antithesis, and the interaction leads to the synthesis, "early Catholicism."

Recent careful evaluations of the materials for Palestinian Christianity (primarily the Gospels and Acts) and of Paul's claims about the sources for his gospel, together with a new sensitivity to Paul's use of quotations of hymns and liturgical formulas, have led to the surprising conclusion that sacramentalism, a fair degree of metaphysics, and indeed the structure of cosmic redemption theology were already part of the church's preaching by the time Paul came upon the Christian scene. To use the memorable terminology of Shaw with which we began Chapter 7, if the image of Christ crucified was made the figurehead of a Salvationist vessel, and if the dragon of superstition was boldly set on its feet after Jesus had knocked it over, it was not Paul who did it, but those who had walked and talked with Jesus.

The discovery that the opponents who dogged Paul's heels around the periphery of the Mediterranean were in all likelihood not emissaries from the mother church, but Hellenistic Jewish Gnostics, or perhaps not even Jews at all, has placed the whole dynamic of conflict and resolution in earliest Christianity into a new framework. The Jerusalem church was more Hellenistic, and Paul less so, than has been thought by virtually all interpreters of the New Testament. Again, we are having to learn that being Jewish in the first century could mean many, many things.

It may be that in future years the Paul of Luther and Barth, the exposer of the futility of human effort to reestablish the broken relationship with God, will recede a bit into the background, and the traditional Paul, the companion of Peter in organizing and strengthening the church in Rome, will emerge from the shadows to take a place—honored, to be sure, but integrated—in the whole picture of the developing Christian community.

3. Hellenistic Synagogue and Christian Church

John Gager's work provides a sociological grounding for the new theological understanding of Paul's relationship to the Jerusalem church. Gager argues that the relative silence of our sources prior to the second century on matters of church organization does not mean there was not much organization; rather, the church was adopting the structure and much of the customary practice of the synagogue without really thinking about it, since it came so naturally to do so.

Arguments from silence are always suspect, but this one has considerable claim to be taken seriously, since Gager is able to point to specific elements of Christian practice (e.g., methods of biblical interpretation, a liturgy which gave prominent place to reading and preaching) which are almost exact copies of synagogue forms. His suggestion should prompt other scholars to look again at the early Christian sources for further evidence of unconscious adoption or adaptation of the traditions of the synagogue. We may well see in the journals more articles about the synagogue and the church, fewer about the internal developments in the priesthood, diaconate, and episcopate. The attempt to trace the sources of what would become, in the later second and subsequent centuries, the normative Catholic organization, may lead in some unexpected directions.

4. The New Testament as Part of the Bible

The most important single influence on the trend toward appreciating the Jewishness of Christianity is growing interest in and attention to the whole Bible. The study of Christian origins has got away from noticing only the specific use made of particular Old Testament texts by New Testament writers, and is now taking seriously the implications of a central fact about the earliest Christians: they thought of the Old Testament as divine revelation. Until the end of the first century, at least, what we call the Old Testament was the Bible for Christians, and for persons today to neglect the Old Testament, and to treat the New Testament as if it stands on its own, is the most serious of missteps in the attempt to apprehend and comprehend both the historical reality of early Christianity and the New Testament itself.

When 2 Timothy (3:15) reminds its recipient "how from childhood you have been acquainted with the sacred writings which are able to instruct you for salvation through faith in Christ Jesus," it is referring to the Old Testament, which is commended (v. 16) as being "profitable." New Testaments printed and sold separately from the Old Testament have no historical justification, and they perpetuate a highly distorted view of Christian origins. To pick up on a theme stated earlier in this chapter in the words of H. Richard Niebuhr, we have to look *with* Paul and the Evangelists, not *at* them—and what all of them saw was the revelation of God in the Scriptures of Israel.

C. The Wider and Deeper Context

The waning of existentialism and the increasing appreciation of the Jewishness of Christianity are part of a larger picture. Here the analysis will become somewhat less precise, since as the angle of vision widens, the sharpness of focus on any particular part of the scene diminishes. However, it seems clear that we are entering a period when the trends in New Testament scholarship are going to be set more by general shifts in orientation than by individuals springing some startling new reading of the New Testament on us.

1. Shifting Academic Orientation

The most basic shift is the one referred to in the opening chapter: the shift of the center of gravity of New Testament study from the seminaries to the universities and colleges. There is still plenty of first-rate scholarship in the institutions devoted primarily to the professional training of the clergy, and professors in that environment are reminded daily that they must make sense to women and men who will have to make sense of the gospel in a lifetime of preaching and pastoral care. Still, the proliferation of departments of religion in academic institutions of all kinds, including many state universities, has opened up a wide range of new academic contexts in which the study of the New Testament and Christian origins can be pursued.

The questions and concerns in such contexts tend to be different from those in seminaries, although as I have indicated at several points in this book, it is not at all clear that increasingly "secular" attention to the New Testament necessarily leads to a more "secularized" interpretation. On the contrary, the placing of the New Testament in a wider context of religious study is leading to a recovery of some of its dimensions that have been lost in the scrambling theological and homiletical effort to keep New Testament interpretation abreast of the latest turning taken by secularized Western persons. A case could even be made that the obsession with theology has blunted our perception of the religious depth and breadth of the New Testament, and that in so-called "secular" departments of religion, where the theological passion is cooled, the rich reality of early Christian experience is being uncovered by means of an analysis that does not have its theological conclusions already formulated. The uncovering of this reality has intellectual significance, and may also have practical benefit for the pastoral interpretation of the New Testament to modern persons, who turn out to be a good deal more complex than some recent theological interpreters have been willing to recognize.

2. New Testament and the Study of Religion

The last hundred years have seen an explosive growth in our knowledge of religions, extended both through space, with researches in remote parts of the world, and through time, with the recovery of whole civilizations hitherto unknown or only dimly perceived. No one can master it all, but some, such as Mircea Eliade, who have mastered a lot of it have detected certain patterns in the mass of data which suggest some basic elements of religious orientation in human nature and culture. In terms of this kind of study, the New Testament displays some of the patterns, particularly in rites of baptism and Eucharist. Healings, nature miracles, acted signs, richly metaphorical language are all characteristic of many religions in many times and places, and questions begin to be raised about the uniqueness of Christianity.

The New Testament does include some exclusivist claims ("No one comes to the Father, but by me"—John 14:6; "There is no other name under heaven . . . by which we must be saved"—Acts 4:12; etc.), but there are also the "openings to the outside" of Paul's Areopagus speech and the first chapter of his letter to the Romans, and there were several second-century Christian writers who wanted to cast the Christian net wide enough to gather in all sound teaching and all virtuous persons. In any case, it is not self-evidently clear that the diminishing of Christianity's uniqueness diminishes its worth. The biblical tradition itself is full of moments when God's truth has to break through the system in which it had been enshrined.

There is an enormous literature on this whole question, growing largely out of missionary experience, and it is not the purpose of this brief mention of the issue to deal with it adequately. It is to the point, however, to note that Donald K. Swearer has recently demonstrated, in *Dialogue: The Key to Understanding Other Religions,* how certain basic New Testament concepts and images—being in the world but not of it, the new creation, self-emptying, faith and works, liberation, community—are given fresh *and specifically Christian* cogency as a result of sustained, serious dialogue with committed Buddhists. Doctrines which on the surface appear contradictory, such as the biblical view of creation and the Buddhist view of the unreality of the world, turn out to cast light on one another instead of annihilating one another when they come into contact in a genuine dialogue between religious persons. Swearer's book confirms a hunch of C. S. Lewis', that "those who are at the heart" of their different traditions "are all closer to one another than those who are at the fringes."[14]

3. New Testament and Myth

The "study of the Bible as literature" has for many years been a device by which biblical study has been "laundered" to make it presentable in certain corners of the academic marketplace, and New Testament scholars have often treated such endeavors as outside the scope of serious study of the subject. Ironically, however, students who learned the Bible *as literature* may have been better served than those who were brought up on one or another theological mode of interpretation.

The New Testament is not "great literature" by any commonly accepted standards, but literary critics, whether they are dealing with stylistic masterpieces or with popular religious tracts (such as the Gospels), are sensitive to the many different ways in which texts speak. Many literary analysts are versed in the theories of Freud and/or Jung, and have antennae that pick up signals that can be conveyed *only* through metaphorical and mythical language. To study the mode of New Testament language—story, symbol, metaphor, image—is to gain an appreciation of the timeliness, as well as of the timelessness, of the mythological frame of mind. The gift that religion can offer people today is not demythologization, but a renewal of the sense of mystery that is conveyed only in myth. If you demythologize the New Testament, people will look elsewhere for what you have eliminated, and the wide popularity of Tolkien's Middle Earth, of Lewis' Narnia, of *Watership Down,* of *Star Wars,* of science fiction itself, suggests that modern persons are quite sophisticated about myth, and hungry for it. Study of the New Testament "as literature" can be a convenient way of evading the religious questions. It can also be a way of bringing genuine religious questions to the surface.

IV. NEW TESTAMENT STUDY AND THE NOBEL PRIZE

New Testament study, like every field, reflects major shifts in society and academic fashion. This book has concentrated on trends that can be illustrated by many examples. It remains true, however, that New Testament study, like every field, goes where it does—indeed, exists at all—because certain persons, for reasons they themselves probably do not fully understand, devote themselves to the mastery and advancement of the field.

There is no Nobel Prize for New Testament study, but two eminent New Testament scholars have been recipients of the Nobel Peace Prize (one for his own work, one for the work of the organization he headed), and this book can fittingly conclude with a look at these two careers. To think about Albert Schweitzer (1875–1965) and Henry J. Cadbury (1883–1974), near contemporaries who both lived to the age of ninety, may serve as a useful reminder that New Testament study is, when all is said and done, the work of students of the New Testament.

Albert Schweitzer was eight years old when Henry Cadbury was born, and had made several of his momentous contributions to New Testament study by the time Cadbury was in college at Haverford. Schweitzer, partly at least, out of his sense that the scholarly investigation of the New Testament was making an intellectual apprehension of Jesus and his significance more and more problematical, chose to heed the call "Follow me" into direct practical medical service to people in need, in the expectation that in such a way one might discover who Jesus is.

Cadbury stayed with the scholarly enterprise throughout his long and productive life. He was at the forefront of New Testament study, but his service at the front was of a special kind. He knew exactly what everyone was doing, and he had an unerring instinct for the dangers of excess in the various schools of interpretation that developed during his career. As a warning to the liberals who would make Jesus into a late nineteenth-century political reformer, Cadbury wrote a book called *The Peril of Modernizing Jesus.* When the neo-orthodox, whether of the right, as with Barth, or of the left, as with Bultmann, tried in their various ways to extract the kerygma from history to confront contemporary persons with it directly, Cadbury published an article called "The Peril of Archaizing Ourselves." Perhaps it was the discipline of Quaker silence that kept Cadbury from being mesmerized by the Sirens calling to this or that side of New Testament studies.

While staying with the scholarly enterprise, Cadbury devoted much energy also to the American Friends Service Committee (he was its chairman 1928–1934 and 1944–1960), and it was in his capacity as chairman of that committee that he accepted, for the AFSC (along with the Friends Service Council of England) the

Nobel Peace Prize in 1947, five years before Schweitzer was to receive it for his lifetime's work at Lambaréné in Africa. Both men, from very different backgrounds (Alsatian Lutheran and American Quaker), gave practical expression to their sense of what the New Testament means, and the award of the Nobel Prize in both instances shows that when the Peace witness of Christianity is made real in act, the world takes notice.

We can never know the full range of reasons why Schweitzer decided to change careers and why Cadbury remained an academic throughout his life, but a clue is offered in a memorial tribute to Cadbury, written by his longtime friend and colleague Amos Wilder.[15]

Wilder points out first of all that many decades before redaction criticism (the study of the Evangelists as creative theologians in their own right) was all the rage in New Testament scholarship, Cadbury was doing just that in his masterful studies of the Gospel of Luke and the book of Acts. If on the one hand Cadbury debunked the commonly held and somewhat romantic assumption that Luke was clearly a physician because of medical terminology in his writings—with a wry sense of humor Cadbury even wrote an article called "Luke Among the Horse Doctors," in which he demonstrated parallels between Luke's language and that of an ancient veterinary manual—on the other hand he established Luke's claim to a place among early Christian theologians.

Wilder goes on from there to make a second, and crucial, point: Cadbury was always aware of the variety of early Christianity, even at its origins. He was constitutionally suspicious of any claim to have found *the* key to the meaning of the New Testament, whether that be the ethic of Jesus or the primitive kerygma or justification by faith or the fight against Gnosticism. Wilder is, in short, crediting Cadbury with a genuine and sustained *historical* understanding of the New Testament and Christian origins—that is, theology grows out of history and is not imposed on it. And since history is by its nature incomplete, subject to revision, full of both promise and peril, so is biblical interpretation a never-ending process of working our way between the twin perils of modernizing the past and archaizing ourselves.

I believe it is because Cadbury found New Testament study to be an experience of opening up and broadening out rather than of closing down and narrowing in, as it appears to have become for Schweitzer, that he was able with commitment and enthusiasm to devote himself to the *intellectual* quest for an understanding of Christian origins while at the same time providing leadership for the eminently practical American Friends Service Committee. Henry Cadbury was arguing for a balanced approach to the New Testament that takes into proper account a whole range of techniques and kinds of questions, and does not expect to find *the* answer by any one of them, or indeed by a combination of them, because the subject matter itself reflects the elusive complexity of experience.

A question which has been both implicit and explicit in this book is that of the relation of the academic study of the New Testament to the role of the Bible in the church—to pick up the titles of two books which served as a focus in Chapter 2, how does "the New Testament in current study" relate to "the church's use of the Bible: past and present"? There is no short answer to the question; if there were, this book would have ended many pages ago. But the study of the New Testament is opening up the New Testament, lowering the power of magnification, so to speak, from the extraordinarily high-powered focus on the kerygma which has dominated both scholarship and the training of pastors. What now appears under the microscope is a variety of forms, indeed of living forms. The New Testament is not a momentary call to decision frozen on a slide, but a drop of water full of living creatures that are influencing one another's behavior. My experience over several years with groups of church people in discussion of biblical and more general religious subjects has persuaded me that this opening up of the New Testament, the admission of variety, the appreciation of the interplay of myth and history both then *and now,* is what persons of this age are calling for as they look to the Bible to help them chart their pilgrimage.

This is not something radically new. Sober and learned persons have known that the academy's commitment to truth cannot but be of service to the church. One of these, preeminently, was Henry Cadbury. What he knew and expressed through a lifetime of productive scholarship, during which he thought of both his writing and his AFSC work as exercises in the interpretation of the New Testament, was a truth put memorably by Matthew Arnold (who,

we might note, was making a lecture tour of America the year
Cadbury was born). In *Culture and Anarchy*, Arnold wrote, "Not
a having and a resting, but a growing and a becoming, is the
character of perfection as culture conceives it; and here, too, it
coincides with religion."[16] We need not make any claims for perfection; our hands balk at writing such terms which flowed rather
freely from nineteenth-century pens. But: "Not a having and a
resting"; rather: "A growing and a becoming." That is what New
Testament study is. That is what study is finding in the New Testament. It is a new direction.

NOTES

Preface

1. John Meagher, *The Gathering of the Ungifted: Toward a Dialogue on Christian Identity* (Herder & Herder, 1972), p. 11.

Chapter One. THE NEW CONTEXT OF NEW TESTAMENT STUDY

1. Theodotus, in Clement of Alexandria, *Excerpta ex Theodoto* 78.2, in J. Stevenson, ed., *A New Eusebius: Documents Illustrative of the History of the Church to A.D. 337* (London: S.P.C.K., 1957), No. 49.

2. Jaroslav Pelikan, *The Emergence of the Catholic Tradition (100–600)*, The Christian Tradition, Vol. 1 (University of Chicago Press, 1971), p. 1.

3. C. S. Lewis, *Surprised by Joy: The Shape of My Early Life* (London: Geoffrey Bles, 1955), p. 195: "I still had all the chronological snobbery of my period and used the names of earlier periods as terms of abuse."

4. Informal discussions of the matter have been the stuff of countless conversations at professional meetings. The first major study is a working paper of the Rockefeller Foundation, "University Divinity Schools: A Report on Ecclesiastically Independent Theological Education," by George Lindbeck in collaboration with Karl Deutsch and Nathan Glazer, and published in 1976. The report acknowledges some benefits in the new situation, but does not view it as positively as I do. Lindbeck provides a summary of the report in the *Bulletin* of The Council on the Study of Religion, Vol. 8, No. 4 (October 1977), pp. 85–89.

5. Augustine, *Confessions* VI.v.8, trans. F. J. Sheed (Sheed ·& Ward, 1943), p. 112; Gregory the Great, *Moralia,* prefatory letter c. 4, J.-P. Migne, *Patrologia Latina* 75.515A.

6. For an introduction to ecumenical developments with implications for New Testament study, see Gerald H. Anderson and Thomas F. Stransky, eds., *Mission Trends No. 3—Third World Theologies* (Paulist Press, 1976), and *Mission Trends No. 4—Liberation Theologies in North America and Europe* (Wm. B. Eerdmans Publishing Co., 1978).

7. Literature of and about liberation theology has become extensive since the "birth" of the movement early in this decade. For a sensitive analysis of its significance for the church (including biblical interpretation), see Monika K. H. Hellwig, "Liberation Theology: An Emerging School," *Scottish Journal of Theology,* Vol. 30, No. 2 (1977), pp. 137–151.

8. See Nicolas A. Nissiotis, "The Theology of the Church and Its Accomplishment," *The Ecumenical Review,* Vol. 29, No. 1 (1977), pp. 62–76. Significantly, the article was the introductory address to the Second Congress of Orthodox Theological Colleges, Athens, August 1976 (the First Congress was held in 1936).

9. James D. G. Dunn, *Unity and Diversity in the New Testament: An Inquiry Into the Character of Earliest Christianity* (Westminster Press, 1977), and *Jesus and the Spirit: A Study of the Religious and Charismatic Experience of Jesus and the First Christians as Reflected in the New Testament* (Westminster Press, 1975). For an interesting illustration of a more general dynamic movement within conservative evangelicalism, see Jack Rogers, *Confessions of a Conservative Evangelical* (Westminster Press, 1974). Rogers is professor of theology at Fuller Theological Seminary in Pasadena, California, an institution that has made some significant moves in an ecumenical direction.

10. Reginald H. Fuller, *The New Testament in Current Study* (Charles Scribner's Sons, 1962), pp. 134–135.

11. Barth used this image in 1927 (*Die Lehre vom Worte Gottes: Prolegomena zur christlichen Dogmatik,* p. ix) to describe what had happened in 1919; the passage is rendered in English by Paul L. Lehmann, "The Changing Course of a Corrective Theology," *Theology Today,* Vol. 13, No. 3 (1956), p. 334.

Chapter Two. THINKING HISTORICALLY

1. Interview with Henry Ford in the *Chicago Tribune,* May 25, 1916; quoted in John B. Rae, ed., *Henry Ford* (Prentice-Hall, 1969), pp. 53–54. As Rae points out, there is no authentic record of Ford's ever having made the unequivocal statement often attributed to him, "History is bunk."

2. Rae, *Ford,* p. 54, cited from State of Michigan, Circuit Court for the County of Macomb, Transcript of Testimony, *Henry Ford* v. *Chicago Tribune Co.,* VIII, 5277. For an extended account of the trial, which became something of a national sensation, see Allan Nevins and Frank Ernest Hill, *Ford: Expansion and Challenge 1915–1933* (Charles Scribner's Sons, 1957), pp. 129–142.

3. "Dover Beach," in Archibald L. Bouton, ed., *Matthew Arnold: Prose and Poetry* (Charles Scribner's Sons, 1927), p. 495. The Bible as literature is the theme of much of Arnold's prose, especially *Literature and Dogma: An Essay Towards a Better Apprehension of the Bible* (1873; 5th ed., London: Smith, Elder and Co., 1876).

4. Van A. Harvey, *The Historian and the Believer: The Morality of Historical Knowledge and Christian Belief* (Macmillan Co., 1966).

NOTES TO PAGES 29–34

5. The cornerstone: College Church of Christ, Abilene, Texas. The cornerstone could be read, of course, in a way that takes history seriously; I believe the implication of the wording, however, is that what was erected in 1951 houses a fairly direct copy of what was established in A.D. 33. Rudolf Bultmann, *Faith and Understanding, I,* ed. Robert W. Funk (Harper & Row, Publishers, 1969), p. 132.

6. Roland H. Bainton, *Here I Stand: A Life of Martin Luther* (Abingdon-Cokesbury Press, 1950), p. 185, notes that the words "Here I stand, I cannot do other," although in the earliest printed version of the Diet of Worms, were not recorded on the spot; he suggests, however, that they may well be genuine. In any case, they are very much "in character" for Luther. *Fiddler on the Roof,* book by Joseph Stein, music by Jerry Bock, lyrics by Sheldon Harnick (Pocket Books, 1965), pp. 73 and 124.

7. Samuel Butler, *Erewhon Revisited* (E. P. Dutton & Co., 1910), ch. 14, p. 169. It is only fair to add that the following sentence reads: "Painters, my father now realized, can do all that historians can, with even greater effect."

8. Henry Chadwick, "The Bible and the Greek Fathers," in D. E. Nineham, ed., *The Church's Use of the Bible: Past and Present* (London: S.P.C.K., 1963), p. 26. In this passage Chadwick, in the manner of the church fathers, deftly weaves together allusions to Ezek. 37:1–14 and Heb. 11:4.

9. Samuel Sandmel, *The First Christian Century in Judaism and Christianity: Certainties and Uncertainties* (Oxford University Press, 1969), pp. vii–viii.

10. Leopold von Ranke, *Geschichten der romanischen und germanischen Völker von 1492 bis 1535* (1824), preface ("wie es eigentlich gewesen"). Georg G. Iggers and Konrad von Moltke, eds., Leopold von Ranke, *The Theory and Practice of History* (Bobbs-Merrill Co., 1973), "Introduction," pp. xix–xx, argue that Ranke has been seriously misunderstood, especially in America, because *eigentlich* has been traditionally translated "actually," but really means "essentially," so that the statement becomes "how, essentially, things happened" (p. 137). The important point for our purposes, however, is how Ranke has been understood, whether correctly or not.

11. Sandmel, *First Christian Century,* p. 7.

12. Sandmel, *First Christian Century,* p. 37 (italics added).

13. The remark was made by Professor George A. Kennedy, Paddison Professor of Classics at the University of North Carolina, during a session of the "Colloquy on the Relationships Among the Gospels" held at Trinity University, San Antonio, Texas, May 26–29, 1977, under the joint sponsorship of the university and the Southwest Commission on Religious Studies. Kennedy was responding to a question about his use of the evidence from a second-century Christian writer, Papias, as a credible source in his paper "Classical and Christian Source Criticism," published in the Colloquy volume, *The Relationships Among the Gospels: An Interdisciplinary Dialogue,* ed. William O. Walker, Jr. (Trinity University Press,

1978), pp. 125–155, at pp. 147–152. Kennedy reminded the New Testament scholars that "ancient writers sometimes meant what they said and occasionally even knew what they were talking about" (p. 126). While some at the Colloquy expressed reservations about the details of his argument (Wayne A. Meeks, the official respondent, called his own paper *"Hypomnemata* [Notes] from an Untamed Sceptic: A Response to George Kennedy" [pp. 157–172]), everyone agreed that "as a result of Kennedy's essay and the subsequent discussion, New Testament scholars have been challenged to take more seriously the external evidence regarding the origin of the Gospels than they have been wont to do in the recent past" (Reginald H. Fuller, "Classics and the Gospels: The Seminar," pp. 173–192, at p. 183). (I wish to thank Professor Albert C. Outler of Southern Methodist University, who was the keynote speaker at the Colloquy, for calling these matters to my attention, and especially for his reminiscences of the discussion following the paper.)

14. This story, which I heard reported in an undergraduate course lecture twenty years ago, may be apocryphal—but like most such stories, it highlights (even if it caricatures) a genuine aspect of the person concerned.

15. Walter C. Sellar and Robert J. Yeatman, *1066 and All That: A Memorable History of England* (E. P. Dutton & Co., 1931), p. vii.

16. Augustine speaks often of memory, piling up (and mixing) metaphors to convey his sense of its vastness and mystery; see, for instance, *Confessions* X.viii.15, where *thesaurus* ("treasure chest") and *aula* ("hall, chamber") are mixed with the idea of depth (*quis ad fundum eius pervenit?* —"who has plumbed its depths?") (Loeb Classical Library, Augustine, *Confessions,* Vol. 2, pp. 96–99).

17. Paul J. Achtemeier, *An Introduction to the New Hermeneutic* (Westminster Press, 1969), pp. 18–19.

Chapter Three. QUESTIONS ANCIENT AND MODERN

1. On the extent of the Marcionite church, see E. C. Blackman, *Marcion and His Influence* (London: S.P.C.K., 1948), p. 3.

2. Irenaeus, *Against Heresies* I.27.2, in Stevenson, *A New Eusebius* (above, Ch. 1, n. 1), No. 73. The sources for Marcion are not entirely consistent; some suggest he taught a "just" creator, others say his creator was portrayed as "vindictive." It is likely that this illustrates a spectrum of views within the Marcionite church.

3. Leander E. Keck, *A Future for the Historical Jesus: The Place of Jesus in Preaching and Theology* (Abingdon Press, 1971), argues strongly against portrayals of Jesus that depend on methods which put him *by definition* at direct odds with his Jewishness.

4. Marcion's wealth: Tertullian, *On Prescription Against Heretics* 30, in Stevenson, *A New Eusebius,* No. 75.

5. There is a growing literature on "Jewish-Christianity," concerned

with definitions as well as with assessments of the evidence. Dunn, *Unity and Diversity* (above, Ch. 1, n. 9), ch. 11 (pp. 235–266), provides a thorough survey of evidence and developments. For a more succinct account, see Aloys Grillmeier, S.J., *Christ in Christian Tradition,* 2d rev. ed., Vol. 1: *From the Apostolic Age to Chalcedon (451),* trans. John Bowden (John Knox Press, 1975), pp. 37–41.

6. Justin Martyr, *Dialogue with Trypho* 47.1–4, in Stevenson, *A New Eusebius,* No. 43.

7. Concerning the 318: *Letter of Barnabas* 9.8, in Loeb Classical Library, *Apostolic Fathers,* pp. 372–373. Justin accusing Jews of bad faith in their use of the Hebrew Scriptures: *Dialogue with Trypho* 84–85, in Fathers of the Church, *Writings of Saint Justin Martyr,* pp. 281–285.

8. For Origen, the best introduction is still the article by B. F. Westcott in *Dictionary of Christian Biography,* now a century old. See also Jean Daniélou, *Origen,* trans. Walter Mitchell (Sheed & Ward, 1955). For Origen as biblical interpreter: R. P. C. Hanson, *Allegory and Event: A Study of the Sources and Significance of Origen's Interpretation of Scripture* (London: SCM Press, 1959).

9. Origen, *On First Principles* IV.iii.5, ed. G. W. Butterworth (Harper Torchbooks, 1966), p. 297. Augustine, *City of God* XVII.3, ed. David Knowles, trans. Henry Bettenson (Penguin Books, 1972), p. 715; see also XVI.2, pp. 652–653. Thomas Aquinas, *Summa Theologiae* Ia.1.10, appeals to Augustine in support of his own view that "nothing necessary for faith is contained under the spiritual sense that is not openly conveyed through the literal sense elsewhere" (Latin text and English translation; McGraw-Hill Book Co., Blackfriars Edition, pp. 38–39).

10. Origen, *Homilies on Joshua* 21.1, in R. B. Tollinton, trans., *Selections from the Commentaries and Homilies of Origen* (London: S.P.C.K., 1929), p. 148 (italics added).

11. I have presented the evidence for this, and have argued for its significance, in "Plutarch and Origen on Theology and Language," to be published in the Proceedings of the Seventh International Conference on Patristic Studies.

12. Rudolf Bultmann, *Primitive Christianity in Its Contemporary Setting* (London: Thames and Hudson, 1956; currently available as a Meridian–New American Library paperback).

13. Schubert M. Ogden, "On Revelation," in John Deschner, Leroy T. Howe, and Klaus Penzel, eds., *Our Common History as Christians: Essays in Honor of Albert C. Outler* (Oxford University Press, 1975), pp. 261–292. There is a reference in the text to Gen. 1:31, but only to illustrate a Lutheran and Reformed position. Early in the article Ogden states (p. 262) that the test of a systematic theological statement is its "congruence with the witness of faith of the New Testament."

14. Sandmel, *First Christian Century* (above, Ch. 2, n. 9), pp. 28–33.

15. There is no better way to get a sense for the variety of Christian literature in the second century than to dip into Edgar Hennecke and

278   NOTES TO PAGES 52–56

Wilhelm Schneemelcher, eds., *New Testament Apocrypha,* trans. R. McL. Wilson, 2 vols. (Westminster Press, 1963). On the question of the canon specifically, and of the influence of Marcion on it, see Vol. 1, ch. 2 ("The History of the New Testament Canon"), pp. 28–60. For a fresh and theologically compelling analysis of the continuing function of the New Testament canon, see Dunn, *Unity and Diversity,* pp. 374–388.

16. Elaine H. Pagels, *The Gnostic Paul: Gnostic Exegesis of the Pauline Letters* (Fortress Press, 1975). Pagels considers the question how Paul, who is treated by Irenaeus as being staunchly anti-Gnostic, could have been seen by the Gnostics as one of their own teachers. "To read Paul either way—as hypergnostic or hyperorthodox—is to read unhistorically, attempting to interpret the apostle's theology in terms of categories formulated in second-century debate. On the other hand, whoever takes account of the total evidence may learn from the debate to approach Pauline exegesis with renewed openness to the texts" (p. 164). I will attempt to show, in Chapter 7, that the Gnostics distorted Paul more than the orthodox did.

17. George Moore, *The Apostle: A Drama in Three Acts* (Dublin: Maunsel and Co., 1911): Paul: "O blasphemy! blasphemy! Jesus of Nazareth, the great mediator between God and man, sitteth at the right hand of his father, and it is in his name that I strike thee down. (Jesus falls; Paul draws back shocked by the rash blow. He advances towards the body and perceives that it is a dead man. After a moment's pause he speaks.) It is well that he died, though the blow was not of my motion, but came from God even as the lightning. . . . If that man has spoken a lie he is worthy of death, and Christianity is saved by his dying; but if he spake the truth?" (pp. 99–100). In *The Brook Kerith* (Macmillan Co., 1917), a long novel, Moore develops his basic idea (with more attention to Jesus), and at the end Paul does not kill Jesus, but receives assurances from Jesus that the true story will remain hidden. This then becomes the conclusion to a revised edition of *The Apostle* (London: William Heinemann, Ltd., 1923). Moore's idea is fundamentally different from that of Hugh J. Schonfield, who, in *The Passover Plot* (Bantam Books, 1967), has Jesus' survival of the crucifixion part of a deliberate scheme on Jesus' part. (There will be considerable discussion of the Essene sect in Chapter 4.)

18. Irenaeus, *Against Heresies* III.11.8, in Stevenson, *A New Eusebius,* No. 98.

19. Irenaeus, *Against Heresies* III.11.7, in Cyril C. Richardson, ed., *Early Christian Fathers,* Library of Christian Classics, Vol. 1 (Westminster Press, 1953), pp. 381–382.

20. Augustine, *The Harmony of the Gospels (De consensu evangelistarum),* trans. S. D. F. Salmond, in *Nicene and Post-Nicene Fathers,* Vol. 6 (Christian Literature Co., 1888), pp. 67–236.

21. Jaroslav Pelikan, *Development of Christian Doctrine: Some Historical Prolegomena* (Yale University Press, 1969), p. 12: "Even more than the related problem of authority, doctrinal development may be seen as the

question at issue between Roman Catholic dogma and the several theological positions within Protestantism."

22. Heracleon: Elaine H. Pagels, *The Johannine Gospel in Gnostic Exegesis: Heracleon's Commentary on John,* Society of Biblical Literature Monograph Series, No. 17 (Abingdon Press, 1973). Ptolemy: selections from his Letter to Flora, in Stevenson, *A New Eusebius,* No. 69. Tertullian on arguments with heretics over Scripture: "A controversy over the Scriptures can, clearly, produce no other effect than help to upset either the stomach or the brain," *On Prescription Against Heretics* 16–19, in *The Ante-Nicene Fathers,* Vol. 3, pp. 251–252.

23. Origen, *On First Principles* IV.ii.9–iii.5 (pp. 285–297).

24. *De Doctrina Christiana,* usually translated as *On Christian Doctrine,* as by D. W. Robertson, Jr., trans. (Library of Liberal Arts; Bobbs-Merrill Co., 1958). Augustine states his program at the beginning (I.i.1): "There are two things necessary to the treatment of the Scriptures: a way of discovering those things which are to be understood, and a way of teaching what we have learned" (p. 7). That, briefly put, is the task of the scholar—and Augustine demonstrates that it is not as easy as it looks.

25. For a sharp and timely critique of the influence of the human potential movement in our culture, see William Kilpatrick, *Identity and Intimacy* (Delta Books, 1975). Kilpatrick notes that existentialism, with its insistence that we are *deciding* creatures, works against the ideal of the "fluid" self; but there is, in both ways of thinking, inattention to our links with tradition and community.

26. Achtemeier, *New Hermeneutic* (above, Ch. 2, n. 17).

27. Achtemeier, *New Hermeneutic,* pp. 162–164.

28. I do not pretend to a full understanding of Structuralism, which has developed a highly technical vocabulary and produced an immense literature. I do believe, however, that I have properly understood some of its chief implications for New Testament interpretation. For a more thorough treatment, see Daniel Patte, *What Is Structural Exegesis?* Guides to Biblical Scholarship Series (Fortress Press, 1976); also Alfred M. Johnson, ed. and trans., *The New Testament and Structuralism,* Pittsburgh Theological Monograph Series, No. 11 (Pickwick Press, 1976).

29. The Ricoeur bibliography is already vast; there is a useful guide by Loretta Dornisch, "Paul Ricoeur and Biblical Interpretation: A Selected Bibliography," in *Semeia,* Vol. 4 (1975), pp. 23–26. The discussion of Ricoeur in the remainder of this chapter will draw on *Philosophical Hermeneutics and Theological Hermeneutics: Ideology, Utopia, and Faith* (Berkeley: The Center for Hermeneutical Studies in Hellenistic and Modern Culture [Protocol of the seventeenth colloquy, November 4, 1975], 1976).

30. Ricoeur, p. 16.
31. Ricoeur, p. 45.
32. Ricoeur, pp. 3,6.
33. Ricoeur, p. 47.
34. Ricoeur, p. 54.

35. Ricoeur, p. 40.

36. Inside front cover of Protocol No. 17 (above, n. 29).

37. *Semeia,* Vol. 8, p. vii. (*Sēmeia,* sing. *sēmeion,* is the Greek word for "sign"; in the New Testament it is particularly prominent in the Gospel of John, where Jesus' actions, such as the turning of water into wine at the wedding feast in Cana, are often designated as *sēmeia.*)

Chapter Four. THE JEWISH MATRIX

1. George Foot Moore, *Judaism in the First Centuries of the Christian Era: The Age of the Tannaim,* 2 vols. (Schocken Books, 1971) (orig. published by Harvard University Press, 1927, 1930, in three vols.; the third vol. contained the notes; in the Schocken edition the notes are divided and published with each volume of the text). There is no relation between this Moore and the dramatist/novelist George Moore, cited above, Ch. 3, n. 17.

2. Josephus, *Antiquities* XVII–XX; *Jewish War* II; *Life* 2, 38 (Loeb Classical Library, *Josephus,* Vols. I, II, VIII, IX).

3. Sandmel, *First Christian Century* (above, Ch. 2, n. 9), pp. 33–34, and esp. n. 69.

4. Sandmel, *First Christian Century,* p. 68.

5. Richard L. Rubenstein, *My Brother Paul* (Harper & Row, Publishers, 1972), p. 117.

6. Raymond E. Brown, *The Gospel According to John (i–xii)* (The Anchor Bible; Doubleday & Co., 1966), pp. lxx–lxxiii: "John is not anti-Semitic; the Evangelist is condemning not race or people but opposition to Jesus" (p. lxxii).

7. Sandmel, *First Christian Century,* p. 54, n. 65; also pp. 127–128.

8. Pelikan, *Emergence* (above, Ch. 1, n. 2), p. 12.

9. Edmund Wilson, *The Scrolls from the Dead Sea* (Oxford University Press, 1955); most of the material had appeared previously in *The New Yorker.* A revised edition, *The Dead Sea Scrolls 1947–1969,* was published (London: W. H. Allen) in 1969.

10. S. T. Bindoff, *Tudor England,* The Pelican History of England, Vol. 5 (Penguin Books, 1950), p. 23.

11. Mark Vonnegut, *The Eden Express* (Praeger Publishers, 1975).

12. For an analysis of the disputes over the influences at work on the Gospel of John, see Linwood Urban and Patrick Henry, " 'Before Abraham Was, I Am': Does Philo Explain John 8:56–58?" in *Studia Philonica,* 6 (1979). We argue there for a partial revival of the recently muted theory that there is Philonic influence in John.

13. Sir W. M. Ramsay, article "Travel" in *Hastings Dictionary of the Bible,* quoted in Adolf Harnack, *The Mission and Expansion of Christianity in the First Three Centuries,* trans. James Moffatt (Harper Torchbook, 1962), p. 369, n. 1. Pages 369–380 of Harnack's book concern the extraordinary amount of travel by Christians in the early centuries.

14. W. D. Davies, "Apocalyptic and Pharisaism," *The Expository Times,*

59 (1948), pp. 233–237, reprinted in Davies, *Christian Origins and Judaism* (London: Darton, Longman and Todd, Ltd., 1962; reissued in series The Jewish People: History, Religion, Literature, Arno Press, 1973), pp. 19–30.

15. Sandmel, *First Christian Century,* pp. 23–24.

16. Martin Hengel, *Judaism and Hellenism: Studies in Their Encounter in Palestine During the Early Hellenistic Period,* trans. by John Bowden (from the 2d rev. and enlarged ed. of the German, 1973), 2 vols. (2d vol. is the notes) (Fortress Press, 1974), Vol. 1, p. 1.

17. Hengel, *Judaism and Hellenism,* Vol. 1, pp. 4–5.

18. Sandmel, *First Christian Century,* pp. 20–21.

19. Arnaldo Momigliano, review of Hengel in *Journal of Theological Studies,* n.s. Vol. 21 (1970), pp. 149–153; Momigliano questions whether we know enough about the Judaism that underwent Hellenization to detect when it has in fact been Hellenized. Momigliano's book: *Alien Wisdom: The Limits of Hellenization* (Cambridge University Press, 1976).

20. Hengel, *Judaism and Hellenism,* Vol. 1, p. 105.

21. Meeks, "Response to Kennedy" (above, Ch. 2, n. 13), pp. 163–164, with references to the main literature on the subject.

22. Hengel, *Judaism and Hellensim,* Vol. 1, p. 104.

23. Hengel, *Judaism and Hellenism,* Vol. 1, pp. 300–301.

24. Hengel, *Judaism and Hellenism,* Vol. 1, p. 312.

25. Hengel, *Judaism and Hellenism,* Vol. 1, pp. 311–312.

26. The historical case for the novelty of Jewish and Christian insistence on conversion in the ancient world has been brilliantly made by Arthur Darby Nock, *Conversion: The Old and the New in Religion from Alexander the Great to Augustine of Hippo* (Oxford University Press, 1933; paperback, 1961).

27. Josephus, *Antiquities* XX.9.1, in Stevenson, *A New Eusebius* (above, Ch. 1, n. 1), No. 1. The new high priest, Ananus, delivered James and some others to be stoned. "But those who seemed the most equitable of the citizens, and accurate in legal matters, disliked what was done," and they succeeded in having King Agrippa remove Ananus from office after he had held it only three months.

28. Pelikan, *Emergence,* p. 14.

29. Steven Runciman, *The Eastern Schism: A Study of the Papacy and the Eastern Churches During the XIth and XIIth Centuries* (Oxford: Clarendon Press, 1955), p. 4: "In fact, the state of schism only came into being when the average member of each Church felt it to be there; and that feeling developed slowly over a period of years and cannot be attached to any single date."

Chapter Five. THE GNOSTIC CHALLENGE

1. The literature on Gnosticism in general, and on Nag Hammadi in particular, is vast and getting vaster. A recent introduction for nonspecialists is John Dart, *The Laughing Savior: The Discovery and Significance of the*

Nag Hammadi Library (Harper & Row, Publishers, 1976). For the specific question of the relationship of Gnosticism to the New Testament, see R. McL. Wilson, *Gnosis and the New Testament* (Fortress Press, 1968).

2. While the Nag Hammadi materials have made possible some corrections of the portrayal of Gnosticism in the anti-Gnostic writings of the church fathers, it is increasingly evident that the fathers did not fabricate their opponents' views; what distortion there is comes from selection, not from invention. It is still legitimate to use materials from the writings of the fathers to characterize Gnosticism.

3. Basilides, as reported by Hippolytus, *Refutation of All Heresies* VII. 23.3, 24.3–4, in Stevenson, *A New Eusebius* (above, Ch. 1, n. 1), No. 53. Basilides identifies the Second Archon with the God of the Old Testament.

4. Theodotus (above, Ch. 1, n. 1).

5. Hans Jonas, "Delimitation of the Gnostic Phenomenon—Typological and Historical," in Ugo Bianchi, ed., *Le origini dello gnosticismo: Texts and Discussions of the Colloquium of Messina, 1966* (Supplements to *Numen*, XII; Leiden: E. J. Brill, 1970), pp. 90–108. This article is the best brief analysis of Gnosticism that I know. See also Jonas' book, *The Gnostic Religion: The Message of the Alien God and the Beginnings of Christianity*, 2d rev. ed. (Beacon Press, 1963).

6. Irenaeus, *Against Heresies* V, Preface (*Ante-Nicene Fathers*, Vol. 1, p. 526). The same notion was expressed classically for Greek Christianity by Athanasius of Alexandria in the fourth century: "He became man that we might become divine," *De Incarnatione* 54, in Robert W. Thomson, ed. and trans., *Athanasius Contra Gentes and De Incarnatione* (Oxford: Clarendon Press, 1971), pp. 268–269.

7. Irenaeus, *Against Heresies* I.24.4 (concerning the teaching of Basilides), in Stevenson, *A New Eusebius*, No. 58. For a discussion of this and similar Gnostic accounts of the crucifixion, see Dart, *The Laughing Savior*, ch. 16 ("The Laughing Jesus"), pp. 107–113.

8. Valentinus, as reported by Clement of Alexandria, *Stromateis* II.7.59.3, in Stevenson, *A New Eusebius*, No. 68.

9. Basilides, as reported in Hippolytus, *Refutation of All Heresies* VII. 26.3, in Stevenson, *A New Eusebius*, No. 54.

10. Gospel of Thomas, Introduction and Logion 13, in Hennecke and Schneemelcher, *New Testament Apocrypha* (above, Ch. 3, n. 15), Vol. 1, pp. 511–512.

11. An example of Gnostic passwords: Origen, *Contra Celsum*, trans. Henry Chadwick (Cambridge University Press, 1953), VI.31 (pp. 346–348), and Chadwick's notes to the passage.

12. Gospel of Thomas, Logion 77, p. 519.

13. Basilides, as reported in Hippolytus, *Refutation of All Heresies* VII. 27.1–4, in Stevenson, *A New Eusebius*, No. 57.

14. This is a frequent theme in *Contra Celsum;* see, for example, III.13 (p. 136) and VI.27–33 (pp. 342–349).

15. Pagels, *Johannine Gospel* (above, Ch. 3, n. 22), esp. chs. 5 and 6.
16. See note to No. 79 in Stevenson, *A New Eusebius* (quoting Harnack).
17. Ignatius of Antioch, Letter to the Trallians 9:1–2, in Richardson, *Early Christian Fathers* (above, Ch. 3, n. 19), p. 100. Note the reference to Mary here; it illustrates the often overlooked truth, that in the early church the point of the doctrine of the Virgin Birth was not to assure that Jesus had a divine parent, but rather to assure that he had at least one human parent.
18. Walter Schmithals, *Paul and the Gnostics,* trans. John E. Steely (Abingdon Press, 1972), p. 62.
19. James M. Robinson and Helmut Koester, *Trajectories Through Early Christianity* (Fortress Press, 1971).
20. Tertullian, *On Prescription Against Heretics* 17–19, in *Ante-Nicene Fathers,* Vol. 3, pp. 251–252; Origen, *Contra Celsum* VI.39 (pp. 354–355).
21. Robinson and Koester, *Trajectories,* p. 118.
22. Robinson and Koester, *Trajectories,* pp. 186–187.
23. Schmithals, *Paul and the Gnostics,* p. 63.
24. For recent studies of the variety of kerygmata in the early church, see Howard Clark Kee, *Jesus in History: An Approach to the Study of the Gospels,* 2d ed. (Harcourt Brace Jovanovich, 1977); Stephen Neill, *Jesus Through Many Eyes: Introduction to the Theology of the New Testament* (Fortress Press, 1976); and Dunn, *Unity and Diversity* (above, Ch. 1, n. 9), especially chs. 2 and 3.
25. Richard H. Drummond, "Studies in Christian Gnosticism," *Religion in Life,* 45 (1976), pp. 7–21, at pp. 10–11.
26. Drummond, "Studies," pp. 17, 1–2, 13.
27. Drummond, "Studies," p. 19.
28. T. S. Eliot, *The Complete Poems and Plays* (Harcourt, Brace and Co., 1952), p. 124 (from Section I of the poem "East Coker").

Chapter Six. JESUS: HOW MUCH HISTORY IS ENOUGH?

1. Howard Clark Kee, Franklin Young, and Karlfried Froehlich, *Understanding the New Testament,* 3d rev. ed. (Prentice-Hall, 1973); Norman Perrin, *The New Testament: An Introduction: Proclamation and Pareness, Myth and History* (Harcourt Brace Jovanovich, 1974). Readers are free to make what they will of the fact that the Jesus chapter is in the exact middle of this book.
2. Perrin, *Introduction,* p. 5.
3. Much has been written on the "new quest"; see, for example, Joachim Jeremias, *The Problem of the Historical Jesus,* trans. Norman Perrin (Fortress Press, 1964) (Facet Books, Biblical Series No. 13), and Ferdinand Hahn, Wenzel Lohff, and Günther Bornkamm, *What Can We Know About Jesus? Essays on the New Quest,* trans. Grover Foley (Fortress Press, 1969).

4. Eccl. 1:2, 9 (and *passim*); *Macbeth,* V.v.26–28; Robert L. Short, *The Gospel According to Peanuts* (John Knox Press, 1964), p. 77; Percy Bysshe Shelley, *Adonais,* LII.462–463, in *The Complete Works,* ed. Roger Ingpen and Walter C. Peck (Gordian Press, 1965), Vol. 2, p. 404; 2 Cor. 5:17.

5. *Harvard Dictionary of Music,* 2d ed. (Belknap Press of Harvard University Press, 1969), pp. 26–27.

6. Kee, *Jesus in History* (above, Ch. 5, n. 24), pp. 293–300.

7. Wilhelm Wrede, *The Messianic Secret* (1901), trans. J. C. G. Groves (Cambridge: J. Clark, 1971).

8. Every introductory book on New Testament study written in the past forty years has something to say about form criticism. For a classic statement of the method, see Rudolf Bultmann and Karl Kundsin, *Form Criticism,* trans. F. C. Grant (Harper Torchbooks, 1962) (includes Bultmann, "The Study of the Synoptic Gospels," and Kundsin, "Primitive Christianity in the Light of Gospel Research").

9. Robert Buckhout, "Eyewitness Testimony," *Scientific American,* Vol. 231, No. 6 (December 1974), pp. 23–31, at p. 24.

10. Buckhout, "Eyewitness Testimony," pp. 25, 26–27, 31.

11. "The Great Span," *The New Yorker,* April 14, 1975, pp. 29–31.

12. Kee, *Jesus in History,* p. 297.

13. Kee, *Jesus in History,* p. 117.

14. Kee, *Jesus in History,* pp. 161–163. Kee has carried through his analysis of Mark in detail in *Community of the New Age: Studies in Mark's Gospel* (Westminster Press, 1977).

15. Dunn, *Unity and Diversity* (above, Ch. 1, n. 9), p. 339 (italics his).

16. Kee, *Jesus in History,* p. 211.

17. Fuller, *Current Study* (above, Ch. 1, n. 10), p. 26.

18. Bruce Barton, *The Man Nobody Knows: A Discovery of the Real Jesus* (Bobbs-Merrill Co., 1925); S. G. F. Brandon, *Jesus and the Zealots: A Study of the Political Factor in Primitive Christianity* (Manchester University Press, 1967); John Howard Yoder, *The Politics of Jesus: Vicit Agnus noster* (Wm. B. Eerdmans Publishing Co., 1972).

19. Keck, *Future* (above, Ch. 3, n. 3).

20. Keck, *Future,* pp. 109, 68, 185.

21. Perrin, *Introduction,* pp. 287–288; compare the rather similar conclusions of Kee, *Jesus in History,* pp. 298–299.

22. Perrin, *Introduction,* pp. 281–282; Perrin notes the remarkable congruence between his criteria and those arrived at independently, and from different bases and biases, by Reginald Fuller.

23. This is a major theme throughout Keck, *Future.* As a corrective to this abstraction, Keck suggests (p. 265) that we look again at the work of two pioneering students of religion in its relation to society, Shailer Mathews and Shirley Jackson Case, who taught at the University of Chicago in the early part of this century. "They surmised, I believe, that a self deciding always and repeatedly against the world was no real self but an abstracted self turned inward. They perceived that man is social and that he

NOTES TO PAGES 148-155

lives his life in structures and institutions that cannot simply be designated 'world' to be overcome by deciding selves."

24. Perrin, *Introduction,* pp. 300–301.

25. Perrin, *Introduction,* p. 301.

26. Kennedy, "Source Criticism" (above, Ch. 2, n. 13), p. 142. Kennedy argues in addition that there may have been an intermediate stage of "taking written notes" on the apostolic preaching before the writing of the Gospels. Every teacher knows that no two students' notebooks are identical, but that does not mean the students were absent from class.

27. Perrin, *Introduction,* p. v.

28. Albert Schweitzer, *The Quest of the Historical Jesus* (1899) (Macmillan Co., 1968), p. 403.

29. I make the case for this understanding of Origen in "Plutarch and Origen" (above, Ch. 3, n. 11).

30. This is the important conclusion of *Jesus and the Spirit* (above, Ch. 1, n. 9), where Dunn, aware of all the problems involved in getting into Jesus' "self-consciousness," shows how to get at least some way round these problems by asking what the New Testament *language* which can be form-critically attributed to Jesus implies about religious experience. One might even credit Dunn with a *"new* new quest of the historical Jesus," one that applies very general analytical techniques for the study of religion (as distinct from strictly historical techniques) to the study of the New Testament.

Chapter Seven. PAUL: ENIGMA VARIATIONS

1. Many of the citations in this chapter will be from the very useful Norton Critical Edition of *The Writings of St. Paul,* ed. Wayne A. Meeks (W. W. Norton & Co., 1972). In addition to providing annotated texts of the letters in the Revised Standard Version, Meeks also gives selections from major writings about Paul from the second century to the present. George Bernard Shaw, "Preface on the Prospects of Christianity" to *Androcles and the Lion* (1913), in Meeks, *Writings,* pp. 299–300. Adolf Harnack, *What Is Christianity?* (Engl. trans., 1901), in Meeks, *Writings,* p. 302. The terminology of "enigma" for Paul is suggested by Henry Chadwick, *The Enigma of St. Paul,* The Ethel M. Wood Lecture, Feb. 27, 1968 (London: Athlone Press, 1969).

2. Adolf Harnack, *History of Dogma,* trans. from 3d German edition by Neil Buchanan (reprint; Dover Publications, 1961), Vol. 1, p. 89.

3. From "The Ascents of James," of uncertain date, as paraphrased by Epiphanius, Bishop of Salamis (4th century), in Meeks, *Writings,* pp. 177–178.

4. "The Acts of Paul and Thecla," from Hennecke and Schneemelcher, *New Testament Apocrypha* (above, Ch. 3, n. 15), Vol. 2, in Meeks, *Writings,* pp. 199–207. For a treatment of Paul's attitude toward women, within a

very wide perspective, see Denise Carmody, *Women and World Religions* (Abingdon Press, 1979), Ch. 5.

5. F. F. Bruce, "Is the Paul of Acts the Real Paul?" *Bulletin of the John Rylands University Library of Manchester,* 58 (1976), pp. 282-305.

6. Adolf Harnack, *History of Dogma,* Vol. I, p. 136, quoted in Meeks, *Writings,* p. 436.

7. Justin Martyr, *Dialogue with Trypho,* in Fathers of the Church, *Writings of St. Justin Martyr* (Christian Heritage, 1948), pp. 147-366. There are a few possible allusions to Paul's writings in the *Dialogue,* but no direct use.

8. See especially Martin Buber, *Two Types of Faith* (London: Routledge and Kegan Paul, 1951) (currently available as a Harper Torchbook).

9. W. D. Davies, *Paul and Rabbinic Judaism: Some Rabbinic Elements in Pauline Theology,* 2d ed. (London: S.P.C.K., 1955).

10. Hans Joachim Schoeps, *Paul: The Theology of the Apostle in the Light of Jewish Religious History* (Engl. trans., 1961), in Meeks, *Writings,* pp. 349-360, at p. 360. A very recent major contribution to the study of Paul and Judaism is E. P. Sanders, *Paul and Palestinian Judaism: A Comparison of Patterns of Religion* (Fortress Press, 1977). By a patient working through the sources for Rabbinic Judaism, Sanders challenges head on the generally accepted view that the rabbis (and the Pharisees before them) championed a theology which required good deeds as a way of *earning* the covenant. Sanders shares Schoeps's judgment that Paul misunderstood the meaning of the covenant, but Sanders grounds the misunderstanding at a much deeper level than that of dependence on the Greek translation. He sees Paul and the rabbis as working within two fundamentally different religious patterns, each with its own logic and psychological consistency.

11. Sandmel, *First Christian Century* (above, Ch. 2, n. 9), pp. 173-174.

12. Bruce, "Paul of Acts."

13. Meeks, *Writings,* pp. 321-322.

14. Schmithals, *Paul and the Gnostics* (above, Ch. 5, n. 18), esp. ch. 1 ("The Heretics in Galatia") and ch. 2 ("The False Teachers of the Epistle to the Philippians").

15. Dunn, *Unity and Diversity* (above, Ch. 1, n. 9), pp. 252-257, portrays the conflict between Paul's Christianity and that of the Jerusalem church as protracted and very bitter. Dunn is clearly not persuaded by the recent reassessments of the evidence. I believe his own position depends too much on arguments from certain silences in Acts.

16. From *Kerygmata Petrou* ("Preachings of Peter"), perhaps about A.D. 200, in Meeks, *Writings,* p. 181.

17. Meeks, "Epilogue: The Christian Proteus," in Meeks, *Writings,* p. 440.

18. Meeks, "Epilogue," p. 442.

19. Meeks, "Epilogue," p. 435.

20. Krister Stendahl, "The Apostle Paul and the Introspective Con-

science of the West," *Harvard Theological Review,* Vol. 56 (1963), in Meeks, *Writings,* pp. 422–434, at pp. 425–426.

21. Rubenstein, *My Brother Paul* (above, Ch. 4, n. 5), p. 11.

22. Rubenstein, *My Brother Paul,* pp. 90, 73. The reference to Freud is to *Moses and Monotheism,* trans. Katherine Jones (Alfred A. Knopf, 1939), p. 110. The specific illustrations Rubenstein provides here will be dealt with in some detail in Chapter 9.

23. Rubenstein, *My Brother Paul,* p. 22.

24. Schweitzer's book, *The Mysticism of Paul the Apostle* (Seabury Press, 1968), is not in vogue in Pauline studies these days, but it remains a profound study, and bears as much attention as many more recent treatments of Paul. Also of note is the fact that Gershom Scholem has devoted attention to Paul in his pathbreaking studies of Jewish mysticism. See, for example, *On the Kabbalah and Its Symbolism* (Schocken Books, 1969), pp. 74–75: "the most outstanding example known to us of a revolutionary Jewish mystic."

Chapter Eight. THE SOCIAL REALITY OF THE NEW JERUSALEM

1. John G. Gager, *Kingdom and Community: The Social World of Early Christianity,* Prentice-Hall Studies in Religion Series (Prentice-Hall, 1975). Since Gager's book is treated extensively in this chapter, most references will be indicated by page number in the text.

2. In order to avoid unnecessary confusion, we should note Gager's explanation of his use of the terms "millennium" and "millenarian"—"in the extended sense of movements that expect a new order of reality in the near future; my use bears no relation to the narrower sense of a thousand-year reign that is to occur in the indefinite future" (p. 57, n. 1).

3. Gager, *Kingdom and Community,* pp. 28–29, quoting Peter Worsley, *The Trumpet Shall Sound: A Study of Cargo Cults in Melanesia* (Schocken Books, 1968), p. xii.

4. Gager, *Kingdom and Community,* p. 40, citing L. Festinger, H. W. Riecken, and S. Schachter, *When Prophecy Fails* (Harper & Brothers, 1956).

5. Gager, *Kingdom and Community,* p. 95. The Pliny-Trajan correspondence is conveniently available in Howard Clark Kee, *The Origins of Christianity: Sources and Documents* (Prentice-Hall, 1973), pp. 51–53. For a corrective to Gager on certain points of detail and interpretation, see Robert M. Grant, *Early Christianity and Society* (Harper & Row, Publishers, 1977).

6. Gager, *Kingdom and Community,* p. 108, citing A. H. M. Jones, "The Social Background of the Struggle Between Paganism and Christianity in the Fourth Century," in Arnaldo Momigliano, ed., *The Conflict Between Paganism and Christianity in the Fourth Century* (Oxford University Press, 1961), pp. 17–37, at p. 37.

7. Gager, *Kingdom and Community,* pp. 107–108, citing Jones, "The

Social Background," and Max Weber, *The Sociology of Religion* (Beacon Press, 1964), pp. 95–99.

8. Gager, *Kingdom and Community,* pp. 80–88, referring frequently to Lewis Coser, *The Functions of Social Conflict* (Free Press, 1956).

9. Gager, *Kingdom and Community,* p. 68, refers to Weber's "pure-type analysis." For a brief discussion of the place of "ideal types" in Weber's thought, and beyond that in sociology generally, see Reinhard Bendix, article "Max Weber" in *International Encyclopedia of the Social Sciences,* Vol. 16, pp. 499–500.

10. Kee, *Jesus in History* (above, Ch. 5, n. 24), pp. 1–8, indicates his indebtedness to several of the social scientists on whom Gager draws.

11. Pelikan, *Emergence* (above, Ch. 1, n. 2), p. 55.

Chapter Nine. WATER, BREAD, WINE: PATTERNS IN RELIGION

1. Carl G. Jung, *Aion: Researches Into the Phenomenology of the Self,* Bollingen Series XX, Vol. 9, Pt. 2 (Pantheon Books, 1959), pp. 34–35.

2. In a recent lecture at Swarthmore College, Dr. Eberhard Bethge, Dietrich Bonhoeffer's close friend and eminent interpreter, pointed out that Bonhoeffer's use of "religionless" is directed particularly at the situation of Christianity in Germany, where lines between "religion" and "state" are fuzzy. But Bonhoeffer's critique does cut very deep, and he has certainly been widely cited as an advocate of a thoroughgoing divorce between Christianity and religion.

3. Mircea Eliade, *Rites and Symbols of Initiation: The Mysteries of Birth and Rebirth* (Harper Torchbooks, 1965), pp. 115–116.

4. Eliade, *Rites,* p. 118.

5. John Moschus (early 7th century), *Pratum spirituale,* J.-P. Migne, *Patrologia Graeca* 87.3044B–3045D. On the treatise generally see Henry Chadwick, "John Moschus and His Friend Sophronius the Sophist," *Journal of Theological Studies,* n.s., Vol. 25, No. 1 (1974), pp. 41–74, including a reference to a critical edition in progress by Philip Pattenden.

6. Mircea Eliade, *Patterns in Comparative Religion* (Sheed & Ward, 1958), p. 188. Such generalizations get one's "exception-hunting juices" flowing, and it is possible to argue with Eliade on the point. But what New Testament scholarship needs to do is to take seriously how strong Eliade's basic position is.

7. Eliade, *Patterns,* pp. 188–189.

8. Rubenstein, *My Brother Paul* (above, Ch. 4, n. 5), pp. 26–27.

9. Rubenstein, *My Brother Paul,* p. 57.

10. Rubenstein, *My Brother Paul,* pp. 66–67.

11. Rubenstein, *My Brother Paul,* p. 29.

12. Rubenstein, *My Brother Paul,* p. 99. In these terms we might see some lines of connection, at a deep level, between Paul and the letter to the Hebrews.

13. Rubenstein, *My Brother Paul,* p. 100.

14. Rubenstein, *My Brother Paul,* pp. 112, 101.

15. Rubenstein, *My Brother Paul,* pp. 103–104.

16. Justin Martyr, *First Apology* 46, in Richardson, *Early Christian Fathers* (above, Ch. 3, n. 19), p. 272; *Second Apology* 10 and 13, in Fathers of the Church, *Writings of St. Justin Martyr* (above, Ch. 7, n. 7), pp. 129–130, 133–134.

17. Eliade, *Patterns,* p. 28.

18. Eliade, *Patterns,* pp. 11–12: "Indeed, we cannot be sure that there is *anything*—object, movement, psychological function, being or even game—that has not at some time in human history been somewhere transformed into a hierophany."

19. Eliade, *Patterns,* p. 26.

20. Carl G. Jung, *Answer to Job,* in *Psychology and Religion: West and East,* Bollingen Series XX, Vol. 11, 2d ed. (Princeton University Press, 1969), pp. 463–464; also in *The Portable Jung,* ed. Joseph Campbell (Penguin Books, 1976), p. 642.

21. Jung, *Aion,* pp. 13, 30.

22. Jung, *Aion,* p. 37.

23. Jung, *Aion,* pp. 32–33.

24. Jung, *Aion,* ch. 5: "Christ, A Symbol of the Self."

25. Gager, *Kingdom and Community* (above, Ch. 8, n. 1), pp. 51–57.

26. Jung, *Answer to Job,* chs. xiii–xvii, pp. 435–459; also *Portable Jung,* pp. 607–636.

27. Clement of Alexandria, *Stromateis* VI.124.6, and Gregory the Great, *Moralia* XX.1; both cited by Robert M. Grant, *A Short History of the Interpretation of the Bible,* rev. ed. (Macmillan Co., 1963), p. 123.

28. Cited in Grant, *Short History,* p. 87, but without reference.

29. Patrick Vandermeersch, "The Archetypes: A New Way to Holiness?" *Cistercian Studies,* Vol. 10 (1975), pp. 3–21, at p. 16.

30. Rubenstein, *My Brother Paul,* p. 93: "In our times, when men are rediscovering the body and learning once more the real power of touching and tasting, the Christian Lord's Meal may serve as an example to other religious traditions of the fact that not prayer but sacrificial communion is the decisive mode of human fellowship and worship." Jung, *Answer to Job,* ch. xix, pp. 461–469, at p. 464; also *Portable Jung,* pp. 639–648, at p. 642: "the dogma of the Assumption— which, by the way, I consider to be the most important religious event since the Reformation"—and he means important in a positive sense.

31. Gager, *Kingdom and Community,* p. 55.

32. Thomas Mann, "Freud and the Future," a speech delivered in Vienna, May 9, 1936, on Freud's eightieth birthday, in Mann, *Essays of Three Decades,* trans. H. T. Lowe-Porter (Alfred A. Knopf, 1947), p. 422.

Chapter Ten. THE APOSTOLIC BOOK AND THE APOSTOLIC SEE

1. Papal encyclicals are identified by their opening words, which do not necessarily indicate precisely the subject of the text. Most of the pro-

nouncements relevant to biblical study are printed in *Enchiridion Biblicum,* 4th ed. (Naples and Rome, 1961).

2. George Bernard Shaw, Preface to *Saint Joan: A Chronicle Play in Six Scenes and an Epilogue* (1924) (Penguin Books, 1951), p. 39.

3. *The Spiritual Exercises of St. Ignatius,* trans. Anthony Mottola (Doubleday & Co., Image Books, 1964), pp. 140–141.

4. My account of developments between Vatican I and Vatican II draws heavily on Thomas Aquinas Collins and Raymond E. Brown, "Church Pronouncements," ch. 72 in *The Jerome Biblical Commentary,* 2 vols. bound as one (Prentice-Hall, 1968), Vol. 2, pp. 624–632. See also Grant, *Short History* (above, Ch. 9, n. 27), ch. 13, "Roman Catholic Modernism," pp. 165–173.

5. *Providentissimus Deus,* in *Enchiridion Biblicum,* par. 113. The image of gnawing the bark is taken from Gregory the Great, *Moralia* XX.ix.20 (on Job 30:3–4), J.-P. Migne, *Patrologia Latina* 76.149A, where the reference is specifically to heretics.

6. James Bryant Conant, *Science and Common Sense* (Yale University Press, 1951), pp. 27–31 (section on "Science and Reality: A Skeptical Approach" in ch. 2, "What Is Science?").

7. Raymond E. Brown, in *Jerome Biblical Commentary,* Vol. 2, p. 625.

8. *Jerome Biblical Commentary,* Vol. 1, p. xvii.

9. *Jerome Biblical Commentary,* Vol. 1, p. xviii.

10. John S. Kselman, "Modern New Testament Criticism," *Jerome Biblical Commentary,* Vol. 2, ch. 41, pars. 46–70, esp. par. 47.

11. "Dogmatic Constitution on Divine Revelation," in Austin Flannery, ed., *Vatican Council II: The Conciliar and Post-Conciliar Documents* (Liturgical Press, 1975), pp. 750–765, at pp. 757–758. Chapters 12 and 13 include quotations from or allusions to the Council of Trent and the First Vatican Council, to the encyclicals of Benedict XV and Pius XII, and to the writings of Jerome, Augustine, and John Chrysostom.

Chapter Eleven. OPENING UP AND BROADENING OUT

1. *The Drummer* (an independent weekly newspaper published every Tuesday by Tixeon, Inc., in Philadelphia), Feb. 1–8, 1977.

2. *Newsweek,* July 25, 1977, p. 58.

3. Bultmann in Hans Werner Bartsch, ed., *Kerygma and Myth: A Theological Debate* (Harper Torchbook, 1961), p. 4.

4. Hal Lindsey with C. C. Carlson, *The Late Great Planet Earth* (Zondervan Publishing House, 1970), pp. 174–175.

5. Rudolf Steiner, *The Occult Mysteries of Antiquity* (originally published as *Christianity as Mystical Fact and the Mysteries of Antiquity,* 1961) (Rudolf Steiner Publications, 1972), p. 139.

6. Steiner, *Occult Mysteries,* p. 193. Steiner places himself within the Gnostic tradition, but he has slightly misconstrued the Gnostics. They were more radical in their conviction of humanity's lost condition than

Steiner is. For the Gnostic, human beings could gain knowledge of their true condition, their true nature, only through a revealer. Steiner is more like Origen, who considered that Christ's function was that of teacher, or helper along the road to knowledge that human beings would eventually have taken on their own.

7. I have developed the theme of pilgrimage as the way of the life of faith in "A Song of Worshiping Pilgrims," *Occasional Papers* of the Institute for Ecumenical and Cultural Research (Collegeville, Minn.), No. 5 (March 1978). I owe the expression "spirituality of the long haul" to my colleague in co-chairing the Institute's ongoing inquiry into "Confessing Faith in God Today," the Rev. Thomas F. Stransky of the Paulist Fathers. For the theme of pilgrimage in wide perspective, see Victor and Edith Turner, *Image and Pilgrimage in Christian Culture,* Lectures on the History of Religion Series (Columbia University Press, 1978).

8. Dunn, *Unity and Diversity* (above, Ch. 1, n. 9), p. 336.

9. H. Richard Niebuhr, *The Meaning of Revelation* (Macmillan Co., 1941), p. 41.

10. Niebuhr, *Meaning,* pp. 73, 83.

11. Niebuhr, *Meaning,* pp. 113, 137.

12. Section "The Flight Into Egypt," IV, in *The Collected Poetry of W. H. Auden* (Random House, 1945), p. 466.

13. Søren Kierkegaard, *Concluding Unscientific Postscript,* trans. David F. Swenson, completed by Walter Lowrie (American-Scandinavian Foundation, Princeton University Press, 1941), p. 49.

14. Donald K. Swearer, *Dialogue: The Key to Understanding Other Religions,* Biblical Perspectives on Current Issues (Westminster Press, 1977). C. S. Lewis, *Letters to an American Lady* (Wm. B. Eerdmans Publishing Co., 1967), p. 11. On this whole question see the thoughtful articles by Lesslie Newbigin, growing out of a lifetime's experience as a missionary in India: "The Basis, Purpose and Manner of Inter-Faith Dialogue," and "Christ and the Cultures," *Scottish Journal of Theology,* Vol. 30 (1977), pp. 253–270; and Vol. 31 (1978), pp. 1–22.

15. *New Testament Studies,* Vol. 21, No. 3 (1975), pp. 313–317.

16. Matthew Arnold, *Culture and Anarchy: An Essay in Political and Social Criticism* (published together with *Friendship's Garland*) (Macmillan Co., 1883), p. 11.

A NOTE ON BRITISH PUBLISHERS

British publishers of the main titles mentioned in the text are:

Bartsch, H. W. (ed.), *Kerygma and Myth*, SPCK 1972
Beare, F. W., *The Earliest Records of Jesus*, Blackwell 1962
Bultmann, Rudolf, *Faith and Understanding*, SCM Press 1969
Dunn, James D. G., *Jesus and the Spirit*, SCM Press 1975.
Dunn, James D. G., *Unity and Diversity in the New Testament*, SCM Press 1977
Eliot, T. S., *Complete Poems and Plays*, Faber and Faber 1969
Fuller, R. H., *The New Testament in Current Study*, SCM Press 1963
Grillmeier, Aloys, *Christ in Christian Tradition*, Volume 1, Mowbray ²1975
Harvey, Van A., *The Historian and the Believer*, SCM Press 1967
Hengel, Martin, *Judaism and Hellenism*, SCM Press 1974
Hennecke, E., *New Testament Apocrypha* (two vols), SCM Press 1963, 1965
Keck, Leander E., *A Future for the Historical Jesus*, SCM Press 1972
Kee, Howard C., *Community of the New Age*, SCM Press 1977
Kee, Howard C., and Young, F. W., *The Living World of the New Testament*, Darton, Longman and Todd 1972 (US title: *Understanding the New Testament*)
Kümmel, W. G., *The New Testament: The History of the Investigation of Its Problems*, SCM Press 1973
Neill, Stephen, *Jesus through Many Eyes*, Lutterworth Press 1976
Sanders, E. P., *Paul and Palestinian Judaism*, SCM Press 1977
Schweitzer, Albert, *The Quest of the Historical Jesus*, A. & C. Black ³1954
Schweitzer, Albert, *The Mysticism of Paul the Apostle*, A. & C. Black ²1956
Sellers, W. C., and Yeatman, R. J., *1066 and All That*, Methuen 1930
Stephenson, J. (ed.), *A New Eusebius*, SPCK 1956
Wilson, R. McL., *Gnosis and the New Testament*, Blackwell 1968

SUGGESTIONS FOR FURTHER READING

The indispensable tool for keeping in touch with developments in New Testament study is *New Testament Abstracts: A Record of Current Literature* (begun in 1956), published three times a year by Weston School of Theology, Cambridge, Mass., in cooperation with the Council on the Study of Religion. This publication provides brief accounts of the contents of articles appearing in about 400 journals and of the contents of about 450 books a year. It can be found in most academic libraries; it would be highly appropriate for church libraries, for the use of both clergy and laity, particularly those who teach in the church's educational program. Many of the articles and books abstracted are of more than technical scholarly interest. (Subscription information: Executive Office of the Council on the Study of Religion, Wilfrid Laurier University, Waterloo, Ontario, Canada N2L 3C5.) Of similar value for church libraries is *Old Testament Abstracts* (begun in 1978), published three times a year by the Catholic Biblical Association. (Subscription information: Old Testament Abstracts, The Catholic University of America, Washington, D.C. 20064.)

NOTE: In the suggestions that follow, books that are currently available in paperback are marked with a single asterisk (*); those currently available in hardcover are marked with a double asterisk (**).

For the history of New Testament scholarship: Stephen Neill, *The Interpretation of the New Testament 1861–1961* * (Oxford University Press, 1964); and Werner G. Kümmel, *The New Testament: The History of the Investigation of Its Problems* **, trans. S. MacL. Gilmour and Howard Clark Kee (Abingdon Press, 1972). The books provide insight not only into their subject but also into the different styles and temperaments of British and German scholarship.

The works of Samuel Sandmel are among the most clearheaded available; see his *The First Christian Century in Judaism and Christianity: Certainties and Uncertainties* ** (Oxford University Press, 1969); *A Jewish Understanding of the New Testament* * (KTAV Publishing House, 1974); *Judaism and Christian Beginnings* * (Oxford University Press, 1978).

Of books mentioned in the text or in the notes to this book, I would single out as particularly significant the following: James D. G. Dunn,

Unity and Diversity in the New Testament: An Inquiry Into the Character of Earliest Christianity ** (Westminster Press, 1977); Howard Clark Kee, *Jesus in History: An Approach to the Study of the Gospels* 2d ed.* (Harcourt Brace Jovanovich, 1977); Leander E. Keck, *A Future for the Historical Jesus: The Place of Jesus in Preaching and Theology* ** (Abingdon Press, 1971); the Norton Critical Edition of *The Writings of St. Paul* *, edited by Wayne A. Meeks (W. W. Norton & Co., 1972); John Gager, *Kingdom and Community: The Social World of Early Christianity* * (Prentice-Hall, 1975); Donald K. Swearer, *Dialogue: The Key to Understanding Other Religions* *, Biblical Perspectives on Current Issues (Westminster Press, 1977).

One way to get the New Testament into proper perspective is to get away from specific focus on the New Testament. Useful collections of sources are provided by Howard Clark Kee, *The Origins of Christianity: Sources and Documents* * (Prentice-Hall, 1973); Cyril C. Richardson, ed., *Early Christian Fathers* * (Macmillan Co., 1970); J. Stevenson, ed., *A New Eusebius. Documents Illustrative of the History of the Church to A.D. 337* * (Alec R. Allenson, 1957). For the story of early Christianity, see Henry Chadwick, *The Early Church* * (Penguin Books, 1968), and Jaroslav Pelikan, *The Emergence of the Catholic Tradition (100–600)* *, The Christian Tradition, Vol. 1 (University of Chicago Press, 1971).

It goes without saying—although perhaps it needs to be said—that the New Testament itself should not be neglected by one who wants to understand New Testament study. There is no better way to get a feel for the doing of serious study of the New Testament than to work through some sections of *Gospel Parallels: A Synopsis of the First Three Gospels* **, ed. Burton H. Throckmorton (Thomas Nelson & Sons, 1957); a very useful companion to such "working through" is F. W. Beare, *The Earliest Records of Jesus* ** (Abingdon Press, 1962), which is keyed to the specific sections of the *Parallels.*

Finally, anyone who is concerned about the question of New Testament study and the understanding of revelation should read H. Richard Niebuhr, *The Meaning of Revelation* * (1941; Macmillan Co., 1967); this book, although written nearly forty years ago, has not even begun to go out of date.

INDEX